MAKING STANDARDS WORK

How to Implement Standards-Based Assessments in the Classroom, School, and District

Douglas B. Reeves, Ph.D.

ROBERT MORRIS UNIVERSITY
LIBRARY

Center for Performance Assessment

ISBN #0-9709455-0-7

Advanced Learning Press books are available for quantity discounts with bulk purchases for education systems, professional organizations, or sales promotion use. For more details and discount information, contact Advanced Learning Press at (800) 844-6599 or fax (303) 504-9417.

Editor: Allison Wedell Schumacher

Printed and Bound in the United States of America

Published by:
Advanced Learning Press
1660 South Albion Street, Suite 1110, Denver, CO 80222
(800) 844-6599 or (303) 504-9312 • Fax (303) 504-9417
www.makingstandardswork.com

Distributed by:
Center for Performance Assessment

Library of Congress Cataloging-in-Publication Data

Reeves, Douglas B., 1953–
    Making standards work : how to implement standards-based assessments
in the classroom, school, and district / Douglas B. Reeves.—3rd ed.
        p. cm.
Includes bibliographical references and index.
    ISBN 0-9709455-0-7
    1. Education—Standards. 2. Educational tests and measurements. I.
Title.
    LB3060.82 .R44 2001
    379.1'58—dc21

2001058624

ROBE

Y

Dedication

Jean and Julie Reeves
who never lost faith

and

Brooks
who still makes me the luckiest father in the world.

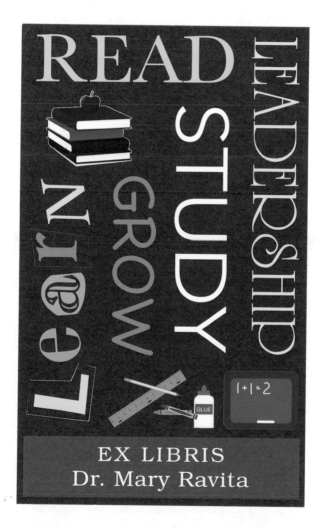

Acknowledgments

Every book is a collaborative process, and credit is due to many more people than the one whose name appears on the cover. In particular, I would like to thank my colleagues at the Center for Performance Assessment who have provided valuable critiques and suggestions. The thanks expressed here are insufficient recognition of their intellectual energy and friendship.

This third edition of *Making Standards Work* reflects significant improvements and revisions from the first edition. I am especially grateful to a small group of hardworking, dedicated individuals who provided substantial editing and technical assistance and contributed creative and intellectual insights to this edition. Special thanks are owed to Allison Wedell Schumacher, who painstakingly reviewed and edited the original manuscript for spelling, grammar, and coherence.

A number of leaders in the field of standards-based performance assessment have provided valuable insights and contributed to the ideas expressed in this volume. Dr. Joyce Bales, one of the nation's most innovative and successful superintendents, has devoted her life to transforming the statement "all children can learn" from a slogan to a reality. Dr. Stan Scheer provides thoughtful challenges when theory must confront reality. Dr. Deanna Housfeld is a singularly effective educational leader whose demands for detail, practicality, and real-world effectiveness set the standard by which every educator, consultant, and leader should be evaluated. Karen Young and her colleagues at Learning 24/7 set the standard for innovation in the field of professional development. In recent years, they have been unique among national organizations by providing not only the motivation of intellectually rich conferences, but also the implementation of those ideas at the classroom and school levels.

Students in my graduate research classes frequently heard the words that references must be cited, not simply because the style manual requires it, but because we have an ethical obligation to acknowledge the shoulders on which we stand. Five people in particular deserve this acknowledgment, for their writing and thinking have shaped much of my intellectual life. Howard Gardner, Ruth Mitchell, David Perkins, Robert Slavin, and Grant Wiggins have written cogently for a generation of teachers, educational leaders, and policy makers about the profound need for thinking about learning, intelligence, and achievement in new ways. They have elevated public debate from the exchange of labels and attribution of motives – an all-too-typical occurrence in the past – to a respectful dialogue about ideas and the imperative that the world has to better educate its children.

Finally, Professors Audrey Kleinsasser and Alan Moore have provided me and countless other students with just the right combination of encouragement, skepticism, good humor, and challenge. This expression of thanks is woefully inadequate.

As usual, this attempt to share credit does not constitute an attempt to share blame, and the mistakes, whether intellectual or typographical, are ones for which I alone bear responsibility.

Douglas Reeves
December 2001

About the Author

Douglas B. Reeves, Ph.D., is the chairman and founder of the Center for Performance Assessment, an organization that works with governmental organizations and school systems to improve standards, assessments, and accountability systems. Schools in 49 states and 5 continents are transforming their approach to assessment, teaching, learning, and achievement through the active implementation of Dr. Reeves' practical and popular books and seminars. The author of ten books and many articles, Dr. Reeves'  recent publications include *Accountability in Action: A Blueprint for Learning Organizations* (Advanced Learning Press, 2000); *101 Questions and Answers About Standards, Assessment, and Accountability* (Advanced Learning Press, 2001); *Crusade in the Classroom: How George W. Bush's Education Reforms Will Affect Our Children, Our Schools* (Simon & Schuster, 2001), *The Twenty Minute Learning Connection* (Simon & Schuster, 2001), and *Holistic Accountability* (Corwin Press, 2001).

A frequent keynote speaker for educational and leadership groups, Dr. Reeves has been featured at the Harvard Leadership and Policy Forum, the Brown University Literacy Conference, the Columbia University Literacy Project, the National Standards Conference, the Effective Schools Conference, and many other national and international organizations.

A video series accompanies this book. It shows students, teachers, and school leaders implementing the ideas of effective standards-based performance assessment. The *Making Standards Work* video series is available through the Video Journal of Education from the Center for Performance Assessment. Order volume numbers 802 and 803. For volume 803, please specify elementary or secondary edition.

Contents

Part Three: Making Standards Work in the District

Part Four:

Preface

As these words are written, our nation and its allies are at war against terrorism and the world remains in mourning for thousands of lives cut short by violence. School children who live thousands of miles from the field in Pennsylvania and the sites of the World Trade Center and Pentagon attacks are anxious, distracted, and emotionally affected by the notion that so many parents and children could be lost in an instant. As parents, teachers, and caregivers, we grieve not only for the loss of life but also for the sense of insecurity and fear that our children and students will likely live with for a very long time. We feel inadequate because there is neither rational assurance nor an easy answer that can adequately confront pervasive and continuing fear. In this emotional climate, we seek to improve teaching and learning.

Among the few comedic moments in the aftermath of these tragedies has been the ridicule justly heaped on those who have sought to link the nation's focus on terrorism to their own agenda. As politicians associated their pet programs with the war on terrorism, we expected to see on our grocery store shelves "anti-terrorism" deodorant and dishwashing detergent. Politicians and the manufacturers of consumer goods do not have a monopoly on opportunism, and participants in educational debates will soon follow suit. New textbooks will breathlessly claim to be more relevant than their competitors because of a publication date after September 11, 2001. New programs and proposals will claim to be linked to the special needs of children in light of the tragedies, as if emotional care and intellectual rigor were alien concepts prior to that date.

Rather than attempt to make some tenuous link between academic standards, performance assessments, national tragedies, and international wars, I will focus on what has not changed. While the world may be a different place in geopolitical and psychological terms today than it was when I first put pen to paper in the hills of southern China while writing the first edition of this book, the bedrock principles on which this book is based remain vital and contemporary. These principles include the following:

1. Fairness is a transcendent value that should be the basis on which educational decisions are made. Whether Congress and state legislatures are analyzing the performance of millions of students or a 3rd grade teacher is evaluating the work of a single child, the principle of fairness demands that the definition of success be clear. Student achievement in a fair system stems from meeting a standard rather than wading through mysterious and changing expectations. While there is value in freedom and creativity by teachers and school leaders, that discretion

does not extend to the freedom to expect less of children or the freedom to ignore the standards which educators, parents, community members, and policy makers have established as the essential requirements for student learning. When claims of freedom tread on fundamental fairness for student opportunities to learn, fairness wins.

2. Critical thinking and academic rigor are best promoted through frequent assessment that demands analysis and clear communication. Annual multiple-choice tests do not promote these requirements. Thinking and rigor are best promoted through frequent classroom performance assessments, with clear standards and the demand for students to edit and revise work that is less than proficient.

3. Analysis, reflection, and factual knowledge are all equally essential. The events of September 11, 2001 have not elevated discussions of current events over a study of history. As surely as students must study the new war on terrorism, they must also understand a context that includes military and political leaders from Churchill to Charlemagne.

4. Educational accountability must be a constructive method of improving teaching and learning. As a moral principle, we dare not ask children to be more accountable than the adults in our schools. This means that a commitment to comprehensive accountability requires more than a litany of test scores. Rather, it demands a thorough exploration of the leadership, teaching, and curriculum strategies in each school.

With these enduring principles in mind, the path to standards-based performance assessment outlined in this book rests on twin pillars of fairness and effectiveness. Neither the rationale for fairness nor the path toward excellence has changed. In a time of dramatic and sometimes daily change, we would do well to remind ourselves and the children we serve of those values and principles that endure.

On a personal note, there are a few additional things that have not changed since the first edition. Brooks still makes me the luckiest father in the world, even as he pursues an independent life in college and the world. My gratitude for the confidence and inspiration of my parents, the late Jean Reeves and Julie Reeves, endures with every class I teach and every page I write. My colleagues at the Center for Performance Assessment provide challenge and companionship, and I am proud to call them partners in this lifelong endeavor of improving student achievement. As I head home from yet another road trip, my footsteps are lighter and my heart more full because I will be greeted by James, Julia, Alexander, and Shelley. When Wordsworth wrote, "My heart leaps up when I behold a rainbow in the sky," he described my feelings each time I walk in the door.

Douglas B. Reeves, Ph.D.
Swampscott, Massachusetts
October 2001

How to Get the Most Out of This Book

This volume is designed not simply to be read, but to be used. It is written principally for use by classroom teachers and administrators at the building and district level. However, many of those interested in effective educational strategies, including students of educational leadership and assessment, parents, board members, and policy makers may find this book useful.

Part One

Part One addresses why standards matter. The central rationale for standards-based assessments is that they provide a means of evaluation that is accurate and fair. An essential component of fairness is consistency: Students and teachers must have a fixed target at which to aim. In contrast to norm-referenced measures frequently in use by school districts, the standards-based academic target does not change.

We do not expect airline pilots to be "above average," but instead expect them to meet a consistent standard of safety and proficiency. The same is true with a standards-based approach in school. If, for example, students are expected to demonstrate proficiency in the application of the Pythagorean theorem (Figure I.1) after a ninth grade geometry class, they can take scant comfort in being better than other students. Proficiency is more than beating other students. It is insufficient to be better than 50% of the other ninth graders in the nation by successfully answering—or guessing—the responses to a multiple choice test, and then claiming that one is "above average."

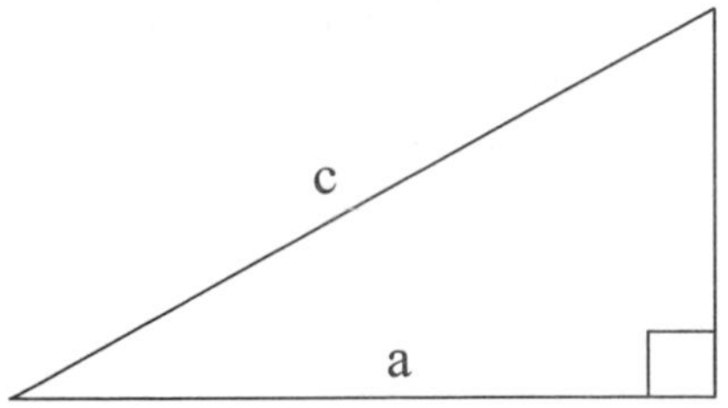

A standards-based system will require the student to demonstrate the application of the Pythagorean theorem—perhaps by using pencil and paper, perhaps by using blocks of wood, or perhaps by using a videotaped oral presentation. In none of these cases can a student guess the right answer. In this

FIGURE I.1
Pythagorean Theorem $a^2 + b^2 = c^2$

respect, standards-based assessments are inevitably more rigorous and more demanding than traditional multiple choice tests. Moreover, the requirement to demonstrate that the sum of the square of two sides of a right triangle is equal to the square of the hypotenuse ($a^2 + b^2 = c^2$) does not change, while the national average does change from year to year. Part One will address why this method of assessment is the appropriate way to implement standards and what the roles of classroom teachers, principals, and district officials are with respect to implementing such a system.

Part Two

Part Two of this book addresses, in a step-by-step manner, the process of making standards work in the classroom. All too frequently, the model of educational innovation has been that of a single teacher who attends a workshop, comes back to school full of innovative ideas and enthusiasm, and implements those ideas *in one classroom*. Sometimes, though rarely, these ideas are shared with others. Even more rarely are they implemented by others. But on the whole, innovation is sporadic and inconsistent.

The process of implementing standards-based performance assessments demands a collegial effort. The requirement for collegiality is not merely a social or political necessity. Effective assessments require consistent evaluation and the application of several disciplines at the same time. If a school system has a writing standard, for example, and teachers create assessments in mathematics, science, and social studies without regard for the writing standards, chaos ensues. Students recognize these inconsistencies and will be the first to tell us that the standards emperor has no clothes. If, on the other hand, standards are consistently applied in assessments in which the evaluation criteria do not change from one discipline to the next, student performance responds accordingly. Such a move from idiosyncrasy to consistency requires cooperative work by teachers. Only with this consistency will policy makers, taxpayers, and, most importantly, students understand that standards have moved from slogans and speeches to clear and unambiguous practice in the classroom.

The issue of consistency invariably raises the issue of teacher independence and discretion. Let us not mince words here: In few other professions do practitioners of all levels of experience and education have such broad discretion to make critical decisions throughout the vast majority of the day. The adoption of standards, consistently applied in standards-based performance assessments, retains large amounts of this discretion, freedom, and individual judgment. But this freedom has limits. The widespread practice of teachers defining curriculum and choosing not to teach critical subjects based on little more than their personal preference will, in a standards-based school system, go the way of the Dodo bird. Changes in teaching practice and experiments in learning activities are one thing; choosing to omit fractions for a third grade class because, in the words of one teacher, "I don't like fractions," is an intolerable abuse of discretion.

The need for consistency in the application of standards is based on more than a bureaucratic imperative for control or the psychometric zeal for statistical reliability. Consistency is required by our commitment to fairness. Any reasonable notion of fairness requires that educational strategies, particularly assessments, must be consistent within a school system. This means, as a practical matter, that "spelling counts" in math class as surely as it does in English class. It implies that "math counts" in a graph provided to the social studies or economics teacher as surely as it does were the graph submitted to the science or math teacher. Although the development of standards-based performance assessments permits an extraordinary amount of creativity by individual teachers, the standards themselves remain fixed guiding stars by which educators and administrators can navigate.

The Ten Steps described in Part Two comprise the heart of this book. The application of these steps to a single assignment and a single standard by every teacher in a district can, over the course of two or three years, completely change the way educational strategies are developed, delivered, and assessed.

Part Three

Part Three addresses the broader policy issues involved when making standards work in the district. Accountability, recognition, and response to challenges are among the critical issues of this section of the book. These chapters offer concrete and specific ideas helpful to superintendents and other educational leaders at the district level.

Part Four

Finally, the reader will find reproducible handouts for easy review of key information, detailed sample assessments and assignments (including a sample format for assignments), a handy glossary, and a brief bibliography. School reform does not take place with books or speeches. School reform takes place through the actions of individual parents, teachers, and administrators who are willing to change what happens in the classroom. The standards movement can have an enormous influence on a national commitment to excellence and equity, but it will inherently be the culmination of the efforts of teachers and school leaders working together, rather than a march in lock-step fashion to a uniform drumbeat. At the Center for Performance Assessment, we continue to gather stories of successful and unsuccessful innovations, and we hope that you might take a moment to share your stories with us. We look forward to an engaging, challenging dialogue with each of our readers and encourage you to contact us.

Center for Performance Assessment
1660 South Albion Street, Suite 1110, Denver, CO 80222
(800) 844-6599 or (303) 504-9312, fax (303) 504-9417
www.makingstandardswork.com , e-mail dreeves@makingstandardswork.com

PART ONE

Why Standards Matter

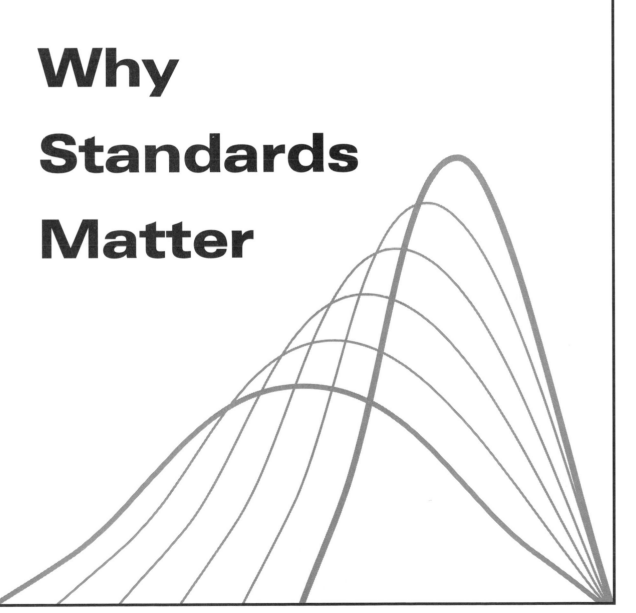

CHAPTER ONE

Tying the Bell on the Cat

The implementation of standards brings to mind a classic story.

> Once upon a time a council of mice gathered to consider how to deal with their deadly enemy, the cat. After much deliberation, the council decided that the best thing to do would be to tie a bell around the neck of the cat so that the mice would be warned whenever the cat approached. Amidst their general back slapping and self-congratulation, a small young voice uttered the telling question, "But who will tie the bell on the cat?"

This book is about "tying the bell on the cat." The national standards movement now faces a similar dilemma. There appears to be general agreement across the political spectrum that academic standards should:

- Be rigorous and challenging.

- Be related to the technological forces that will mold the 21st century in which today's students will work.

- Provide a fair and equitable basis for evaluation.

However, there is widespread disagreement about how schools will be held accountable for the implementation of these standards. Without accountability and without comprehensive and meaningful assessments, the standards movement contains little more than platitudes. While high expectations are certainly an important part of successful academic achievement strategies, expectations alone are insufficient. Assessment and accountability drive every other element of the education delivery system, including instructional design, classroom technique, allocation of resources, administrative practice, and central office decision making.

Linking Standards to Assessments: An International Challenge

This issue crosses national boundaries. In August of 1997, I addressed a policy roundtable at the International Conference on Technology and Education in Oslo, Norway. Representatives of 57 countries heard speeches from leaders, including a Prime Minister, several cabinet-level education officials, and a large number of leaders from universities and school systems. They appeared to be united on the necessity for high standards and placed particular emphasis on the need for technological literacy, student collaboration, and "higher order thinking skills." The most frequent comment from the delegates of the many nations was, "The same speech could have been delivered by educational leaders in our country." I then asked the group a simple question: If there is such unanimity on the need for high standards in thinking skills, collaborative work, and technological literacy, can any of the 57 nations here claim to have an assessment system that reflects these philosophies? In fact, can any nation claim to have an assessment system that doesn't reflect the opposite of what we claim to believe? One American community college dean said that they require performance assessment in technology. A few delegates said that they were experimenting with individual proficiency tests at the university level.

These noble efforts notwithstanding, the state of assessment is now little different than it has been for decades. School leaders and national policy makers frequently talk about laudatory goals, such as teamwork and cooperation among students. Indeed, business leaders frequently cite these characteristics as essential for a successful participant in the work force of the 21st century. Unfortunately, typical assessment practices do not match these goals. Few assessments encourage meaningful teamwork and cooperation; in fact, tests based on the Bell Curve actively oppose cooperation among students because the gain of one student is invariably at the expense of another. The most frequently-used tests encourage memorization of narrowly defined fact patterns or vocabulary words, and rarely require students to explain or justify their answers, analyze and synthesize information, or apply general principles to new and unfamiliar information. These are the skills required in the never-never land of political speeches, but rarely assessed in the classroom.

At the dawn of the 21st century, there is a significant backlash against standards in general and mandatory testing in particular. Here is the dilemma: Critics of standardized tests note that the tests are poorly aligned to curriculum and standards. In reaction to this criticism, a few states have expanded the scope and method of assessment to include writing, problem solving, and other academic areas. These assessments are more complex and time-consuming, but are better related to the standards than the formerly used "quick and dirty" standardized tests. The critics, rather than celebrating the fact that they influenced assessment for the better, are now enraged because the tests take too much time and are so directly related to state standards that teacher creativity has been inhibited. In the absence of a perfect test, what are school leaders and state legislators to do? The extreme options appear to be the abandonment of tests or the exclusive reliance on a single nationally standardized test. Neither extreme is worthy of our students. A balanced approach to standards-based assessment will continue the quest for improved assessments, with multiple testing methods that include multiple-choice, short-answer, extended response, problem solving, and demonstration. Most importantly, the result of these assessments will not be the terrorizing of children nor the threatening of adults, but clear and meaningful feedback on how to improve teaching and learning. While that vision departs significantly from present reality, educational leaders will never achieve the goal of meaningful and fair assessment if we remain mired in the acrimonious debate that now prevails. We should be able to acknowledge the flaws inherent in any human-made test and use those flaws as a basis for improvement. This will help us avoid a retreat to the pre-standards era of mystery grading, idiosyncratic judgments, and the Bell Curve.

The Central Issue: How to Make Standards Work

Despite this discouraging reality, the voices demanding change are gaining national and international attention. As far as voters and most board of education members are concerned, the issue is not whether to create effective accountability and assessment. The question is how to do it. There are a few hold-outs remaining who regard accountability and assessment as inherently improper, unfair, demeaning, and even unprofessional, but these voices are rarely taken seriously in most debates over educational policy. The new voices in the debate demand accountability and assessment systems that are based on high academic standards and that reflect the consensus of their communities about what students should know and be able to do. These voices lack the patience to debate endlessly *whether* we should have effective assessment – they demand to know *how* to implement effective assessment. It is to these energetic, innovative, and frustrated voices that this book is addressed. Their central question is: Now that we have standards, how do we make them work?

What Makes the Standards Approach Different From Business as Usual?

Many school systems across the United States and abroad have endured the arduous process of establishing academic standards. This has been no easy task, particularly in the politically charged areas of social studies, economics, and literature. As difficult as these tasks have been, however, even more difficulty lies ahead when transforming standards into assessments. If standards are to be successfully implemented, then many of the traditional ways of doing things must cease.

Examples of traditional activities that can no longer take place under a standards-driven environment include the following:

- **Attendance (or "seat time") is sufficient to gain credit.**

  This issue frequently leads to a debate over "social promotion" versus "high standards," with the implication that high standards invariably lead to flunking students. In fact, high standards are founded on the core belief that all students can perform at high levels given the opportunity to learn, and with appropriate teaching and assessment strategies. Therefore, the practical impact of the application of high standards is neither high failure rates nor social promotion. It is rather the use of multiple opportunities for students to demonstrate proficiency and the steadfast refusal of teachers and administrators to label students "proficient" when they are not.

- **A "D" is a passing grade.**

  I know of no classroom in America in which a "D" represents anything other than the failure of the student to demonstrate proficiency and the failure of the teacher to acknowledge it. The availability of a "D" is simply the policy option that allows a school to explicitly acknowledge that a student failed to demonstrate proficiency in the subject, while refusing to require the student to do so. In a genuinely standards-based school system, the grade of "D" should not exist. Either students are proficient (usually a grade of at least an "A" or "B" and, sometimes, a "C") or they are not. The failure to be proficient should, in most circumstances, result in a grade of "incomplete" while the student is afforded more opportunities to learn and demonstrate proficiency. Should the student refuse to do so, a failing grade, not a "D," is the only accurate grade.

- **A great high school is measured by the quantity and creativity of its elective offerings.**

  There is not a shred of evidence to suggest that the proliferation of non-academic electives has improved student learning. But there is a growing quantity of statistical and narrative evidence that an emphasis on core academic disciplines promotes student learning, not only in traditional test scores, but also in complex performance assessments. Nevertheless, there are hundreds of high schools that have academic standards for statistics and economics, but offer no classes in these subjects, while the same schools devote time and resources to classes for which they have no academic standards. **Note well:** This does not make a brief for a curriculum based only on the "three R's," but rather insists that every class, regardless of its label, owes a duty to the student and community to reinforce academic standards in math, language arts, social studies, and science. Classes in music, cooking, wood shop, and physical education offer extraordinary opportunities to teach math, science, history, and language arts. We cannot squander the talents and time of these teachers, nor can we afford the inconsistent message that such subjects are "soft" because they are not really academic. The defensiveness of teachers (and more commonly, some professional associations) on the subject of academic emphasis in elective subjects is misplaced.

- **Academic core curriculum classes are identical in structure and length for every student.**

   The common practice requiring that every ninth grade student should take identical math classes (typically algebra) is absurd. In a diverse district (that is, any district without a small and neatly identical group of students), some students come to the ninth grade ready for trigonometry while others require basic mathematical skills in order to avoid catastrophic failure. Some students are ready for the challenges of literary criticism and advanced composition, while others need work on the fundamentals of spelling and grammar. A standards-based approach to education begins with the premise that all students can learn and achieve at high levels, *but that does not imply that all students learn in the same way and at the same pace.* Standards-based districts expect that all students will achieve. That does not mean that they should expect that all students will learn in an identical manner and at the same pace. The practical impact of standards implementation is more than a series of community meetings in which everyone exclaims how nice it would be if all students learned math, English, history, and technology. This will remain the stuff of Rotary Club lunch speeches unless it is transformed into specific curriculum reforms.

It is likely that many school districts that began establishing standards would never have completed the journey had they realized that the elimination of these notions is the practical outcome of standards implementation. A standards-driven district, however, cannot afford the luxury of paying lip service to academic standards by implementing a system based only upon attendance (or "seat time"), hourly credit, and ancient definitions of satisfactory. Let us consider each of these implications in some detail.

It Is Proficiency, Not Seat Time That Matters

Standards implementation depends on a demonstration of proficiency. Traditional means of assessment, such as a letter grade associated with "seat time," are hardly ever an indication that a student has met standards. Indeed, most teachers would agree that students to whom they have given a "D" grade do not meet the standards for that class, and the teacher would have regarded the "D" as an unsatisfactory grade. Nevertheless, for the purposes of awarding a high school diploma the "D" is regarded as satisfactory.

If standards mean anything, they mean that students must demonstrate proficiency in order to obtain credit for classes and, ultimately, in order to obtain a high school diploma from that school system. This means that the era of credit for attendance and class participation is over. Students gain credit through a demonstration of proficiency. This can be done either at the beginning of the class, in the middle of the class, or at the end of class. For students who demonstrate proficiency early, the classroom teacher has the responsibility of providing enrichment opportunities that allow those students to indicate that they have exceeded standards. For students who have difficulty achieving standards, the teacher has the obligation to provide multiple opportunities and constructive feedback for those students to make progress towards standards and, ultimately, to meet the standards. For students who, at the end of the term, fail to meet standards, the teacher has an obligation to forthrightly indicate that the student does not meet standards, and hence was awarded no credit for the achievement of that standard. Along with this obligation to tell the uncomfortable truth, teachers have the obligation to continue to help the student work toward the achievement of that standard.

Standards Lead to Curriculum Reform

Standards implementation inevitably leads to curriculum reform, including the provision of intensive assistance for small groups of students who are not initially meeting standards. Another essential element of curriculum reform is the systematic use of standards in the description of courses. At the very least, this means that every class (particularly in a middle school, junior high, or high school) is listed in a course catalog and is associated with one or more standards established by the district. Some districts, for example, have standards in statistics, but no classes in it. On the other hand, they have classes in psychology, sociology, and photography, but no standards are associated with those classes.

If standards are to become more than a slogan, then one of two things must happen. Either the classes that are not associated with standards are no longer taught, or – a better alternative – the teachers of those classes creatively identify ways their classes can help students achieve academic standards. For example, statistics standards can clearly be met in a number of sociology, ethnic studies, psychology, and social studies classes. The same is true of many language arts and civics standards. The photography class could be linked to standards in mathematics, visual arts, science, language arts, and civics. The bottom line remains, however, that classes not linked to standards do not make a contribution to the goals of the district and should not be taught.

Standards implementation requires a compartmentalized curriculum. By compartmentalization, I mean the reduction of some academic subjects into smaller blocks. There should be no such thing as "ninth grade mathematics" or "tenth grade English." Rather, standards that these classes have traditionally comprised should be taught in units ranging in size from a few weeks to a full semester. It might be possible that some students would take two classes to complete all those requirements – the time traditionally used for a full class. Other students, however, may need four, five, or even six units to achieve the same level of standards.

This is most evident in mathematics classes. The notion that every ninth and tenth grader should take the same algebra class is simply preposterous. A number of students enter high school without knowing multiplication tables, not to mention having any preparation for algebra class. The traditional system requires that these students take a class for which they are hopelessly ill-prepared and then brands those students as failures in mathematics. A better approach is to permit these students to achieve high school mathematics standards through a number of different classes, including not only traditional academic classes, but also application classes, vocational classes, and interdisciplinary classes. Those students still have to achieve the algebra standard, but they do so by taking a variety of classes, not by taking a "dumbed-down" curriculum.

The goal of a standards-based curriculum is not to tell students how to achieve standards, but rather to provide a broad menu of alternatives that meet the needs of students who require additional instruction, as well as those who have already achieved the standard and appreciate further enrichment. The practical effect of this system is that students who need to spend more class time to accomplish the graduation standards will take fewer electives. Does this mean that a student who needs extra math and English classes in order to achieve high school graduation might not have time in his or her curriculum for band and drama? That is precisely what it means. This leads to the next issue. Standards implementation almost invariably implies fewer electives.

What About "Non-Academic" Electives?

One of the many ill-considered trends in secondary school education in the last twenty years has been the proliferation of non-academic electives. Although many of these classes have earned high marks for innovation and creativity, they have done little to contribute to the academic achievement of students. Even in districts that claim to be standards-based, many of these electives continue to thrive in ignorant bliss of any responsibility the teachers of these electives should have with regard to standards implementation. Although I acknowledge the social importance of many electives, these are times of limited resources and falling academic achievement in many districts. Such times call for making choices with regard to available time and resources. Although it may not be necessary to eliminate electives in instrumental music, chorus, journalism, drama, social sciences, and creative writing (just to name a few), it is essential that these electives be available only to students who have already achieved the standards appropriate for their grade level, or that those classes are directly used to help all students achieve academic standards. In addition, the teachers of these elective subjects bear a responsibility for either demonstrating that their classes can, in fact, help students achieve specific academic standards, or accepting the fact that the activities in which they are engaged are more appropriate as after-school extracurricular activities. To be sure, there are a number of teachers of music, shop, home economics, and many other electives who can be splendid mathematics and English teachers if only given the chance to use these subjects, which they so creatively teach, to help students achieve academic standards.

There is substantial controversy on the subject of whether "non-academic" subjects should have their own standards. Many professional groups associated with music, physical education, and vocational education advocate this position. They argue that separate standards make these subjects part of the standards movement. In my view, these arguments are wrong because they diminish the very subjects they seek to promote. The contention that music, physical education, and art, to name a few examples, should not be part of academic content standards but should have completely separate standards distances these subjects from core academic subjects and may doom them to irrelevance when the next round of budget cuts inevitably comes. A better approach is to integrate these traditionally "non-academic" subjects with academic standards. For example, woodworking and cooking become ways to teach math and science. Music and art become ways to teach history and literature. This integration will elevate the status of music, art, woodworking, home economics, and subjects that are too frequently placed on the chopping block during budget difficulties. In sum, the importance of these subjects is best recognized, not by their isolation, but by their integration into the core academic content standards of our schools. This is not merely a theoretical ideal, but has been applied in practice to the hundreds of schools I have visited. Art classes routinely capitalize on the visual learning styles of students to build vocabulary and enhance thinking skills. Music classes give students not only a joy of rhythm and tunes, but also a better understanding of fractions and intervals. Art and music classes collaborate to give students a deeper understanding of social studies subjects, relating culture to history. Physical education classes integrate the joy of movement and games with measurement and strategy. Administrators bear a particular burden to incorporate all faculty members into the standards discussion. When, after all, was the last time we invited the physical education teacher to a discussion of math achievement? When did we last ask the art teacher to participate in a discussion of thinking skills and vocabulary development? Effective faculty collaboration depends upon administrators who will take the initiative to be deliberately inclusive of all faculty members in all discussions of academic standards and student achievement.

Standards and High School Graduation Requirements

Standards implementation implies different graduation requirements. The myth of the "gentleman's C" (or given today's grade inflation, the "gentleman's A-") holds that mere attendance without an excess of disruptive behavior qualifies a student for a passing grade in a class. If standards are to have meaning, then a demonstration of proficiency must be linked to the awarding of high school diplomas. Many progressive districts are moving toward a certificate of completion for students who have been able to pass the attendance requirements for graduation but were unable to demonstrate proficiency in academic standards after the normal number of high school years. Typically, these students are offered a fifth year of instruction, at no charge, either in the secondary school setting or in an appropriate post-secondary institution.

Standards Call for Courage

For most, "tying the bell on the cat" requires courage, just as it did for the council of mice. Districts that seek to undertake standards must be prepared to face the political firestorm that accompanies a restriction on student choices and a diminution of the widespread emphasis on non-academic elective subjects. Moreover, criticism will inevitably come from those who believe the application of curriculum blocks is too close to "tracking." As a result, they will brand the implementation of standards as unfair, sexist, racist, and other appellations that say more about the level of educational and political discourse than they do about the targets of the labels.

Finally, criticism will come from teachers themselves, who appreciate performance-based assessments of standards in theory, but who are less than enthusiastic when they discover that the primary responsibility for the creation and year-round administration of these assessments rests with the classroom teacher. Only those districts willing to risk the wrath of all of these criticisms, and many more, are going to be able to successfully implement standards. The result will certainly be worth it in academic achievement, fairness, equity, educational opportunity, professional development for teachers, public accountability, and in many other ways. But only the most innovative and courageous districts will endure the pain and discomfort of these criticisms in order to achieve those long-term results.

CHAPTER TWO

Getting to Know Your Standards

"We've been working on standards for three years, and I still don't know what they mean."

This sentiment, expressed by teachers, administrators, parents, and board members, grows largely from the failure of the advocates of standards to be precise in their language. This chapter addresses some of the causes of this confusion and suggests a means to bring some order to the chaos that frequently surrounds the discussion of school standards.

Forty-nine states have already adopted academic standards. In Iowa, each school district establishes standards. Thus, every child in every public school in the nation is now learning in a standards-based curriculum. The same is true for students in the vast majority of industrialized nations, whether curriculum and assessment are governed by national, regional, or local standards. Unfortunately, the word "standards" means vastly different things to different people. In some school systems, standards describe general expectations for student knowledge, while in others, standards describe very specific performance requirements. When the same word is used to describe very different concepts, some confusion and frustration is inevitable.

After working with hundreds of schools on this subject, I am convinced that the use of the word "standards" to mean many different things is confusing and potentially destructive. Therefore let me suggest vocabulary that will be clear and unambiguous:

- *Academic Content Standards*: The general expectations of what a student should know and be able to do. These are typically few in number and general in scope. Examples include:

  - Students will be able to design, conduct, analyze, evaluate, and communicate about scientific investigations.

  - Students will know and understand properties, forms, changes in, and inter-relationship of matter and energy.

  - Students will communicate clearly and effectively about science to others.

- *Benchmarks*: The specific expectations of student performance at a grade or continuum of grades. Some states use other terms, such as "frameworks" or "curriculum objectives" to describe grade-level expectations. Whatever the terminology, the key is that this level of description is more specific than the general academic content standard but less specific information than teachers and students need to evaluate individual pieces of student work. Examples of benchmarks include the following:

  - By Grade 4, students will identify and describe science-related problems or issues, such as acid rain and weather forecasting.

  - By Grade 4, students will relate scientific information to local and global issues, such as world hunger and ozone depletion.

  - By Grade 8, students will analyze the risks and benefits of potential solutions to personal and global issues.

  - By Grade 12, students will analyze the costs, risks, benefits, and consequences of natural resource exploration, development, and consumption, such as resource management of forests and ground water pollution.

  - By Grade 12, students will design, communicate, and, when possible, implement solutions to personal, social, and global problems, such as school noise pollution or school recycling.

- *Scoring Guides*: These are the very specific descriptions of student proficiency for an individual standards-based assessment. Many writers have used the word "rubric" rather than "scoring guide." I use the terms interchangeably. Examples of passages from scoring guides include the following:

  - To earn a score of "proficient," the student will produce an informative essay with no spelling, grammar, or punctuation errors. At least two graphs that include data points and relationships that support the conclusions of the essay will accompany it. The graphs will be mathematically accurate, properly labeled, and clearly related to the essay. (**Note:** Students will have at least three opportunities to submit work, make changes, and re-submit it in their pursuit of a score of "proficient.")

  - To earn a score of "exemplary," the student will meet all the requirements for a "proficient" essay and will also include research from two primary and three secondary sources. The research citations will conform to the Modern Language Association format in the back of the English textbook.

There are several additional examples of scoring guides in the assessments in Appendix A.

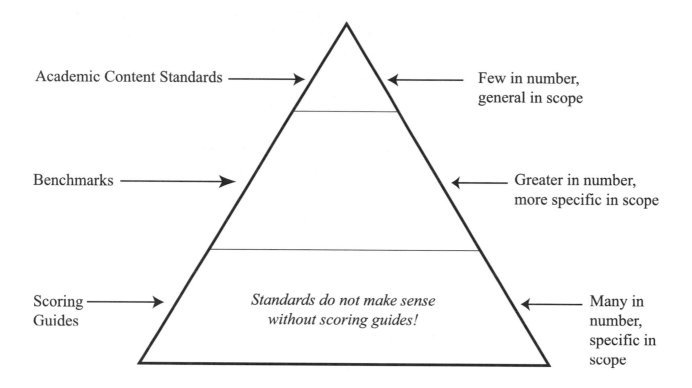

FIGURE 2.1
Standards Vocabulary

Academic Content Standards → ... ← Few in number, general in scope

Benchmarks → ... ← Greater in number, more specific in scope

Scoring Guides → ... *Standards do not make sense without scoring guides!* ← Many in number, specific in scope

The Relationship Between Standards, Benchmarks, and Scoring Guides

Figure 2.1 illustrates the relationship between scoring guides, benchmarks, and academic content standards. It might take several different assessments, and hence several different scoring guides, for a student to demonstrate that she has achieved a benchmark. It will take several different benchmarks, all completed with proficient performance, for a student to demonstrate that she has achieved an academic content standard.

If you have not already done so, please take time to become familiar with the standards in your state and district. If your district chooses to create its own standards, it is important to bear in mind that states require that districts establish academic standards at least as challenging as those adopted at the state level. Therefore, it is imperative that educators, administrators, and policy makers take some time to become familiar with their state academic content standards. A list of state web sites with all academic content standards has been provided in Appendix B.

Where Do I Start?

The academic standards can appear to be overwhelming at first glance. After all, they represent the collective efforts of your community or your state to articulate what students should learn. Many teachers and parents initially respond, "I'm swamped with work already! How can they expect me to do all this stuff too?" The rule, when confronted with such a large body of information, is "one handful of mud at a time." Start with a content area with which you are comfortable, and then look at the description of the standards for one area within that field. Then ask this question: "What evidence would assure me that a student meets that standard?" Equipped with your response to this question, you can then begin to design standards-based performance assessments that will provide you with the evidence you need. Such a detailed and analytical approach is overwhelming when one considers the sheer quantity of academic standards. As a result, I recommend that you avoid the Herculean task of creating a separate assessment for each standard. Rather, you and your colleagues should create a few assessments – perhaps half a dozen for each nine-week quarter – and each assessment should be rich in content, addressing several academic content standards.

Why Are Standards for Several Grades Mixed Together?

In some states, standards are not articulated for individual grades, but rather established as the culminating expectation for groups of grades. There are usually three such groups: kindergarten through fourth grades, fifth through eighth grades, and ninth through twelfth grades. Many people looking at standards for the first time find this baffling. "How can you expect a third grade student to be doing the same work as a first grade student?" The reason is that our traditional groupings of children into grades has been a reflection of our need for order and convenience more than it has been a reflection of how children learn and behave. In fact, it is quite common for a single classroom in a primary grade to have children who are working below, at, and above the level traditionally associated with that grade. The standards, when described for a group of grades, acknowledge that we must address a continuum of learning covering many different activities, not just traditional grades and not just an isolated set of skills traditionally associated with a single age or grade.

Standards Are Concerned With the Reality of Student Achievement, Not Artificial and Meaningless Time Requirements

The traditional approach has held that children have a fixed amount of time to learn something and assumes that the learning will be variable. For example, "Kids should learn to add and subtract in first grade, but let's face it, some kids just won't make it." Inevitably, those children fall farther behind with each successive year. A nation that expects its children to compete in the twenty-first century can ill-afford such a primitive and unrealistic approach to education. In fact, the learning expectation must be fixed: Children will learn to add and subtract; students will learn to read and summarize a passage of nonfiction text; students will learn to write a paragraph that expresses a clear idea and is free of errors in grammar, spelling, and punctuation. The time it takes to learn these skills may be shorter for some children and longer for others, but it is not acceptable that "some kids just won't learn it." At the very heart of the standards movement is the change from fixed time, variable learning, to variable amounts of time to learn fixed educational standards. Standards-based districts understand that some students will learn to read in one year, while others may need three years. They understand that some ninth grade students can complete algebra in six months, while others may need two years. Standards-based districts are committed to the principle that all of their students will read, and that all of their ninth grade students will learn algebra. These school systems care about achievement, not about time requirements of a bygone era. Chapter 3 will provide greater elaboration on this important concept.

Translating Standards Into Activities

Let us consider a sample content standard:

> Students will relate physical materials, pictures, and diagrams to mathematical ideas.

Whatever your mathematical background, you can imagine some ways students can demonstrate that they meet this standard. For a student in the early grades, this might include working and playing with blocks and creating some elementary mathematical relationships with them. For older students, this might include drawing pictures of a house and calculating the dimensions of their drawings. The point is that students demonstrate that they have met this standard not by responding to artificial (and boring!) multiple choice questions involving pictures and mathematical concepts, but by engaging in realistic, interesting, and thought-provoking activities.

Obviously, there is much more to the creation of standards-based performance assessments than we have described here. The entire process includes the development of a scoring guide, several rounds of critiques by colleagues and students, and the deliberate inclusion of other disciplines into the exercise so that each assignment is a rich tapestry of different activities. Part Two of this book deals at length with the creation of standards-based performance assessments and Part Four provides several illustrations of how standards can come to life.

What Happens if Students Do Not Meet the Standards?

Parents, teachers, and administrators ask this question, perhaps, more than any other. "Some kids just don't get it," they argue. It would be more precise to say, "Using our present methods of instruction and our present notions of curriculum and grades, some kids don't have much of a chance to 'get it'." The straight answer to the question of, "What happens if students don't meet the standards?" is that the student does the assignment again or has additional opportunities in other contexts to meet the standards. Indeed, revision and improvement is one of the distinguishing features of a standards-based performance assessment. It is not a "one shot" ordeal. To people who regard such advice as unworkable and extraordinary, I would recommend a few hours with a typical music or physical education teacher. When the student clarinetist squeaks through the B-flat scale, the typical response is neither a note home nor a low grade awarded many weeks later. Rather, the student plays the B-flat scale again – and again, and again, until he gets it right. Effective coaches and physical education teachers routinely do the same thing, knowing that skills in that subject are acquired with practice. Thus when I ask teachers to give students multiple opportunities for success and when I insist that the consequence of poor performance should not be a low grade but rather the requirement for more work, I am only asking them to take reading, math, social studies, and science just as seriously as they take music and physical education.

From "Saturday Night Specials" to Continuous Improvement

In the traditional model, students have one shot at performance: the typical final exam. But in real life, we are constantly working on problems, making modifications, improving our work, and then examining it to see if it meets the needs of our colleagues or if it needs yet more improvement. Far better work is done in college (and, I would argue, in business) by students who are used to the process of continuous improvement than by those who have been conditioned to make every project a "Saturday night special" with one attempt at perfection and without the process of revision, reflection, and improvement.

Grading and Standards

In the traditional model, the price of not meeting the standard has been a "D" (or with today's grade inflation, perhaps a "C" or a "B"). These marks tell the parents, "This student really can't do the work, but I'm not going to go through the political hassles associated with holding the child back a year or getting sued. Hey, he's really unsatisfactory, but let's call it passing." Sometimes this is done under the mistaken notion of building a student's self-esteem. In fact, there is only one thing to call such a practice, and that is a lie, and a particularly destructive lie, too. The worst damage done to students' self-esteem is not when they are told that they do not meet a standard. Rather, it is when they find out that, although teachers told them that they could "get by" through all the years of school, now prospective employers, college professors, professional licensing boards, and others are telling students that they do not have what it takes to succeed.

How do we break this cycle of deceit? How do we stop lying to children when we tell them that they are meeting standards when, in fact, it is manifestly clear that they are not? One of the principal advantages of the standards-based approach is that it begins with the premise that all children can learn. This is not an empty slogan, but a fact. Contemporary educators have much to learn in this respect from the field of special education. Here, a generation of teachers using a methodical, interdisciplinary, standards-based approach has demonstrated that children on whom the traditional educational system had given up were able to learn, and to learn at high levels.

Because learning is a complex activity, a single grade never tells the whole story and it certainly does not give students and parents the information they need to improve academic performance. In a standards-based system, grades should not merely evaluate student work, but should give specific feedback on which standards have been met and where improvement is needed. The ideal vehicle for this is the Standards Achievement Report discussed in Chapter 9. This device saves teachers time when compared to the traditional grade book, and provides much clearer guidance for students and parents so that they can work together for improved achievement.

The fundamental issue of grading in a standards-based system is the purpose of grades. If the purpose of grading is merely evaluation, then a single grade will suffice. If the purpose of grading and assessment is rating, ranking, and sorting, without any illumination of student needs or consideration of future improvement, then a single test will suffice. But if our purpose in grading is the improvement of learning and teaching, then we have an obligation to provide information that is accurate, meaningful, and relevant to student improvement. The fraudulent "D" that confers a passing grade on wholly inadequate work does not achieve such a purpose. The "B" that provides an apparently good grade does not achieve such a purpose either, particularly if that "B" is an amalgam of attitude, performance, time management, and academic success. Using standards as our guide in the awarding of student grades, we can answer the questions, "What does the grade mean?" and "How can I do better next time?"

What Do We Do When Students Do Not Meet Standards?

In practical terms, this means that when children first attempt a standards-based assessment and fail to meet the standards, they are not given a low grade and then pushed onto the next assignment. Rather, they revise their work and submit it again, and again, and again. In a classroom in which standards are clearly ingrained into the students' learning behaviors, it is not unusual to see a child on the way to the teacher's desk and then, noticing the standard on the bulletin board, stop, return to the desk, and make an important revision. This is the process we wish to encourage in our writers, engineers, scientists, accountants, attorneys, and, one might hope, teachers and professors.

CHAPTER THREE

Standards and Norms: What Is the Difference?

"There are already high standards in my class! Only a few get an 'A' and more than 40% can't pass!" (Ninth grade math teacher)

"I'm not ready for algebra but it's no problem. I got a 'B+' because I'm better than most of the other kids in my class." (Eighth grade math student)

At the very core of the concept of academic standards is the principle that student achievement is measured against a fixed objective, not in comparison to other students. It seems obvious: Standards-based systems use standards. In fact, a decade after most schools have supposedly implemented a standards-based approach to education, the comparison of student work to the average of other students remains the prevailing model of evaluation. School officials, board members, teachers, and parents who have been exposed to standards and have expressed their hearty approval of them will nevertheless ask the question, "But, how are the students doing compared to the average?" In a district genuinely committed to standards-based achievement, the answer is, "We don't know, and we don't care."

This chapter outlines the differences between standards and norms as the reference point for evaluating student achievement. We will also consider the reasons that this distinction is critical to the understanding and implementation of a successful standards-based education program. The following differences are paramount.

Standards Are Fixed. Norms Move.

Consider a mathematical standard in which students are expected to "find the area of a triangle." In a standards-based system, the student has not achieved the standard until she can successfully determine the area of a triangle. If a student is able to accomplish the task successfully, along with the vast majority of other students in the class, that one student is not heaped in the middle of a distribution and labeled as the "fiftieth percentile." Rather, the student has achieved the standard. This is the only thing that matters.

Consider the situation in which there is only one student in the class who is progressing toward the standard, but still has not achieved proficiency in that standard. The other students are not progressing toward the standard. The one student who is making progress toward the standard should not be recognized as achieving the ninety-ninth percentile with all the glory and honor associated with such an exalted position. Rather, that student, along with all the students in that class, has not yet met the standard and every single one of them needs additional work to achieve the standard. This is precisely the situation that prevails in student writing, where few if any students produce essays that match the level of proficiency required by state standards. Rather than accepting work that is demonstrably short of the standard, we should reward the honest teachers who say, "None of my students meet this standard yet, so it appears that we have some work to do." Unfortunately, we are more likely to hear, "Of course my students don't meet the standard, but they are much better than those students in the school across town, so their writing must be pretty good."

The norm, or average student performance, may change from year to year as testing companies publish data with different numbers of "average" achievement by students, but the standard is immutable. The academic standards of every state require that students must add, subtract, multiply, divide. These standards do not change no matter how many or how few of the students can perform these calculations. It would, after all, be scant comfort to an engineering company (and to the tenants of the building which that engineering company might construct) if its newest hire were unable to properly calculate the load-bearing ability of the parking lot, but the engineer was proudly able to say "but my math abilities are better than those of most of my peers!" In the real world we are much less interested in how people fare relative to one another. What matters is only the central question: "Can they do the job?"

Former Colorado Governor Roy Romer, a leader in the standards movement as chair of the National Governor's Conference Education Committee and Superintendent of Los Angeles Unified School District, uses the example of airline pilots to make the point. Like me, Governor Romer is a pilot. We have a standard that one should have an equal number of takeoffs and landings. We gain scant comfort from pilots who assert that their performance is "above average." If they do not meet the standard, their lives and the lives of their passengers are in peril.

Standards Are Cooperative. Norms Are Competitive.

My observation of students in graduate and professional schools across the country would indicate that not much has changed in twenty-five years. The movie *The Paper Chase* illustrates the insidious nature of competition among first year law students. In the movie, students who have compiled outlines that will assist them in taking their final exams are unwilling to give them to other students unless they can gain something back of equal value. After all, they reason, there will be only one top A in the class, and there will only be a fixed number of people in the top ten percent. The only thing that matters in the mind-set of these students is their comparison to one another, not their mastery of the law.

Does this mean that competition is bad? Of course not. I was a competitive – some of my friends and colleagues would say hyper-competitive – debater in college and high school. My oldest son has qualified for the national finals three times in high school forensics. All of my children enjoy some sort of competitive activity. The problem is not competition itself; the problem is that teachers, parents, and students confuse competitive success with proficiency. Academic standards make it clear that students cannot become complacent merely by "beating" a competitor; they must persist, work, and learn until they meet the standard.

In a standards-based educational system, the first year law students would need to know the elements of a contract. There may be a number of opportunities to distinguish themselves: writing law review articles, participating in moot court competitions, and perhaps even helping other students master the intricacies of contract law. However, the evaluation of a student's proficiency in a course on contracts would be determined by whether or not the students could, given a typical law school final exam scenario, identify the elements of the contract, whether it is enforceable, and what its strengths and weaknesses might be. Students are not graded along a continuum of how well they do compared to each other, but on whether or not they can analyze the contract. If they cannot, they must, as Professor Kingsfield said in *The Paper Chase*, "Take a dime, call your mother, and tell her you will not be a lawyer after all." If, on the other hand, students have demonstrated their mastery of contracts, then the exercise of distinguishing one student from the other based on arcane and meaningless distinctions is of no value to students, professors, employers, or future clients.

Perhaps the best models for measurement of performance against a standard are the training programs for our most delicate surgical specialties. When one is certified as a brain surgeon, there is not much differentiation between the top ten percent and the bottom ten percent. If a physician has such a certification and is ready to put a knife in the skull of his or her patients, then the patients have a right to assume the physician has met the standard and is competent. The competition among brain surgeons is of tiny consequence compared to the fundamental issue of whether or not the physician is competent to wield the knife. If that is the standard we apply to brain surgeons, pilots of airplanes, and most people in highly sensitive and demanding jobs, then why should not the same high standards be applied to math students in middle school?

Standards Measure Proficiency. Norms and Their Counterparts (Grades) Measure Behavior.

Either the subjective opinions of teachers or the pseudo-objectivity of multiple-choice tests typically identify norms, and they are a classic example of distinctions without a difference. The notion that, after four years of education, a 3.9 GPA (Grade Point Average) is "better" than a 3.85 GPA is ludicrous. And yet what student with a 3.9 GPA would stop for a moment to conduct a test of significance, demonstrating that the difference between 3.85 and 3.9 is very likely due to random variation and hence is not a meaningful or "statistically significant" difference?

Distinctions Without a Difference

Is the attribution of differences based on meaningless distinctions the exclusive province of education? Certainly not. Business people make the same silly distinctions all the time. They believe the Fortune 500 is a meaningful group, not thinking for a moment that it is indistinguishable from the Fortune 501 to any observer except, perhaps, the president of the 501st company on the list. The three best runners in the world receive medals in the Olympics, but the fourth best runner in the world is regarded as a loser.

For centuries we have bred a bone-deep belief that competition has intrinsic meaning and value. Certainly there is nothing wrong with competition. It is fun to watch. It is fun to be a participant. One can even argue that some of the winners of such competitions create appropriate role models for children. But even if all of these premises were accepted as true, it does not logically follow that the competitive model is appropriate for the educational setting.

Cooperation and Effective Educational Practice

In a comprehensive review of research on educational innovations, Ellis and Fouts (1997) found that the one innovation with the most clear and unambiguous link to improved student achievement was the use of cooperative learning. The nation's premier researcher of cooperative learning effects is Robert Slavin of Johns Hopkins University. It is important to note that Slavin's models of cooperative learning are not the ambiguous and ill-defined practices that frequently bear the label of "cooperation"— as if anything without a teacher's supervision deserved that label. In fact, structured cooperative learning groups insure that all students have the opportunity to assume different responsibilities and learn all aspects of solving a particular problem. Slavin's research is rigorous in linking cooperative learning techniques to individual performance and thus provides the best of all worlds: team skills, cooperative behavior, and individual results. The unfortunate conception that "cooperative learning" is the 1960's educational equivalent of "peace and free love" in the classroom makes for entertaining criticism, but does not square with the facts. The cooperative learning that Ellis, Fouts, Slavin, and many others have studied leads to rigor and realism. Most importantly, it produces better mathematicians and writers than does a system based on competition.

Standards Promote Flexible Grouping. Norms Promote Segregation of Students by Ability.

Many modern teachers sneer at the "blackbirds and bluebirds" reading groups of the 1950's, and recall the insidious impact such labels had upon children. Nevertheless, strong and vocal constituencies remain who support the concept, if not the names, of ability groups. The evidence, however, is strikingly in favor of flexible student grouping (*Harvard Education Letter*, June 2000). Not only does the performance of less able students improve when they are matched with students who can serve as peer coaches, but also the performance of the peer coaches themselves improve. With mixed ability groups, these coaches are in a position to articulate their knowledge, help another person, and think through the cognitive steps of a solution. Without the challenge of mixed ability grouping, this variety of ideas might not have occurred to them. This conforms to common experience: One tends to master a subject better when one is forced to teach it, rather than to study it.

There are, to be sure, times when ability grouping makes sense. On the athletic field, some students need more practice in free-throw shooting than others do. In the chorus or orchestra, some students need more practice on certain musical passages. In the classroom, some students need more work on vocabulary or math facts. However, in all of these endeavors, students and teachers can be sufficiently flexible to move from individual practice for improving particular skills to mixed groups that have all students performing well together. While students in a reading class may benefit from temporary separation to read a story at different rates, some reading independently while others work to decode the words of the story, the same children can discuss together their evaluation of the story, their prediction of what will happen next, and their comparisons of this story to the events and characters that were encountered in the stories they read earlier in the year.

When the objective of the teacher is to have all students achieve a high standard, then the "bluebirds" are not held back and the "blackbirds" are not frustrated by failing to learn essential skills. Flexible grouping allows each student to have the opportunity to perfect basic skills, without segregating students on a permanent basis. When, by contrast, the objectives of the teacher are to confirm the stratification of abilities with which the students began the year, then bluebirds inevitably remain bluebirds, and blackbirds remain blackbirds.

Standards Are Challenging. Norms Provide Excuses for a "Dumbed Down" Curriculum.

One of the more extraordinary political charges made against the standards movement is that it lowers educational expectations. In fact, precisely the contrary is true. A norm-based concept of achievement allows a student who is proficient in arithmetic and has a rudimentary acquaintance with algebra to score very well on standardized high school mathematics tests. Yet such a student would not come close to meeting the standards-based high school graduation requirements many districts have adopted. Those requirements include a demonstration of proficiency in algebra, geometry, trigonometry, statistics, and, in some cases, even calculus. Although it is a rare district, indeed, that has been able to turn out graduates who universally achieve these requirements, the enforcement of high school graduation requirements is the only mechanism by which such challenging and rigorous standards will ever become part of the universal curriculum.

This is a paradox of the Bell Curve mentality. While most critics assume that the norm-referenced tests that result from the Bell Curve create disadvantages for poor and minority children, it is also the case that norm-referenced tests based on the Bell Curve do great damage to those children who have been traditionally "above average" on such tests. The Bell Curve provides a degree of inappropriate complacency for the student who, though he cannot write an essay or analyze a complex piece of literature, is in the 55th percentile on a norm-referenced test of verbal ability. "I'm above average," the student reasons. "What more do you want?" In a standards-based educational system, we want proficiency, and we are unimpressed with the fact that this student scores better than 55% of his peers. Rather than reinforce his indolent complacence, we insist that he take his above-average score, deposit it in the trash can, and get back to work until he can write a competent essay. While the Bell Curve provides comfort to the comfortable, a standards-based approach will, in the words of Finley Peter Dunne, "comfort the afflicted and afflict the comfortable."

As long as districts rely upon norms, mathematically illiterate students with above-average preparation in a suburban district will generally score better on standardized tests than students in urban districts. Because the urban districts are more numerous, suburban districts will be secure in their "above average" label while performing at a mediocre level. This is even more apparent in grade school, where the differentiation among the latter elementary grades is striking, with some students barely able to read and others mastering many number operations. The fifth grade student who is merely a proficient reader and able to perform rudimentary addition, subtraction, multiplication, and division is given a false sense of security by scoring in the upper twenty-five percent on norm-based tests. Yet such a student may not achieve even half the fifth grade academic standards that a standards-based system of achievement would require.

Standards Are Simple. Norms Are Complicated.

A generation of psychometricians has thrived on the complexity that norm-referenced tests and their byproducts have engendered. I am indebted to the Hawaii educational leader Robert LeMahieu for the appellation "recovering psychometrician," a label I gladly accept. Despite the superficial complexity of manipulations of statistical distributions, norm-referenced tests offer the public the artificial simplicity of reducing student performance to a single number. "Your child is a 136," say the norm-referenced advocates with satisfaction, though they have not a clue as to the level of proficiency such a number represents. What they know for sure, however, is that there were very few who scored a 136, which means that a 136 is good. Such labels are comparable to a doctor calling the patient into her office and announcing, "I have good news and bad news — your x-factor is 136, but your y-factor is an 88. Have a nice day." Such a cryptic message from a doctor would be regarded as malpractice. The same misuse of meaningless numbers, accompanied by little or no explanation and carrying implications of grave weight and predictive power, reaches the level of educational malpractice when done by school districts, test vendors, and teachers.

Typical test results from schools are obscure. Neither parents nor principals understand them. The language of stanines, quartiles, and percentiles bring forth dull headaches, as remembrances of college statistics classes and statistics professors elicit memories that are, at best, unpleasant. This is not the case because statistics professors are, by nature, bad people. Some very nice people, including this writer, have taught a few statistics courses, and we still love children, are kind to small animals, and weep at sad movies. These admirable attributes do not, however, excuse us from the penalties that properly accompany deliberate obscurity, and that is precisely the right description for a great deal of norm-referenced test data. Parents and teachers ask a simple question such as, "What percent of my students need extra work on linear and area measurement?" The standardized test report responds with, "139 – have a nice day." As this edition goes to press, I have challenged the publishers of some norm-referenced tests to provide more illuminating information, and their response has been haughty and indifferent. "If we provide more specific information as you request," they sneer, "then we would be compromising the test. We only provide scale scores, and if you want to learn more, there is an interpretive guide you can purchase."

I do not begrudge test-makers the right to make a dollar. However, I insist that they give students, parents, teachers, and school leaders the information that is necessary to improve student achievement. Such information is not an obscure comparison to an average score. It is instead the item-by-item analysis of student achievement. We must displace obscurity with analysis in order to use test information to help students and teachers improve academic achievement.

Standards Reward Improvement. Norms Reinforce Stereotypes.

Standardized tests are frequently associated with racial prejudice. In fact, the history of standardized tests, starting before the First World War, is associated with the eugenics movement – the theory of racial superiority. Fortunately, data from these tests get in the way of prejudice. One of the best illustrations of this issue is provided by an examination of the intelligence scores of Italian-Americans over the past three generations. When a substantial number of Italian-Americans were new to the United States and had limited language facility, limited opportunities for education, and limited social recognition, their exam scores were the lowest among European ethnic groups. This, of course, conformed with the prejudices of the intelligence test bureaucrats prior to the 1920s, who were convinced that southern and eastern Europeans were genetically inferior to northern Europeans.

The test administrators and race purists did not count on one thing: Italian-Americans, as any other ethnic group, would eventually learn the game. Over time and through succeeding generations, Italian-Americans achieved scores that steadily increased to the point that they achieved scores higher than the other average European-American scores and even higher than the average American scores. (Perkins, 1995). Thus the use of norms did not provide a meaningful distinction for Italian-Americans any more than it does today for any other ethnic group whose test scores are compared to others. Such a competitive system provides a false sense of achievement to sluggards who score in the upper third, but who still don't know their multiplication tables. If the evidence of many international math and science student performance tests has demonstrated anything, it is that we should take little comfort from being "above average" in a country whose eighth grade students consistently rank far behind their counterparts in other nations. Finally, competition gives a false sense of inability to those in the lower third who have never been taught their multiplication tables.

Using Test Scores to Improve Teaching and Learning

The other extreme, keeping test scores secret because "parents wouldn't understand them anyway," is equally destructive. What is required is a test data reporting system that clearly answers two questions: "Do the students meet the standard?" and, "What areas need the most focus in planning next year's curriculum?" Incredibly, for the millions of dollars spent on testing in the U.S., these two fundamental questions are rarely answered. Scores are almost invariably reported against a norm or average. On many occasions I have asked the basic question, "How many problems did the student get right and how many did he get wrong?" Only rarely have test directors or national test companies been able to provide an answer. "We're not programmed to do that," they explain. If teachers and leaders cannot analyze individual test items, they cannot plan their classes to improve student performance. Frequently, the only "analysis" comes down to bromides such as, "Math scores are down — let's do more math!"

The board of education, amidst some disgust about kids these days not knowing math the way their grandparents did, votes to increase the number of hours spent in math. But rarely is a strategic analysis of curriculum, learning, assessment, and time undertaken. A standards-based approach would begin and end with one question: "What must students know and be able to do?" Then curriculum, assessment, and time requirements would be based on the answer to that question. Classes and times might change, but learning expectations would remain uniform for all students. Finally, a standards-based approach to test data would include many different assessments and not make curriculum and other strategic decisions based on a single indicator taken on a single spring afternoon.

Standards Address Causes, Intermediate Effects, and Achievement. Norms Reflect Only Test Scores.

The second generation of standards will address not only academic content, but also the antecedents to academic achievement. My colleagues at the Center for Performance Assessment have developed a family support scale, which conveys to parents the importance of their role in the academic achievement of students. Although a breakdown of student mathematical and reading achievement is important, a family support scale that identifies antecedents to achievement of academic standards is even more crucial. Examples include the following:

- I read with my child 15 minutes every day.

- I limit television to no more than two hours every evening.

- I review my child's homework every day.

- I have at least one meal per day with my child, and during this time the television is turned off.

No doubt readers can think of many more. Other creative schools have included standards describing participation in extracurricular activities, development of artistic and musical appreciation, participation in community service projects, and levels of parental involvement. Every one of these antecedents represents not only measurable and standards-based achievements, but also is demonstrably linked to academic achievement.

Because the causes of academic achievement are varied and complex, a meaningful reporting system must consider not only the ultimate effects, but also the causes and intermediate effects. Such a system helps to provide important early warning signals where performance appears to be inadequate.

The Impulse Toward Ranking

Even in a district without norms, ranks, or comparisons, there will remain the inevitable impulse toward competition. Frequently, this is fueled by the academic equivalent of the "little league dad" who must live out his fantasies of academic victories through his children. It is never enough for the demanding "little league dad" that his child is playing ball, having a good time, and enjoying the game. This child must successfully hit every ball, catch every throw, run every base, and accomplish every unfulfilled dream of the frustrated father.

The competitive impulse extends from parents to society. Newspapers love to rank schools. One member of the education research community recently remarked that if we treated psychological tests the same way that we treat educational tests, *USA Today* would be the first to publish the nation's top ten neurotic states, the top ten egomaniac cities, and the best counties for depression. Such rankings supplant substance with ego and elevate the smug self-satisfaction of the victor over the meaning that attaches to achievement. The "little league dads" and their journalistic counterparts give us the worst of both worlds. They confer inappropriate satisfaction on those who are incompetent but better then their peers, and they deny satisfaction to those who have labored long and hard to achieve proficiency, but who are not quite as proficient as their neighbors. In contrast, a standards-based approach to education and to life will validate the hard work of the proficient student, and challenge the complacency of the victor whose superiority is devoid of a foundation of proficiency.

Making the Case for Standards to a Skeptical Public

Successful transformation from norms to standards requires an iron political will – the sort of will that can withstand the abuse of critics who will claim that the failure to publish norms, or even to discover how a district is performing compared to norms, represents hiding from bad news. It requires the will to demonstrate to those critics that, were they infected with a dread disease, their objective to become cured would be paramount. Moreover, if such a cure were to arrive, they would not become dissatisfied if their white cell count showed them to be somewhat less "cured" than a neighbor who had a similar disease. Rather, their only hope would be to be healthy, fully recovered, and cured. Making these arguments requires patience, repetition, and seemingly interminable explanations. Ironically, this is the same effort we expect from the average elementary teacher and that seems appropriate for the average student in the primary grades. We must be at least as willing to pursue such laborious strategies with critics who cannot, or will not, understand the importance of the movement toward standards.

CHAPTER FOUR

Standards-Based Assessments: The Key to Standards Implementation

Every state and most developed nations have either implemented academic content standards or are in the process of developing them. The documents associated with these standards outline a set of expectations for the knowledge, performance, and achievement by students in the public schools of those states. Unfortunately, however, the link between the promise of standards and the reality of their implementation is a tenuous one. States that adopt new standards but retain old assessments should not be surprised that the test content will drive educational practice. Unless standards are linked to assessments, the standards become little more than a political slogan full of good, but empty, intentions.

Chapter 3 outlined the reasons standards are different from norms. These differences are important not just in theory, but also in the day-to-day practice of the classroom teacher. It is in accountability and assessment where the most dramatic differences are evident between a standards-based approach and a traditional approach to education. Standards are not simply a different method of labeling traditional curriculum contents, but are fundamentally different. In this chapter we will contrast these differences.

The Traditional Assessment

1. **The assessment is secret.**

   Consider for a moment the principles that underlie traditional assessment. The assessment is a secret. The contents of the tests are typically locked away and revealed only at the moment when students break the seal on the test booklet. Teachers and principals who fail to maintain the test security lose their jobs. Teachers who teach to the test are regarded as unethical.

The traditional test uses advanced statistical programs to look for patterns of student responses in which a large number of students respond to questions in the same way. This would indicate that the question was not ideal. One might express surprise at this expectation. After all, students who have been in a classroom for 180 days with the same teacher receiving the same instruction might be expected to answer the same questions in the same way. This logic, however, does not penetrate the veil of mysticism that surrounds traditional testing. Students are victims of the immutable Bell Curve and no amount of instruction will change the normal distribution of their answers. Any deviation from this is to be regarded with suspicion.

2. **Traditional tests are associated with average scores or norms.**

Norm-based assessments are predicated on the notion that the objective of every classroom teacher is to beat teachers in other parts of the country. This impulse to be above average is fostered by the test companies themselves, who are able to report data in such a way that nearly every district and state in the nation can claim to be above average, something most people know is an impossibility. Worse yet, the impulse to be above average takes precedence over the demand for knowledge. There are functionally illiterate students who can answer a sufficient quantity of multiple-choice questions to be in the middle band of national test results. It should be worrisome that professional educators, not to mention parents and policy makers, could be satisfied with such an inadequate level of performance. Nonetheless, the traditional approach to assessment takes comfort not in achievement, but in the average.

3. **Traditional assessments seek to discriminate among different students.**

The ideal test item is one that a substantial number of students will get wrong. These are regarded in the test industry as good discriminators, not because they discriminate in a sense of racial or cultural bias, but because they distinguish one student from another. A test item that is answered correctly by every single student is regarded as a poor discriminator, even though such a wonderful performance was due to the hard work of teachers and students. If a test item fails to differentiate among students, it serves no statistical purpose. Of course, the practical result of this process is to systematically discourage students and teachers, a result apparently inconsequential to the traditional assessment advocates.

4. **Traditional assessments are overwhelmingly multiple-choice tests.**

The selection of the multiple-choice method of testing is the result of two factors. First, when tests are given in large numbers they must be graded by computers and only multiple-choice tests readily submit to computer grading. Second, there is a certain statistical neatness to multiple-choice responses. Some answers are clearly wrong and other answers are clearly right. The fact that our complex world rarely offers such neat distinctions is another factor that is lost on the advocates of traditional assessment.

5. **Traditional assessments are typically limited in time.**

Most students are conditioned to expect one week of terror in the spring, when classroom instruction comes to a halt and testing begins. During that week, children are admonished to eat good breakfasts, get plenty of sleep, and pay attention. Class schedules are rigorous, the hallways are silent, and extra attention is paid to every detail. The level of anxiety and tension is palpable. Students and teachers know there is something very different about testing, and it is not at all the same as regular education.

At the very heart of traditional testing is its difference and distance from instruction; at the heart of standards-based performance assessment is its similarity and closeness to classroom instruction. If silent hallways and good breakfasts are nice things for assessment, then they are splendid things for instruction. If good instruction requires immediate feedback from teachers, student respect for that feedback, and the immediate opportunity for improved performance, then good assessment demands the same thing.

Children of all ages know the difference between what adults say and what they do, and the difference between the two displays our hypocrisy for all to see.

One of the most obvious differences between final assessments and real instruction is the issue of time. With good coaching and instruction, time is a variable and students have multiple opportunities to demonstrate success. This encourages perseverance, feedback, and success. In the typical end-of-course test, by contrast, time is limited and student achievement is widely variable. In such a system, we are measuring the speed of a student's response as much as the degree to which the student achieves an academic standard.

Why Standards-Based Assessments Are Important

There are some districts and states that have implemented standards but still maintain the "week of test terror" approach to assessment. Such a change is illusory with little impact on daily instruction and classroom practice. It is as if traditional assessments were the "emperor who wore new clothes," and after many meetings with advisors, having him wear an expensive, ostentatious tie solves the problem of the emperor's apparent nudity.

The fundamental result is the same, but those engaged in the energy and expense to adorn the emperor with a new tie failed to realize that they have not engendered a fundamental change.

Standards are closely linked with expectations, and a large body of evidence suggests that high expectations lead to better student achievement. It is also reasonable to say that expectations alone do not generate fundamental change. Standards without standards-based assessments are merely a very expensive and time-consuming pep talk, one in a string of educational initiatives and innovations that shed more heat than light.

Why Standards-Based Assessments Are Different

1. **Standards-based assessments are open, not secret.**

   One innovative program is in the Milwaukee Public Schools, where standards-based assessments have been in use for more than five years with remarkable improvements in student performance. Similar programs are also in place in several school systems throughout the nation. In the Milwaukee program, teachers are given as many as sixteen standards-based assessments at the beginning of the year. One of these will be used for the springtime assessment. Teachers are encouraged to use the assessments not just as "a practice test" but as part of their daily teaching activities. Students write, read, solve mathematical problems, and generally do things in class that they and their teachers know will be directly related to what they will be doing on the test.

   This may seem to be nothing more than common sense and clear logic, but it is dramatically different from the veil of secrecy that shrouds traditional assessments. In the classrooms in which standards-based assessments have become fully integrated, assessments happen frequently, not as a terror-filled week, but as part of daily classroom activities. The contents of the assessments are not secret, but are known by and discussed among the students. Rather than being locked in a safe, assessments are freely distributed to students, parents, and teachers, so that the expectations about performance are clearly understood by all constituents.

2. **Standards-based assessments are designed so that a large number of students can achieve proficiency.**

   When a large number of students fail to succeed at a particular challenge on a standards-based assessment, that item is not regarded as a good "discriminator." Rather, it is a signal that more work needs to be done in the classroom. Standards-based classrooms are built on a philosophical foundation that every child can learn, rather than the philosophy that every child has a fixed place on the Bell Curve from which movement is unlikely to occur.

3. **Standards-based assessments involve a demonstration of proficiency, not a guess on a multiple-choice test.**

When discussing this subject before workshops and other audiences, I will usually issue the challenge, "Will everyone who has never guessed on a multiple choice test please stand up and holler." In hundreds of workshops and speeches across the country, I have never once had a participant holler or otherwise give any other indication that they have failed to guess. This is an important point because critics of standards-based performance assessments believe that multiple-choice tests are inherently more rigorous and objective than standards-based performance assessments. On the contrary, when students have a choice of A, B, C, or D as a response, there is a 25% chance that they can guess correctly, thereby "demonstrating" proficiency on that test item when they are clearly not proficient.

In a performance assessment, by contrast, students are able to demonstrate proficiency when they have genuinely mastered the subject. This criterion would apply to problems in science, mathematics, social studies, and English. It is impossible to assess student writing with any degree of confidence by having the students take a multiple-choice test about grammar and punctuation. On the contrary, it is indispensable to assess student writing by having them write a passage designed to describe or persuade.

It is evident that the logistics of performance assessments are much more complex than running thousands of answer sheets through an electronic scanner. The supposed need for the efficiency of electronic answer sheets is based on the premise that assessments occur only during one week, and hence thousands of tests must be graded in a very short period of time. In a classroom in which standards-based performance assessments predominate, however, there is no such thing as the week of terror associated with traditional tests. Rather, assessments happen every week of the year. Teachers collaborate on grading, revising, and creating new assessments. When a school district or state conducts large-scale assessments, teachers participate in evaluating the student work so that they can have a clear idea of what other students in the same grade are able to accomplish. This becomes an important professional development activity for the teacher rather than a mindless administrative task in which bubbles on an answer sheet are compared to letters in a scoring guide.

4. **Performance assessments recognize the fact that there is not a single "right" answer on a number of test items.**

Consider the following example for first grade. It makes the point that a computer, or for that matter, a teacher, administrator, or board member who recognizes only one "right" answer would be failing to recognize student achievement. The example in Figure 4.1 is not contrived, but is taken from tests that have been administered within the last twelve months.

FIGURE 4.1
Only One "Right" Answer

Elementary Example

In this example, the first grade student was given the following story problem:

Mary had four balls. John had three balls.
How many balls did they have all together? (Show your work.)

In the traditional method of assessment, the only "right" response was the following:

4 + 3 = 7

One enterprising student, however, took the directions quite literally and responded as follows:

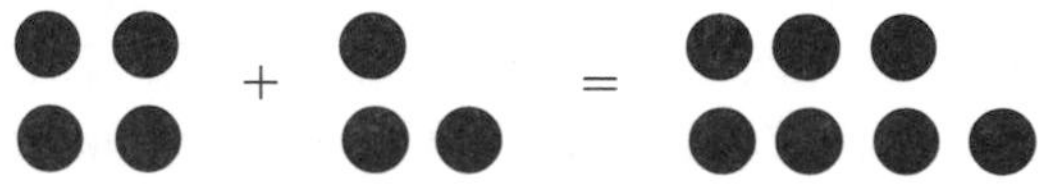

Using a traditional assessment method, the student who answered in the first manner received a satisfactory score, while the student who responded in the second manner received a failing score. Clearly both students understood the directions and responded appropriately.

---

5. **Standards-based performance assessments force educators to come to grips with this central question: What do we expect of our students?**

   If the answer to that question is, "We expect them to color in an oval with a number two pencil in a box that corresponds to the expectations of a test item writer, who may or may not have the slightest clue about the requirements of our curriculum or the conduct of our classes," then traditional assessments will fit the bill nicely. If, on the other hand, the response to this central question is, "We expect students to demonstrate proficiency in the standards that our community, our school district, and our state have established," then only standards-based performance assessments will suffice.

Self-Esteem and Assessment

Much ridicule has been directed toward assessment practices that substitute self-esteem for academic rigor. This criticism is appropriate in many cases where students have been permitted to demonstrate unsatisfactory performance and still receive rewards and recognition from teachers and schools. There is indeed a cult of self-esteem that holds that giving "bad news" about school performance can produce undue damage to

---

children. Therefore, the self-esteem of the child is elevated above the truth. Unfortunately, the response to this sort of nonsense has frequently been equally nonsensical. There are undeniably silly things that have been done in classrooms in the name of self-esteem, but the cure for this silliness is not a retreat to Neanderthal assessment techniques.

Most adults can recognize at least some moments in their lives when they actually enjoyed learning something. Typically, this was associated with their ability to demonstrate performance in something at which they were particularly good, and for which they received a certain amount of external praise and internal satisfaction. Moreover, when it was their time to "perform," they knew precisely what was expected of them. Standards-based performance assessments follow that model and, as a result, students are able to approach the last week of April not with a sense of dread at the impending test week, but rather with a sense of confidence. Ideally, students should be able to open the book of assessments and say confidently to themselves, "been there, done that," and then proceed with the assessment. Properly prepared students see nothing new in the spring assessments. They should see only a slightly different form of the assessments they have been completing every week since school began. Assessment is not a "gotcha!" In the words of one of the nation's leading performance assessment researchers, Dr. Lorrie Shepherd, assessments should be an opportunity for students to "show what they know."

The principal objective of this book is to facilitate the implementation of academic content standards by using standards-based performance assessments in the classroom and home. There is no longer a wall that divides teaching and testing, but rather assessment will become an integral part of the teaching process. Instead of being locked away in safes, tests are scattered about classrooms, lunchrooms, and coffee tables. Instead of being a subject reserved for discussion among the priesthood of psychometricians, assessments are freely discussed by students, teachers, and parents. Most importantly, everyone involved in the educational process has confidence that assessments directly reflect the standards which the school, community, and state have established. People who know what the standards are will also know what the assessments will contain. Rather than regarding "teaching to the test" as an unethical educational practice, teaching within the framework of standards is, by definition, the only sort of teaching that takes place and is directly linked to the standards-based performance assessments that students receive throughout the year.

CHAPTER FIVE

Standards-Based Assessments: How Are They Better?

Consider this hypothetical situation:

> You have just returned from a conference where you were exposed to some exciting new ideas in your field. You are anxious to share this information with your colleagues because it is good for your organization and because you genuinely believe in what you have heard. This may not be a magic bullet, but you believe these ideas will help your company, department, or school. At a meeting of your colleagues, there is not only a remarkable lack of enthusiasm, but the cynicism is palpable. Finally, it is voiced: "We've heard it all before." While a few others chuckle, another chimes in: "This, too, shall pass."

Your enthusiasm crushed, you return home wondering if innovation ever has a chance in this place.

Being enthusiastic is not enough. Ideas competing for the attention of busy teachers, administrators, and policy makers must have merit not only in theory, but also in practice. The simple question, "What is the bottom line?" must be addressed before we can expect educators or anyone else to implement standards and performance assessments. It is not sufficient to simply answer, "It is the law."

Bureaucracies, including educational ones, are notorious for being resistant to change regardless of the mandates surrounding them. Educators are, after all, part of the discipline that developed motivation theory. Therefore, it should not be surprising to them that extrinsic motivators such as carrots and sticks are far less effective than intrinsic motivational forces associated with improving the worth of teachers as professionals and as people. Thus, in an appeal to this most noble and most effective form of motivation, we consider the issue of why standards-based performance assessments are better. Why, after all, is it worth the inconvenience to change the way we have been teaching?

There are four fundamental answers to this question. The answers include fairness, specificity, feedback and improvement, and relevance. These four powerful characteristics are the prime differentials between traditional assessments and standards-based performance assessments.

Fairness

Imagine you were asked to play a game with a group of people. Unfortunately, none of them speak your language. Nevertheless, they insist that you join the game. You notice that red lines surround the area in which you are playing and that there are baskets at each end of this area. Then you are handed a ball. This group communicates with you by their expressions and inflections in their voices. From this communication you deduce that you are a member of the red team and proceed to take the ball and place it in one of the two baskets. The people on the blue team scream with delight, while your teammates look at you in disgust. You notice that the scoreboard displays the number one for the blue team. Again, you have the ball, and this time, learning from your mistake, you place the ball in the other basket. Wrong guess — the blue team is ecstatic, and the score is now two to zero. Next, one of the blue team members comes up to you and, as he takes the ball away from you, knocks you to the ground with a blow that leaves you seeing stars. Before you can get up, you notice that the opposing blue team was awarded another point, apparently for knocking you down. Three to zero. Your teammates are now screaming at you, apparently encouraging you to get back on your feet and get back in the game. You go over to the player who had so unceremoniously knocked you down a moment ago, and return the favor by taking the ball and dispatching him with an elbow to the solar plexus. Now you are sent to the penalty box and the blue team is awarded ten points. Though you cannot understand their language, you discern that your teammates have decided that you are irredeemably stupid and utterly unable to play their game. How do you feel?

If you absorb the physical and emotional imagery of this scene, you might have an inkling of what a child feels when she has brought home reams of papers with smiling faces and high marks, and then takes a test that makes her feel incompetent. You might feel like the student who has graduated from high school with a "C" average and finds out that he cannot get a job at the factory because he cannot complete the application forms and initial testing battery for new employees. You might feel like the student whose cooperative manner has earned him a "B" average in his classes in one school, but after transferring to a high school across town, finds that he is two years behind and is failing every course. You would feel cheated, betrayed, useless, and sick.

These games all have one thing in common: Their primary obligation is not to be fair, but rather to report that there were winners and losers. All of these games perform the function of dividing the participants into two groups: winners and losers.

What Does "Fairness" in Testing Mean?

For a test to be fair it must, above all, conform to the common principle that every child on every playground knows: You must know the rules before you can be expected to play the game. Yet every year in thousands of school districts, millions of children are subjected to the academic equivalent of the mystery game described above. School districts think that they are assessing these students when, in fact, they are learning little about the students' academic achievement. These tests, secretive by nature, are based on general content fields, but are not specifically linked to the curriculum, textbooks, or teaching practices in that district. Therefore, the "winners" on these tests do not demonstrate effective educational strategies, but effective guessing and test-taking techniques.

Standards-Based Tests Are Different

When standards are a public document, making clear to every parent, teacher, and student what is expected, there is a community consensus about what makes one proficient. Then the community develops a commitment to the principle that all students can achieve the standards, though there is an acknowledgment that some students will need more time, assistance, and resources to become proficient. Some students will need more help learning the language. Others will need assistance in basic skills, which their previous school did not provide. Still others may need enough food to allow them to concentrate on their lessons. But all students can eventually meet the standards. Because every student knows what is expected and precisely what the standards are, no student is ever asked to play a game in which the rules are a secret. No child becomes a loser because she guesses wrong. No child is limited to a single opportunity to become a winner. And most importantly, becoming a winner does not depend on a certain number of your classmates becoming losers. Because of the openness of the process and the public ownership of the standards, fairness is inherent in standards-based assessments.

Specificity

The national love affair with "the basics" has a certain appeal. We like to reduce things to their simple elements, such as reading, writing, and arithmetic. But as Albert Einstein wisely said, "Things should be made as simple as possible, but not more so." In fact, these "three R's" do not tell students and parents very much at all about what is expected, while content standards provide a high degree of specificity. Students will know, for example, that fractions and decimals are important for fourth graders, but trigonometry is not. They will know that by high school, they will be expected to understand the properties of plane and solid figures, and also that the understandings that students acquire in the earlier grades will lead directly to higher levels of mathematical understanding. They will also know that math alone is insufficient for their success. They must also be able to effectively communicate their mathematical knowledge in written and oral presentations. The tests these students take in high school are not a mysterious "gotcha!" but an open and public set of expectations for which students have spent years preparing.

Feedback and Improvement

While traditional tests focus on a single product, typically the answers to a set of test questions, the standards-based performance tests focus on the process of continuous improvement through feedback, reflection, focused work, and improved results. A student is not a failure if, during his first attempt to solve a problem, he writes a wrong answer. Rather, an important part of the assessment process is the revision and continuous improvement of the student's work product. One of the most powerful tools teachers can use to improve student writing is editing and rewriting. Tests that allow students to turn in only one draft of a paper (such as many of the essay tests now used in high schools and colleges) discourage reflection and improvement. Rather, such tests encourage the "Saturday night special" mentality, in which students give any assignment their best shot and then move to the next project.

Standards-based performance assessments, by contrast, encourage students to try, revise, improve, and try again. This is the process by which most scientific advancement has been achieved. We hope this process will be ingrained into those who build bridges, fly airplanes, and mend bodies. The most effective workers, from the factory floor to the executive suite, are those who systematically and consistently observe, modify, and improve their performance. Standards-based performance assessments allow students to start this process at a much earlier age.

Process and Accuracy: A Critical Combination

Critics of performance assessment have been quick to ridicule assessments in which process is emphasized because they argue that any consideration of process must de-emphasize the need for accuracy. This is an important argument and it deserves a complete answer. First, there is no dichotomy between accuracy and process; both are essential for a student to demonstrate proficiency. In writing, students must not only have the ability to demonstrate the process of creating an informative essay, but they must also spell and punctuate their essay correctly. In mathematics, students must not only solve the problem in a logical sequence using appropriate processes, but they must also solve it accurately. Any good performance assessment requires both process and accuracy, not one or the other.

Second, if there is a danger of improper emphasis associated with a test format, it is the danger that multiple-choice tests pose when they allow students and teachers to assume proficiency when the right letter is selected, while the student does not understand how the answer was achieved.

Third, our technical, professional, and leadership jobs of the future require the ability to communicate about solutions to problems. That is why the most effective math and science standards, for example, require students to communicate about the application of mathematical and scientific principles to real world problems. Calculation ability alone, or communication ability alone, are insufficient. The challenges of a technological world require students who have mastered process, accuracy, and communication about the problems they are attempting to solve.

Relevance

The tests that many students take are mind-numbingly boring and strikingly irrelevant to the worlds of work and life. It is not uncommon for employers to express shock that students are completely unfamiliar with the world of work. This is largely a reflection of the fact that so little of the language and activity of the work place has been included in school life.

Standards-based performance assessments can change this. They can provide extended assignments, challenging students to engage in real-world activities. Students in science classes do not answer questions about the chemical composition of a compound using pencil and paper. They conduct an experiment and analyze the compound. Students in an English class do not take a vocabulary test. They write an essay demonstrating that they can effectively communicate using the vocabulary words they have learned. Students in a geometry class do not write down page after page of equations involving angles and sides. They design a building showing the application of their skills.

The result is not just greater student interest, though that surely would be sufficient to justify a move toward standards-based performance assessments. Of equal importance is the rebuilding of the bridge between the business community and public education. This relationship has been almost destroyed in the past three decades as educators have regarded vocational endeavors as the polar opposite of education. As a result, business people have allowed their discontent with the products of the educational system to lead them to feelings of unrestrained contempt.

Performance assessments offer both educators and business people the opportunity to stop posturing and to identify the many areas they have in common. Teachers want to make their tests more relevant and interesting. Business people want students to emerge from school acquainted with work place expectations. Together, both parties can help to make that happen. The articulation of standards (and their associated performance assessments) is an excellent foundation upon which those conversations can focus.

CHAPTER SIX

The Role of the Classroom Teacher

It is impossible to address the role of the classroom teacher in the implementation of standards without considering the traditional means by which any initiative is communicated to educators: staff development. Not long ago, I sat at a table with a number of the nation's leading experts on public school standards. After one person spoke at length about the need for staff development in order to implement standards, the moderator, an official from the U.S. Department of Education with many years of experience in both the government and the classroom said, "If we have learned anything in the course of several decades of educational reform, it is that attempting to change behavior through staff development does not work."

Although I travel more than 300,000 miles each year to provide keynotes, workshops, and seminars for educators and school leaders, I must confess that the moderator's contention has merit: Staff development alone does not lead to educational reform. Staff development efforts in districts throughout the nation have consumed an extraordinary amount of resources of time and money, yet these efforts frequently have a minuscule impact on teaching and learning in the classroom. In fact, many professional development efforts are counterproductive, creating such resentment and antagonism among the participants that the program achieves the opposite of the intended result. This is particularly true of the all-too-typical staff development model, which is best described as a "dog and pony show" or, more recently, the "sage on the stage." In this model, an "expert" – always from a distant city – comes in and shares some theory of teaching, analysis, assessment, or other more chic term of educational nomenclature. The presentations are invariably regarded as new and exclusive, known only to the upper echelons of intellectuals, and to make the suggestion that any of these emperors might be wearing no clothes would be to brand oneself as not being sufficiently innovative or reform-minded. The participants who recognize the presentation as recycled or plagiarized must just not "get it" and lack the faith of the true believer necessary for acceptance into the inner circle. The uncritical acceptance that is offered to most professional development efforts allows even the most absurdly unprofessional exercises and wildly exaggerated claims to go unchallenged.

Most readers of this book have probably witnessed many such presentations and would concur, with perhaps a few notable exceptions. These "expert" presentations range from a blinding flash of the obvious to the patently absurd, with notions concocted by people who have not set foot in a real classroom with real children in many years, if ever. The research on recent educational innovations by Ellis and Fouts (1997) has effectively stripped some of these methods of the claim to be "research-based."

It is essential to note at the outset that, although the term staff development may be associated with standards implementation, the traditional "dog and pony show" model will not work. A substantial body of research suggests that, in the area of standards-based assessments, consistency by teachers is not achieved until they have actively participated in at least twenty hours of hands-on workshops. This is consistent with my own experience. In a five-day, standards-based assessment workshop, Monday and Tuesday are typically a mixture of chaos and resentment, with comments ranging from "This too shall pass" — one more reform effort that won't be here a year from now — to "Why are we doing this? You mean to tell me that what we have been doing for the last twenty years has been wrong?" Amidst this frustration, resentment, and cynicism, all of a facilitator's efforts are expended in maintaining a semblance of organization.

But there is a point, typically about Wednesday afternoon, when a significant breakthrough occurs. This is not a gradual process, but a threshold. The laborious process of associating content standards with individual tasks occurs more rapidly once participants become more familiar with standards. Consensus on the type of work that constitutes achievement of standards or progress towards standards is achieved more quickly. Scoring guides are worded more precisely and with greater clarity, with less dissent among the group. The difference between Wednesday morning and Wednesday afternoon is astonishing. Consistency of scoring standards-based assessments jumps from 20-30% all the way to 70-80%. This consistency, frequently labeled "inter-rater reliability," describes the relationship of the scores (ratings) among two or more judges (raters). It can be computed in a variety of ways, from simple correlation to percentage of agreement. Here the larger numbers indicate a greater degree of agreement. As participants in the seminar become more competent at the tasks before them, cynicism, while not completely absent, becomes the exception rather than the rule. Suggestions are made for innovative applications, and extraordinary things start to occur. Most importantly, there is a feeling among the participants that, with this level of initial mastery in standards-based teaching, the whole concept not only has merit, but just might work.

These breakthroughs will never happen as the result of an inspirational speech or an administrative directive. It will happen only with a commitment to many hours in professional reorientation at the classroom level. In most school systems, a five-day seminar is not possible. Thus an equivalent number of hours of faculty meetings, grade-level meetings, department meetings, and professional development sessions must be devoted to the essentials of standards-based instruction: understanding the standards, linking standards to classroom assessment, and most importantly, evaluating real student work compared to the standard. The knowledge and skills that come with such effort develop over time. The first collaborative meeting to evaluate student work is slow and agonizing; the 10th such meeting proceeds with relative ease. Most faculties, however, will never hold the 10th meeting if they conclude that, "we tried collaborative scoring once and it just didn't work." At the end of this chapter (Figure 6.1, pages 55-56) is a model staff development curriculum. Outsiders need not provide every element of this. Indeed, the best professional development experiences are those that are owned by district educators and leaders and ingrained in the local school culture.

In order for standards to make the jump from theoretical discussions during a staff development workshop to actual classroom practice, more than mere training sessions are required. The application of standards requires a commitment on the part of teachers to engage in specific classroom activities relating directly to standards. If this is going to happen, it is necessary to pull the weeds before planting the flowers. (More about pulling weeds is addressed in Chapter 13.) Where are the weeds? They are all around us. Classroom practice is typically full of activities bearing little or no relationship to the district's academic standards. To the extent that there is a link, it is more likely to be made by the publishers of workbooks or textbooks than by principals and teachers.

Student work is typically broken into discreet assignments, more remarkable for their quantity than for their quality. I cannot count the number of times I have heard teachers state, with more than a hint of resentment at even discussing the subject, that they are "of course teaching in a standards-based manner, of course teaching problem-solving techniques, and of course teaching higher level thinking skills." I then ask these teachers for a typical parent packet that contains a week of one student's papers. The packet is often full, and provides the pleasant illusion for both teacher and parent that a great deal of activity and learning is taking place. But an examination of the contents of the packet reveals otherwise. Page after page is devoted to repetitious skills that require thinking at the lowest level. Even more astonishing (and environmentally offensive) is the number of instances the paper is largely comprised of workbook directions, with only a sentence fragment or two of student expression contained on each page. The requirement to cover the subject matter leaves teachers claiming they have little choice, and their commitment to completing the workbook is one designed more to demonstrate comprehensiveness than comprehension.

While skill-building – math facts, spelling words, competence in grammar, and so on – is important in the life of every student, the question we must consider is how best to build those skills. Some drill is necessary; ask any successful music teacher or athletic coach. But the orchestra or athletic team that conducts only drills will never be ready for the performance. Successful educators must balance drills with authentic practice in which the activities of students closely match the expected results during the final performance. Thus the orchestra plays not only scales, but also real music. English teachers provide not merely grammar and spelling drills but also essays with editing and rewriting. Math teachers provide not only the opportunity to master math facts, but also the requirement that students apply these facts in the context of real-world problems.

Pull the Weeds and Prepare the Soil

If administrators wish to give educators the opportunity for the successful implementation of standards-based instruction, then they must take this pledge before their assembled faculty: "I will not ask you to do one more thing unless I first help you identify some things that we can take off the table." This may lead the first round of applause this administrator has received in a while. The clutter that dominates the classroom day is often the result of "initiative fatigue" created by successive generations of administrators whose good ideas led to greater amounts of content to be addressed in the same amount of time. Administrators who are the authors of these requirements will assert, "If we don't require teachers to cover all of this material, then we are short-changing our children!" Their motives are right, but their logic is wrong. This emphasis on coverage by teachers confuses teachers talking with students learning. Over the course of time, the amount of time allowed to teachers remains stagnant while the amount of curriculum grows, and thus the logic becomes even more distorted: Teachers must not only talk, but they must talk quickly, in order to satisfy all the administrative requirements before them.

Administrators and teachers would all benefit from asking a simple question of every activity now thrust into a school day: To what standard does this activity relate? If it does not appear to relate to an academic content standard, then one of two things is true. Either there is a grave omission in the academic standards that should be corrected, or the activity should be discontinued. Such a clear standard would appear to exclude only the pet projects that represent the idiosyncratic preferences of a teacher. While such projects do exist, my observation is that the activities devoid of academic standards are far more likely to come in the form of administrative interruptions, including mandatory assemblies, incessant announcements, and the never-ending parade of well-intentioned people who want "just an hour or two" of classroom time. Collectively these interruptions require teachers to compress the same academic content into fewer minutes.

Does the requirement that the classroom day be focused on academic standards mean that the classroom should be transformed into an academic boot camp with the teacher as a well-educated drill instructor? Certainly not. There are teachers who have devoted many hours to creative and engaging activities that involve deep studies of nature, dramatic representations of historical events, and the relationships of culture, art, music, and history. Many of these activities offer clear links to academic standards and provide models of the synergy between teacher creativity and academic focus. There are other activities, however, that have not the slightest link to academic standards. In other cases, the activities themselves may have promise, but are unrelated to the achievement level for that particular grade. Pulling the weeds is a difficult process, not unlike cleaning out an old closet or emptying a desk containing years of mementos. It can even be painful, but it is necessary. Standards cannot be effectively implemented in a classroom that clings to pre-standards activities.

Identify the Standards-Based Assessments That Will Be Used for Accountability Purposes

In order to gain an appropriate level of focus in the standards-based classroom, teachers must begin with a consideration of assessment. The essential question is this: What is the evidence that my students are proficient at a standard? If we expect teachers to consider this question, then standards must be clear and assessments must be consistent and available for analysis by educators. If the only standards-based assessments that are available are those provided by the state at the end of the year, then teachers should create them. One of the best ways to focus any school on standards-based instruction is for teachers to agree on end-of-course assessments based on academic standards. In some schools, teachers have taken the next step and created end-of-unit assessments for each academic area. Once they have agreed on the standards and the assessments of those standards, individual teachers can vary the curriculum to meet the needs of individual students. Those variations, however, will all remain within the framework of a consistent set of expectations for all students.

Identify the Best Practices in Standards-Based Teaching and Learning in Your Area

I have told audiences on many occasions that the best professional development occurs when the speaker stops talking. If we are to build a culture of success in any school, then workshops are not the answer. Rather, teachers must devote time to both learning and sharing their own success stories. This process can begin with the identification of a single area for the development of your own standards-based activities. You identify a standard, create an assessment, try it with students, and share the results with colleagues. What worked? What would you change next time? What was unexpected? In brief, what have you learned? This sort of discussion can form a part of the agenda of every faculty meeting, professional development workshop, and collaborative meeting at any grade level. The discussion of what teachers learn from assessment makes clear that we assess students not merely to evaluate them, but to improve the entire process of teaching and learning. This may appear to be a slow and tedious process. A reasonable goal is that over the course of four years, teachers might be able to analyze thoroughly the curriculum for which they are responsible. While such a time horizon may seem intimidating, we should ask this question: Where will we be in the process of standards-based education four years from now if we do not start the process one assessment at a time?

Have Students Express Standards and Scoring Guides in Their Own Words

All too frequently, the language of standards and scoring guides is a professional one, designed to allow one educator to speak to another. It is much more important that these standards come alive for our students. One of my favorite examples appeared on a bulletin board in a first grade classroom in a small rural community of a western state. This teacher, among the most professional standards-based teachers I have witnessed, asked her students to put the standards into their own words. The students had, accordingly, identified what they needed to do to get a rating of 4, 3, 2, or 1 representing exemplary, proficient, progressing toward the standard, or not meeting the standard. On the board was the note "I get a 2 if I squish my letters like a fuzzy worm." I have yet to meet a psychometrician who was able to write with such precision.

Conduct Weekly Reflective Evaluations of Your Classroom Practice

Whenever a major change is taking place in one's professional or personal life, the activity of writing reactions, reflections, and observations is invaluable. Too often educational evaluation has focused only on test scores. An essential part of the standards movement is that our concept of effectiveness and our framework for evaluation extends far beyond test scores alone, and includes levels of student engagement in the process, levels of teacher passion for the process, and levels of innovation through the process. Keeping a journal is an excellent means of conducting such an introspective evaluation.

Identify a Small Group With Whom Your Successes and Challenges Can Be Shared

A faculty meeting can provide the forum for this, provided that the administrator will stop the silly practice of reading announcements and devote the time to serious reflection on teaching and learning. In addition, schools should provide opportunities for teachers who are committed to standards and who share a common professional interest to meet on a regular basis. A group of four to six is ideal. Fewer than that does not provide for sustainability, while greater than that number can tend to become overly bureaucratic, with too much listening and not enough sharing.

Share Your Successes With Others

The foundation of effective implementation of standards is the periodic publication of best practices by schools and districts. Effective teachers are willing to contribute to this process. There is no question that there are a variety of impediments to the implementation of standards or to any educational reform. The ones I hear most frequently are lack of support, lack of resources, lack of parental involvement, and so on. But the proverbial bottom line is this: No amount of policies, workshops, and consultants is worth the effort or resources if they are expended on things that do not change classroom practices or do not implement standards at the classroom level.

FIGURE 6.1
Staff Development Curriculum

Knowledge and Skills Required for Teachers	Professional Development Seminar Description	Result
Understand the importance of standards and how to assess in a standards-based environment	*Designing and Developing Standards-Based Assessments* (Two 6-hour seminars)	Participants create a complete standards-based assessment, including four tasks with a scoring guide for each task. The assessment can be immediately used in the classroom and shared with colleagues.
Understand the layers of standards, from general academic content standards to specific classroom requirements	*Unwrapping the Power Standards* (One 6-hour seminar)	Participants begin with an academic content standard and identify the essential questions that must be asked by the teacher and answered by students to provide evidence that the standard has been achieved.
Understand and apply effective teaching strategies in the standards-based classroom	*Effective Teaching Strategies in the Standards-Based Classroom* (One 6-hour seminar)	Participants understand the research foundation behind specific strategies for effective teaching, practice these strategies, and immediately apply them in the classroom.
Understand the relationship between test data at the state, district, and classroom levels and successful curriculum and teaching practices	*Data-Driven Decision-Making* (One 6-hour seminar)	Identify specific goals for student achievement, teaching strategies to achieve those goals, and measurable indicators that allow educators to provide monthly evidence of student improvement.

FIGURE 6.1 (continued)
Staff Development Curriculum

Knowledge and Skills Required for Teachers	Professional Development Seminar Description	Result
Understand aspects of writing instruction and how to establish a cohesive professional development plan to address needs of teachers as they learn effective teaching strategies	*Writing Excellence Part I: Administrators/Curriculum Leaders* (One 6-hour workshop)	Participants understand the research supporting program development and learn what teachers and building principals need to be able to establish and sustain either district or school changes related to improving student achievement in the area of writing.
Understand aspects of writing instruction, assessment, analytic traits, best practices, and effective teaching writing strategies in content areas	*Writing Excellence Part II: Teachers* (Two 6-hour workshops)	Participants understand the research supporting specific and effective instructional and assessment techniques.
Understand and prepare for writing instruction using modes (Persuasion, Descriptive, Expository, Narrative)	*Writing Excellence Part III: Teachers* (One 6-hour workshop)	Participants acquire specific knowledge of different modes of writing, how to create meaningful writing prompts for students, and how to critically assess student writing.

CHAPTER SEVEN

The Role of the Principal

Principals today are under siege. While teachers feel overwhelmed with the multiple demands of students, parents, and administrators, principals must respond to all of those constituencies and more, including central office leaders, state legislators, and community activists. When the suggestion is made that these men and women should be the educational leaders of their schools, some scoff and reply, "I spend from 7:00 a.m. until 7:00 p.m. on paperwork and discipline. If I'm not completely exhausted at that point, perhaps I'll devote an hour or two to instructional leadership."

Despite their workload and the intense pressure of their jobs, principals have an enormous impact on the school environment. A number of studies, as well as careful observations by people who have spent much of their professional lives around schools, confirm this fundamental truth: Even when the budgets, faculty, and students are the same, a change in a single person, the principal, can have a profound impact on the morale, enthusiasm, and educational environment of a school.

Seven Steps for Principals

Principals who believe in the promise of standards can have a dynamic impact on making standards work. If the implementation of standards is regarded as just one more initiative from the central office, it is unlikely to result in more than the most superficial response. The paperwork will be completed, but the classroom will be unaffected. This chapter suggests seven practical steps by which effective school leaders can jump-start the standards implementation process:

- Understand the standards
- Identify faculty leaders
- Create professional development opportunities
- Assess student progress
- Analyze classroom activity
- Recognize outstanding performance
- Reflect, revise, and improve

Understand the Standards

First, take time to become acquainted with your state and district standards, particularly those relating to the grade levels of your school. Perhaps your first reaction will be, "We're already doing this!" If so, great. Then you can use standards as a tool for communicating with parents and the public about what you are teaching. However, you may notice that in some of your classrooms there are differences between what is actually happening and what the standards describe. Some teachers in your school may also note that their textbooks do not include all the content described in the standards. Noticing these disparities is an essential step toward becoming a standards-based school. If you have not already provided every faculty member with a complete set of state and district standards, you should take immediate steps to do so. It is also up to the principal to carefully distinguish between claims to standards adoption and the real thing. Teachers who are simply tough and award high grades sparingly may or may not have "high standards." It is possible that these teachers simply have tests and instructional practices that result in a small number of successful students. A commitment to standards implies that the teacher is creating and using techniques that allow all students to meet standards, not maintaining the status quo in which only a few students are expected to do so.

Before plunging into professional development activities, the first step is to relax, sit down, and read the standards. Everyone in the building should have a working knowledge of the standards. This is a time-consuming process because teachers need to know all the standards, not just those for their grade levels. It is very important for teachers to place their instruction into context. What will be expected at the next level of education? What should have been done before the student came to my class? Finally, it is important to share the standards with students and parents. This certainly does not mean mailing a copy of the typically voluminous state standards document to every parent. Rather, the principal should facilitate the transformation of state standards into clear language that is provided in small pieces – not more than a page at a time – for distribution to parents. In a single page, the document could include a standard, what it means, how we teach it, how we test it, and an activity that parents could do to help students master that particular standard.

Identify Faculty Leaders

Experienced principals know that when implementing any change, the top-down method (changes mandated and enforced from the management) is rarely effective. Rather, systemic change occurs when faculty members emulate the success of their colleagues. It is, therefore, essential that the principal identify faculty leaders who have already accepted the principle that standards-based education is appropriate, important, and vital to the health of our schools. Take some time to nurture these leaders, and ensure that they share a common vision with you and the leadership of your district.

It is important to note that the faculty leaders in standards may not be the traditional faculty leaders who have been committee chairs and organizational leaders in the past. Rather, you want to identify innovative leaders. These are people who lead others not with the power of personality or organization alone, but with the power of ideas. Neither age nor experience is a criterion here. Teachers almost invariably know who the most effective educators are. Effective educators are the ones who earn respect and, ultimately, emulation. If you are new to the building and want to find out who the most effective educators are, just ask; you are likely to find a strong consensus of opinion.

There are some faculties in which the teachers with the most influence are not those who promote excellence and equity, but who safeguard the past and create roadblocks to change. They have been treated well by the Bell Curve and actively oppose standards and, in particular, they oppose the hard work that is involved in helping all students to succeed. When faced with such opposition, I have seen too many principals throw up their hands and sigh, "They've got tenure, so there really isn't much I can do." I wonder what the reaction of the principal would be if the school nurse decided that vaccination standards were unimportant or if the food service staff decided that hygiene standards were just another passing fad. At some point, the principal decides that standards are not optional because the health and safety of students and staff are at risk when employees ignore standards. The question that principals must ultimately resolve is this: Do students who fail in school expose themselves and the community to greater health and safety risks? Ask a high school counselor about the health and safety risks facing dropouts. Student success in school is as serious as vaccination in the nurse's office and hygiene in the cafeteria. If the principal regards standards as important in those areas, then standards are important in the classroom as well. Thus the search for faculty leadership must focus on the leaders who are not merely influential, but who are committed to the best interests of students through the promotion of standards-based education.

Once you have identified these faculty leaders, they must be nurtured and appreciated. Although extra money is seldom available to recognize exceptional performance and risk-taking leadership by faculty members, you can find a number of other means to nurture and appreciate faculty leaders. Time for collaboration (perhaps facilitated by the principal taking the class for a couple of hours), extraordinary professional development opportunities, letters of recommendation for awards, public recognition of ideas and programs, and personal notes and letters are all ways in which effective principals show their appreciation for faculty leaders. Principals know better than many people how lonely leadership can be. When teachers are willing to accept the burden of leadership for the implementation of standards, the teachers deserve support, empathy, and every bit of assistance the principal can manage.

Create Professional Development Opportunities

If we have learned anything in the past few decades of ill-fated educational reform efforts, it is that professional development in the traditional form has not worked. This used to mean hauling all faculty members into a meeting, entertaining them, pleading with them, finally ordering them to "reform" and, at last, sitting by helplessly while things continue to function just as they always have.

Standards-based professional development opportunities must be different. First, these opportunities do not occur in isolation, but must be part of a curriculum (see Chapter 6). Second, professional development is not uniformly provided to every teacher, but rather different levels of professional development are provided to different teachers depending on their background and familiarity with standards. The sample Staff Development Curriculum (Figure 6.1) can be of great help with this. By the end of a two-year cycle, every teacher should have completed the learning objectives of such a curriculum, but not every teacher will have necessarily participated in every element of the curriculum. By taking the time to allocate professional development resources based on the needs and backgrounds of teachers, you not only grant these people the professional respect they deserve, but you also conserve scarce staff development resources.

Assess Student Progress

The most certain way to kill a standards-based approach to education is to establish a wall between standards and assessments. Such a wall is erected when school leaders spend the months of September through March talking about standards. Then, in April, they make students and teachers endure the same tests they have always taken – tests that may or may not be related in any form to the content standards you have been swearing will be the core of educational practice in your school.

To show that standards-based assessments are truly different, do not wait until April to start assessments. Ask every teacher in the building, over the course of the next month, to develop just one standards-based assignment (see Part Four for several models). Then allocate plenty of class time to complete these assignments. Identify how well your students are performing on just the standards associated with this assignment. If this is started early in the school year and continues throughout the year, a persuasive case can be made that the traditional "week of terror" associated with tests is irrelevant, inappropriate, and dispensable. You will also be able to make the persuasive case to parents and policy makers that by eliminating those tests, you are not reducing the amount of meaningful assessment in your school, but increasing it by a wide margin. Documents such as the Standards Achievement Report (see Chapter 9) can also help you make this case.

Analyze Classroom Activity

One of the best school superintendents I know, Dr. Stan Scheer, astounded his colleagues (and, he might admit, himself) when he put himself on the substitute teacher list for his district. In this way, he learned more about what was happening in his district's classrooms than he would have learned in a thousand committee meetings and formal presentations. He learned how hard teachers work, how profound the social and familial problems were, and how primary-grade teachers simply never have a break during the morning hours – not even to use the restroom! During the typically brief observations that administrators usually make of classrooms, there is always some activity going on. But during the sort of extended observations made by Dr. Scheer, it was also obvious that a lot of time is wasted by the interference of outside forces, and even some of the planned activities did not really relate to the educational objectives of his district.

I know what you're thinking. The problem with spending so much time in individual classrooms is that it wouldn't give an administrator enough time to plan and think. On the contrary, it was only by spending extended time in the classroom that Dr. Scheer was able to think systematically about what was really happening in the classroom. These hours allowed him to encourage teachers to challenge themselves to pull the weeds before planting the flowers – that is, to identify classroom activities that can be eliminated in order to make room for substantive standards-based activities. Teachers tend to listen to a leader who has walked in their shoes not years ago, but days ago.

It is fair to note that some leadership professors object to the idea of a school leader getting so involved with individual classrooms. They believe that there is a "role" assigned to the principal and superintendent, and that a violation of that role intrudes on the teachers' areas of responsibilities. It might even indicate that administrators who choose to make such extended observations do not trust the teachers. Such a view, in my judgment, does not conform to today's classroom reality. My conversations with thousands of teachers and hundreds of administrators indicate that the traditional assumptions about the role of school leaders must be challenged. Effective decisions require accurate information, and the statistics delivered to principals and superintendents are not sufficient. There is no substitute for personal observations of hours, not minutes, of classroom time.

You will not analyze classroom activities with a questionnaire or a faculty meeting. You need to be there, without pager or cell phone, completely present in the classroom, down on the floor if necessary, interacting with students and teachers, and perhaps even reminding yourself why you entered this profession in the first place.

Recognize Outstanding Performance

In the course of analyzing classroom activities, many wonderful things will happen, but perhaps the best is that you will have the opportunity to immediately recognize and appreciate outstanding performance. You probably already have some teachers who regularly fill in the gaps left by textbooks and who have developed multidisciplinary assignments that are engaging, interesting, and absorbing for the students. You will see creative ways of dealing with incessant interruptions and disturbances, and you will see an intense focus on academic achievement. Because these images are so contrary to the public image of the classroom, it is imperative that you recognize and publicize these educational heroes. If your work rules and resources permit it, monetary rewards are nice. But never underestimate the power of the personal note, the public recognition, the picture sent to the newspaper, or the commendation placed in a personnel file. Administrators are required to find the time to fill a book with paper when it comes time to reprimand or fire a teacher; a commendation takes only a single page.

Reflect, Revise, and Improve

Principals must walk the talk of standards. One way of doing this is to reflect systematically on how far your school has come, and how far it has yet to travel down the road toward standards implementation. A public display of your "standards implementation report" and a visual indicator of the progress since your last report a few months ago will send an important message. This message says very clearly, "I am expecting students and teachers to be accountable for the implementation of standards only after I have become accountable for their implementation." The seven steps in this chapter are just the start, but they are the first steps on a very rewarding journey.

CHAPTER EIGHT

The Role of the District

Superintendents and board of education members have some of the most difficult jobs in the country. Their tenures are notoriously brief and their public esteem is frequently low. Their critics include people who are quite convinced they could do the job better themselves, but who typically have not spent a millisecond in the shoes of the school leaders and policy makers they so vehemently criticize. When board members and superintendents accept the challenge of implementing standards, they have done far more than simply give their approval to the latest educational reform initiative. They have, instead, committed themselves and their districts to comprehensive and rigorous courses of action which will influence teaching and learning for decades to come. This chapter outlines six key responsibilities of superintendents and board members as they seek to make standards work.

Ownership

Standards cannot be the exclusive product of the outside. Instead, standards must have broad ownership from every major constituency within the community. Even if your state has already adopted standards, each local district typically has the responsibility and the opportunity to develop its own standards that are at least as challenging as the state standards.

The constituencies that should be represented in the standards development process include, at the very least, the following: teachers, parents, community members, business owners and managers, colleges and universities, groups representing significant minority populations in the community, unions, and school administrators. The local history of your district may dictate the inclusion of other key interest groups. In many communities, for example, the American Association of Retired Persons (AARP) is a key voting group for school bond issues, and it would ill-behoove any school district to exclude this group from any major educational policy initiative. Indeed, research on school bond elections indicates that support from the population frequently hinges on a clear understanding that voting "yes" will result in clearly understood educational results. Community ownership of standards is an excellent means to achieve this broadly based understanding.

Congruence

The superintendent and board of education must ensure that the policies they implement involving standards are congruent with other policy initiatives undertaken by the school system. In fact, the litmus test for every other educational initiative in the district should be, "Does this conform with our commitment to standards?" This means that in the selection of textbooks and assessment instruments, conformity to district standards is essential. I know of one district in which a national assessment instrument vendor reviewed every single item in the assessment to determine the correspondence of those elements to the district's standards. This is in marked contrast to the bland assertions of textbook and assessment vendors that their products are "standards-based." In fact, most textbooks and other curriculum materials are designed to meet the requirements of a great many states and thus provide overwhelming amounts of material for any individual teacher. The district leadership should specifically authorize curriculum directors, principals, and classroom teachers to use textbooks as a guide, not as a script. In the end, instructional leaders and educators are not responsible for the words they say but the results they achieve, and thus the senior leadership makes it clear that there is a difference between delivery of prescribed material and the mandate to help all students achieve academic standards.

Congruence must also be assured in personnel decisions. As superintendents and other senior administrators contemplate the hiring, promotion, and tenure of teachers, administrators, and other key decision makers, the issue of standards must be part of these conversations. There are a number of fine teachers and administrators who do not believe in standards or who believe that they are a passing fad of minor significance. There are many places in the country for these people to work, but your district should not be one of them. Because this statement can be regarded by many as inflammatory, let me elaborate.

Standards are not just a good idea. They are essential if we are to achieve our national promise of equity and excellence for all children. If a school had a math teacher who was completely competent, but who sincerely believed that Hispanic children could not do algebra, few superintendents or school boards would hesitate to terminate the teacher. When it comes to matters of blatant discrimination, few people would argue, "Every teacher has the right to an opinion, and all opinions on the mushy field of education are equally valid." In this hypothetical case, we would conclude that competence in math is not enough, and that the teacher must also be able to teach all students without prejudice.

What about a teacher who refuses to take a standards-based approach to education? Is this just a matter of personal opinion and professional independence? If we accept these tired claims based on a twisted notion of professional independence, then any teacher can say, "I can teach the math, and it is the students' responsibility to learn the way that I teach." If such a statement is equated with academic freedom and professional independence, then there is little recourse against the teacher who explicitly confesses a prejudice based on ethnicity or gender. In sum, teachers have a responsibility to teach all students and leaders have a responsibility to make decisions based on the best interests of students. If we fail to lead decisively, then teachers who took the risks and endured the work of implementing standards will soon get the message that the words of their leaders are not congruent with their actions.

Congruence is also essential in the use of external evaluations. The discipline of educational evaluation has too frequently depended on the notion of expertise. This leads to the model in which the designated "expert" evaluates a program based on her individual understanding of what is good and proper rather than the criteria of the district. In a standards-based district, however, the standards have already set the criteria for evaluation, and hence every external evaluator should be expected to develop familiarity with district standards. More importantly, it should be clear in every Request For Proposal (RFP) for external evaluations that the standards of the district – not the personal beliefs and prejudices of the consultant – will be the definitive guide for the evaluation.

Experimentation

One of the most frustrating things for superintendents and board members is the feeling of utter impotence as they implement a policy initiative and then watch as nothing happens. Harry Truman remarked that when General Dwight Eisenhower assumed the presidency, Ike would be immensely frustrated by the contrast to his military days in which every order was followed by a salute and an action. As president, Truman observed, the most powerful man on earth is frequently powerless in the face of the immovable federal bureaucracy.

Systemic change rarely occurs as the result of an order, a resolution, or a policy. Rather, changes in complex systems occur when the multiple key decision makers (in this case, teachers, principals, students, and parents) decide that the new initiative is in their best interest. This conclusion will be reached most frequently by these many decision makers, not on the basis of a persuasive speech by the superintendent, but rather by their direct observations of the use of standards in classrooms and schools they know to be effective. As a result, the use of a pilot program is an important first step for standards implementation at the district level. During the pilot program, you can document your success, gathering testimonials from teachers, students, parents, and administrators. You will have a ready-made answer for every challenge, question, and inevitable complaint that "these ideas just won't work here."

Superintendents are typically action-oriented leaders – that is how they became superintendents. Some of them, along with many board members who must stand for reelection in a short period of time, might ask, "If standards are so great, why not simply implement them throughout the district immediately? A pilot project just seems like a waste of time!" This question deserves a serious response.

1. **Pilot projects create enthusiasm among the key faculty leaders and principals.**

   The best educational innovators in your district have probably already been implementing some version of standards already, and it is essential that they be on your team.

2. **Pilot projects allow the initial bugs to be worked out of a system, which lowers the costs due to errors.**

   Many initial drafts of standards, including those approved at the state level, contain important omissions. Other drafts are not as clear as they should be. The pilot project allows a district to have the second draft of standards implemented on a district-wide level, with the omissions and ambiguities corrected prior to large-scale implementation. Experienced computer users know that you "never buy version 1.0 of anything." The same applies to district-wide implementation of standards: First, work out the bugs with a pilot project.

3. **The justification for pilot projects is leverage.**

   There is an enormous professional development process involved in standards implementation (see Chapter 6). This challenge can best be achieved through the use of teachers teaching teachers. The participants in your pilot project will have local credibility and direct experience in making standards work in your district. In addition, the use of outside consultants can be focused on a fewer number of schools in workshops of a manageable size.

4. **Pilot schools provide an ideal long-term source of mentors for student teachers.**

   Few teacher-training institutions are providing any in-depth preparation for standards-based performance assessments. If this is a skill you expect teachers in your district to have, then it is essential that you build that expectation into the student-teacher training program. It is also important that student teachers are not assigned to mentor teachers who are not actively conducting their classes in accordance with the district's academic content standards.

5. **The use of pilot programs gives the district leadership the opportunity to provide public recognition and rewards for those who are leaders in the standards movement.**

   To create systemic change, you must change the system of rewards. This includes not only appropriate remuneration for the extra meetings and time that a pilot project entails, but also includes public recognition, professional development resources, and special consideration for promotion and advancement. One of the most certain ways to effectively kill standards implementation in your district is for the leadership to talk about the wonders of innovation and academic standards, and then give the Teacher of the Year award to the person whose class had the best test scores on an assessment not related to your district standards.

Support: Time, Money, and Protection

Requests for support probably constitute 90% of a superintendent's in-box. Standards implementation requires support in three specific ways: time, money, and protection. Management theorist Tom Peters has remarked that if he wanted to see what a leader's priorities were, he would look no farther than the leader's calendar. If the days were consumed with meetings and presentations, then the headquarters staff (invariably large) would be devoting its time and resources to preparation and elaborate presentation for those meetings. If, by contrast, the days were largely consumed with community associations, boards, and public posturing, then the leader was probably using the organization to promote his own image rather than using his leadership skills to promote the organization. Finally, if the leader was spending time doing what the organization actually did (make cars, sell toys, teach students) then, (and only then) was the leader devoting the precious resource of time where it belonged.

Time

Surely no superintendent can get through many days without meetings of some kind. But my observation is that too many school leaders are captives, rather than controllers, of their calendars. If school leaders are to provide the time essential for standards implementation, they must devote significant amounts of time for teacher collaboration. This is not simply a longer "planning period," but rather a specifically structured time in which the specific elements of student performance standards are reviewed. Some school districts that are successfully implementing standards devote two to four hours every week to this effort. Just as Peters advocates a minimum of four hours each week of "management by wandering around," the superintendent focused on standards should similarly allocate a minimum of four hours each week to the subject of standards. Some of this time could be spent watching teachers in a pilot project struggle with their evaluation of student work. Other hours could be spent with members of the business community improving their understanding and support for the standards movement in the district. Still other hours could be spent in extended classroom observation, sitting on the floor with some second graders.

The superintendent must be able to articulate what makes a standards-based classroom different. In one standards-focused district, the superintendent required every senior district-level administrator, including himself, to create and teach a block of standards-based instruction. This leader is putting his time where his rhetoric is.

Money

Support for standards by the district also means money. Specifically, standards implementation requires blocks of time (typically half a day per week) for teachers to review student work, create scoring guides, and create new standards-based assignments. Allocating this time will cost money. Given the workload of most teachers, their pursuit of graduate degrees in their non-working hours, their family responsibilities, and the stress associated with a normal school day, it is unreasonable to expect that this half-day block should occur after the school day or on weekends. (I have seen some effective standards implementation teams do this, but the participants ended the school year physically and mentally exhausted.) The best course of action is for the district to provide either long-term substitutes or other organized activities for the classrooms of these teachers so that the teachers can spend these half-day blocks at a consistent time and day. They can then devote their full intellectual energy to the hard work of standards implementation.

Protection

Finally, the support required of the superintendent and board is that of protection of the champions of standards. The resistance to standards implementation can be formidable and emotionally draining. This is particularly true at the secondary school level, where some students will spend more hours and take more classes than has traditionally been the case in order to meet their requirement to demonstrate proficiency in all of the district standards. With more hours devoted to academic content standards, there will be fewer hours devoted to non-academic pursuits. Inevitably, some non-academic classes and popular extracurricular activities will suffer.

Rather than allowing a destructive division to occur between academic and non-academic faculty members, effective district leaders must make clear that there is not such thing as non-academic faculty members. Every teacher, activity, class, and requirement makes a substantive contribution to the achievement of standards by students. Teachers who effectively integrate academic content standards into their classroom activities need support and protection from the cynics who will always allege that some activities are outside the realm of standards. In the standards-based district, there are no such activities.

Leading Reluctant Followers

When a district changes its orientation from seat time to the achievement of standards, it often takes more time for many students to achieve these standards. This leaves some teachers, parents, and students asking, with quavering voices, "Do you mean to tell me what I've been doing all these years isn't valuable because it doesn't meet the district's new standards?" The only response to this query is, "Your work is indeed valuable, because every class and activity including yours (for example drama, music, art, woodworking, etc.), will now be linked to an academic standard. How can you enrich this class so that it will help our students achieve standards?" Some teachers and parents will respond, "But this just isn't an academic class, and never has been!"

Faced with absolute intransigence, the superintendent and board must unhesitatingly make the decision to eliminate those activities or to do them in a strikingly different way. Such a position may make some educators, particularly those who have viewed their fields as non-academic, very apprehensive. Upon further reflection, however, educators in music, art, physical education, technology, and other areas that have been inappropriately stereotyped as nonacademic frills should be delighted that their classes will at last be recognized as possessing academic content and value. They know from experience that many students (particularly those who are kinesthetic learners) can learn fractions, decimals, ratios, and many mathematical standards in home economics, industrial arts, and music classes. There are many students who will learn these standards far better in such a hands-on class than they will in a traditional abstract math class. But some programs supported only by tradition and popularity, rather than a commitment to the achievement of standards, will have constituencies ready to conduct a wholesale attack on the standards movement.

The effective superintendent and board will have no choice but to take swift and sure action to protect the champions of standards from these attacks and, ultimately, to eliminate inappropriate, unproductive, and wasteful activities from the district.

Focus

The final obligation of district leadership is focus. Initially, the school board should consider seriously a one-year moratorium on any new initiatives in the twelve months following the implementation of standards. Implementation of standards is a mammoth project and no complex system should attempt to undertake multiple major changes, particularly if there is a risk that some of the changes are contradictory. In addition, the board and superintendent should build into every agenda a progress report on standards implementation. This should specifically include an action report at the building and classroom level, where particularly effective examples of standards implementation can receive a high level of recognition and appreciation. Just as many board agendas begin with the Pledge of Allegiance and public recognition, so the standards-driven district will give consistent attention and priority to reports of successful standards implementation.

The leadership must ensure broad community ownership of standards. The content of meetings includes more than the words of the participants. Public wall charts in the board and superintendent meeting rooms, containing standards achievement reports for the district and individual schools, will also send a powerful message as these documents receive wide public attention. To implement standards effectively, educational leaders must do more than pass resolutions and articulate policies. They must insist that all policies of the district are congruent, and that the district standards are the filter through which all other policies must pass to ensure a high level of consistency. Leaders must experiment with the early phases of standards implementation and use pilot programs to demonstrate the effectiveness of standards in their district. Support by leaders, including time, money, and protection, is essential in the standards-driven district. Finally, leaders must focus on standards, not only by eliminating distractions, but also by providing consistent attention, in meeting agendas and environments, to the district's focus on standards.

CHAPTER NINE

Measuring Standards Achievement

In a standards-based system, the Standards Achievement Report becomes a useful supplement to the traditional report card. In some cases, the Standards Achievement Report can be used in place of the report card. Given the emotional attachment many parents and communities have to traditional grade cards, school leaders are wise to introduce the Standards Achievement Report as a means by which teachers can provide additional meaningful information to students and parents rather than as a disruption of traditional letter grades.

Why the Standards Achievement Report?

If letter grades were serving the purpose of clear and accurate communication about student performance, no supplementary information would be necessary. Unfortunately, the traditional report card suffers many of the same deficiencies as norm-based assessments. These deficiencies are particularly pronounced for teachers who have been trained (or perhaps required) to grade on the curve. In such cases, teachers do not assign grades on the basis of student performance alone. Rather, they assign grades on the basis of a comparison of student performance to other students. In other cases, the traditional report card does not rely on norms, but simply upon the teacher's judgments regarding the student's ability, along with test results, homework assignments, classroom behavior, timeliness of assignments, neatness, and other matters that inevitably enter into the recipe for determining grades. Can the implementation of standards help make this document more meaningful and less terrorizing? I believe so. As an alternative to the traditional report card, consider the use of the Standards Achievement Report in Figure 9.1.

The Accountability Imperative

Parents demand many things from public schools. Some are reasonable and some are not. It is reasonable, for example, for parents to demand that schools provide their children with challenging and decent educational opportunities. It is manifestly unreasonable, by contrast, for parents to demand (as an astonishing number do) that schools provide their children with values and morals, but, they quickly add, "Make sure you don't talk about any political, religious, ethical, moral, or value issues with which I disagree. And while you're at it, make up for the neglect the child suffered during the first five years of life, straighten out his behavioral problems, and for goodness' sake, do something about his terrible table manners!"

This caricature only slightly exaggerates the frustrations felt by many teachers and educational leaders when dealing with public sentiment, which often borders on contempt toward education. Perhaps the most reasonable demand of parents, however, is that schools provide a coherent response to the question, "How is my child doing in school?" I submit that sending home the mysterious results of a norm-referenced test on the last day of school is close to educational malpractice. This leads to meaningless exchanges such as, "I got a 136. What did you get?" and damaging conclusions such as, "You missed the program (perhaps gifted and talented, resource room, learning disabled, and so on) by only one point. We are so sorry." As reprehensible as is the technique of summing up a child's educational attainment with a single number on a test, the use of the traditional report card is not much better. Saying that Matilda's math performance is a "D+" suggests that she has some work to do this summer, but also suggests that she passed and is ready for the next grade. In fact, the "D+" could mean one of several things. Our conversations with teachers reveal that a final grade of "D+" could mean, among many other things:

- Matilda received average grades of 76 on all of her homework assignments and tests.

- Matilda does not understand the material at all, but she tries very hard, behaves well in class, and her earnestness has impressed the teacher so that a passing grade is appropriate. The "D+" is the teacher's attempt to provide Matilda with some self-esteem, which the teacher understands is important for "slow" children like Matilda.

- Matilda excels at math and is perhaps the brightest student in class. But she repeatedly turns in her homework assignments late and is missing some assignments entirely. The point system used by the teacher, which was announced at the beginning of the school year, penalizes students for missing assignments. "Matilda is just not responsible," the teacher concludes, "Perhaps getting a 'D+' will teach her a lesson."

- The teacher simply does not like Matilda, and Matilda makes it quite clear that the feeling is mutual. This, of course, is the explanation most frequently embraced by students who receive low grades.

The list could go on and on. Parents frequently do not know what a "D+," or any other grade, really means. The conventional letter grade system certainly does not answer the question "How is my child doing?" Moreover, the system for awarding grades might include student behavior, timeliness, neatness, and many other considerations. The grading system may change drastically from one class to another. Thus the notion of adding grades together to arrive at the much-vaunted GPA (Grade Point Average) makes as much sense as averaging the number of pounds of weight, inches of height, and points of IQ to come up with an HCA (Human Characteristic Average). Howard Gardner has articulated the theory of multiple intelligences. His theory suggests that there is a multiplicity of intelligences, including spatial, musical, and interpersonal intelligence, to name a few. His research also indicates that there is no relationship between the IQ as measured by traditional intelligence tests and the existence of other types of intelligence. Daniel Goleman has articulated the idea of emotional intelligence and offers persuasive evidence that this is more important for future success than traditional test scores. Perhaps, the cynic would suggest, we should average grades, IQ, emotional intelligence, and a score on each of Gardner's intelligences to describe student performance. Such a computation would be meaningless and would never be taken seriously. Yet educators frequently compare the incomparable – grades from different classes – without substantial questioning about their intended meaning.

A Better Way: The Standards Achievement Report

If report cards and grades fail to respond to parents' reasonable demand for accountability, then what is the answer? Several schools across the country are using the Standards Achievement Report as a supplement to, or replacement for, the traditional report card. An example of the Standards Achievement Report is provided in Figure 9.1.

Ideally, the Standards Achievement Report should be printed on a file folder, with the four surfaces of the folder allocated to the four core academic areas of language, math, science, and social studies. Inside the file are documents – assignments, assessments, teacher observations, student reflections – that support the conclusions in the Standards Achievement Report on the surface of the folder.

Figure 9.1 provides an example of what one page of the report might look like. Across the top of the table are the standards that are most important for student success. This is not a comprehensive listing of every standard, but those that the teachers in this school or district know to be the most important. In the left-hand column are the assignments, assessments, and activities that were evaluated by the teacher. Some assignments indicate student proficiency in many standards, while others assess student proficiency in only a few standards. By reviewing the columns, students, parents, and teachers can quickly determine where the student is strong and where the student needs additional assistance. When this report is used as a supplement to the traditional report card, two students might both receive the same letter grade, but have quite different levels of standards achievement. In the example in Figure 9.1, the student is quite proficient in most of the academic content standards, yet deplorable in his ability to get work handed in on time.

In a realistic Standards Achievement Report, several columns will be blank, indicating that the student has not yet attempted this standard. But, by the end of a course of study, each student should have completed every one of the listed standards (not every conceivable state standard, but only those most important ones listed on the Standards Achievement Report) with a rating of proficient or higher.

The use of the Standards Achievement Report does not necessarily require more effort by classroom teachers. Consider the number of marks in Figure 9.1, and then compare that number to the typical number of marks in the traditional grade book in which each student's scores are listed in a line. Teachers make literally thousands of marks in their grade books, particularly at the secondary level. Unfortunately, the details of this documentation are rarely shared with parents, and the circumstances of such sharing are typically when a grade is challenged. In that case, the teacher offers abundant evidence to support the grade. When the Standards Achievement Report is used, teachers communicate proactively with students and parents.

From a building and district point of view, the aggregate of Standards Achievement Report data will allow administrators to identify with far greater precision the strengths and weaknesses of their curriculum and instruction programs. For example, rather than simply having a grade point average for middle school math students, administrators will know that there is a particular problem in the study of ratios and decimals in fourth and fifth grade classes. Instead of hearing reports of failures by ninth grade English students, curriculum strategists can identify issues in vocabulary and written expression in sixth and seventh graders. This makes the Standards Achievement Report a most effective tool for professional development and data analysis.

What About Behavior?

One of the most frequent criticisms of the standards-based approach to education is that it emphasizes the achievement of standards without appropriate emphasis on the behavior of students. If a student is proficient in quadratic equations but never turns in assignments on time and is uncooperative in class, should the teacher be allowed to reflect dissatisfaction with such a student? Of course, parents should certainly know if their child is disorganized, late, uncooperative, or unpleasant. But they will rarely gather such information by intuition or through the mechanism of the traditional report card. Behavioral standards can be made explicit in a Standards Achievement Report just as academic standards can be explicit. If, in our earlier example, Matilda excels at math but not in the category so rarely observed in today's report cards, deportment, then the Standards Achievement Report allows the teacher to be explicit about Matilda's strengths and weaknesses. Moreover, such specificity helps avoid the tragedy of placing very bright students in remedial classrooms because their grades are low, only to discover (typically much later) that low grades reflected boredom, distraction, or breaches of decorum, rather than intellectual deficiencies.

This is Too Hard!

Another frequent criticism of the use of the Standards Achievement Report is that it is too detailed, time-consuming, and difficult. Precisely! Assessing the educational achievement of a child is detailed, time-consuming, and difficult. Two observations might help overcome this objection. First, teachers frequently have the documentation to justify the grades they assign. The vast majority of teachers are not arbitrary and capricious in their grading policies, but the documentation of precisely what lies behind the "B" or "D+" is frequently known only to the teacher. Thus no matter how rational the grading policy might be, if it is shrouded in mystery, it appears irrational to parents, students, and the public. I would argue that if the documentation is readily available (and it usually is whenever a grade is challenged), then it makes much more sense to provide it in a format that makes clear how the student was evaluated.

Second, it is disgraceful that emotional and professional energy, as well as extraordinary financial resources, are inappropriately allocated to programs for children whose educational achievement has been "diagnosed" through poor grades. Thus we have the spectacle of school districts in which more than 50% of ninth grade students take an introductory math course more than once because a student who receives a "failing grade" must take it again to meet grade-based graduation requirements. Anecdotal evidence suggests that the vast majority of students (teachers estimate more than 70%) who repeat introductory high school math classes fall into one of two categories: those who were never prepared in the first place for the class, or those who failed because of attitudinal and behavioral reasons. In the case of the first group of students (those not prepared), a Standards Achievement Report from the previous year would have made it clear why the student required more preparation. Even if the student had a "passing grade of D+," the Standards Achievement Report would make clear why the student needed more preparation. It was not necessary to waste a year of time and resources forcing the student to receive a failing grade in order for him to finally get help.

What about the students with attitude and behavior problems? A Standards Achievement Report would document that their math proficiency was acceptable, but their conduct was not. Therefore, the appropriate strategy for these students is not to reinforce their bad behavior by allowing them to repeat the process of rebellion, but rather to place them in a class with a math content that is more challenging, using instructional strategies designed for disruptive students.

What About Parents?

Perhaps the greatest advantage of a Standards Achievement Report is the opportunity for parents to participate in the educational process of the child in an explicit and tangible way. Report cards typically provide a small space for the parent to sign the document and, occasionally, to provide one or two sentences of comments. Such opportunities for parental feedback usually expire in the late elementary grades. An effective Standards Achievement Report, by contrast, will include two critical pieces of information for parents. First, the report makes clear what standards the student has yet to achieve. Parents thus have the opportunity to do much more than say, "Do more math homework," but can work with their children on specific content areas. Second, the parents have the opportunity not only to sign the document, but also to apply some standards to themselves.

Another page of the Standards Achievement Report folder might look something like Figure 9.2. The Standards Achievement Report folder sends the clear message that parents are critically important members of the educational team, and they should be as reflective about their own contribution to this team as are students and teachers. In this part of the report, parents respond to such standard questions as, "I review homework with my child every day," or, "I limit the amount of television my child watches on school nights."

While parental responses are not a component of student evaluation and are not intended to be intrusive, they can help a teacher understand whether or not there is at least minimal engagement by parents in the educational performance of the child. Such a list also allows the parents to model for their children the importance of accountability and goal setting. The Standards Achievement Report reinforces the instrumental role of the parent in the educational success of the child.

Obviously, the content will vary with the age of the child, but it is my contention that if schools expect more parental involvement in the education of students, they must do more than ask parents to attend meetings, sell candy bars, and support the athletic teams. Rather, they must seek the direct involvement of parents in the daily educational activities of children.

Too frequently, the standards movement has been discussed only among administrators and teachers. The use of the Standards Achievement Report transforms the movement to one involving parents and students in a meaningful and tangible way. It makes standards a part of daily classroom practice as well as a part of the conversation between students and their parents. And, perhaps most important of all, it makes the parental contribution to education explicit and accountable.

The Most Important Rule: Tell the Truth

In the course of my many opportunities to speak with groups of teachers, administrators, and parents, I am often asked to sum up the most important element of my standards and assessment philosophy. This book has 26 chapters, reproducible handouts, and sample performance assignments, and much remains unsaid. Nevertheless, when challenged to be concise about what effective standards and assessment are all about, I respond with three words: "Tell the truth." That is, indeed, the essence of effective standards and assessment. We tell the truth about what we expect of students. We tell the truth about the differences between their present performance and those standards. We tell the truth about the time and effort required to close that gap. And we tell the truth about the progress that students make toward the goals the community has established. Neither cryptic statistics nor percentiles nor evasive platitudes nor bromides about student self-esteem can meet this simple test of truth. Only a clear and direct statement about expectations and performance can meet such a test.

Unfortunately, the truth hurts. Many schools have officially established their expectations of student performance, but tremble at the thought of telling the public about the difference between those expectations and the reality of student performance. They say that they want accountability, but what they report is a hodge-podge of test scores only distantly related to the standards that the community has adopted. Standards and assessment are inextricably linked. Standards without new assessments, new report cards, and new accountability systems are little more than castles in the air – lovely to contemplate but utterly without a foundation.

For school leaders and policy makers, telling the truth about standards, expectations, and performance will be difficult, but it might sound something like this:

"We expect every student to read complex directions, write persuasively, and calculate compctently. We expect every teacher to apply consistent standards, evaluate student performance accurately, and coach students with diligence and compassion. We expect every parent to support teachers and students in their mutual quest for excellence. And we cannot afford, nor will we tolerate, practitioners or leaders who believe that failure is inevitable. We know that if a choice must be made between essential truth about student performance and the subordination of our standards to convenience, we will choose truth, however inconvenient, unpopular, or challenging it may be. We didn't engage in a rigorous program of academic standards because it was popular or because it was a fad. We took this course because it was the right thing to do. Educational progress can never happen without truth as its foundation, and it is to the wonderful truth of student potential and the challenging truth of student performance that we are unalterably committed."

FIGURE 9.1
Sample Standards Achievement Report

Washington High School
Standards Achievement Report 2001-2002

Student Name: Alex Roseman   Class: Biology I   Teacher: Sackett

E = Exemplary; **P** = Proficient; **IP** = In Progress; **N** = Not Meeting Standard

Please note: A complete description of all standards and assignments is available from the instructor and on our web site: www.washingtonhigh.org/sackett.

Assignment	Standard 1: Biodiversity	Standard 2: Genetics	Standard 3: Cell Structure	Standard 4: Environmental Interrelationships	Standard 5: Explains Scientific Conclusions	Standard 6: Teamwork	Standard 7: Submits Work on Time
Lab 1	P			P	P	E	N
Analytical Paper 1	P				P		IP
Lab 2		P			P	E	IP
Analytical Paper 2		P			P		IP
Lab 3			E		E	E	N
Analytical Paper 3			E		E		IP
Synthesis 1	P	E	E		E		IP
Lab 4				P	P	E	IP
Analytical Paper 4				P		P	IP
Lab 5		P		P	P	E	N
Analytical Paper 5		E		E	E		IP
Lab 6				P	E	E	P
Analytical Paper 6				E	E	E	P
Synthesis 2	E	E	E	P	E		P

Explanatory note: Not every assignment encompasses every standard, but every assignment addresses several of the most important standards for this class. Moreover, the teacher has clearly identified that there are both academic and behavioral standards for students. This particular report is the profile of a student who is "proficient" or "exemplary" in every academic standard, but who displays a rather consistent inability to turn work in on time. The feedback that is provided by this report is far more revealing than the letter grade.

FIGURE 9.2
Standards Achievement Report, Parent Contribution

Parent Contribution

Standard	Never	Sometimes	Always
We/I review homework every day.			
We/I restrict television viewing on school nights.			
We/I enforce a bedtime on school nights.			
We/I read with our child at least three times a week.			
We/I encourage our child to write letters.			
We/I discuss current events with our child at least once each week.			

Comments:

CHAPTER TEN

Validity and Reliability in Performance Assessments

The fundamental requirements of any assessment in any form are validity and reliability. Although these terms are used quite commonly, they are frequently misunderstood. The purpose of this chapter is to identify what validity and reliability mean in the context of standards-based performance assessment.

Validity and Reliability: What Is the Difference?

In order for a measure to be reliable, it must be consistent. For example, imagine that I am stepping on a scale at the doctor's office. The first time I step on the scale, it shows that I weigh 250 pounds. The second time I step on the scale, just a moment later, it shows 200 pounds, and the third time I step on the scale, it reads 150 pounds. This lack of consistency, or lack of reliability, means that the physician was using an unreliable instrument – in this case, a faulty scale. The diagnosis might have ranged from obesity to anorexia, depending on which reading of the scale the physician decided to use, and thus the use of an unreliable scale could have very serious consequences. The greater our reliance on a single reading from a single scale, the greater the risk of grave error due to the lack of reliability. Because the consequences of an unreliable scale can be so significant, reliability is the first issue when considering any measurement. No matter how valid the reason was for learning about my weight, the use of an unreliable scale removes any utility that the physician might have gained from taking such a measurement.

The analogy is appropriate. Teachers, administrators, and policy makers have good reasons for wanting to know if students and schools are successful, just as the physician has good reasons for wanting to know the weight of a patient. The quality of their reasoning behind a request for information, however, does not legitimize any measurement. Only those measurements that consistently – that is, reliably – provide information are worthy.

Too frequently, in the context of education, we allow our desire for information to overwhelm our inhibitions against using faulty and unreliable instruments. Because we earnestly want to know how a student performs in mathematics, we administer tests without asking whether or not those tests provide us with information that is reliable. We justify the use of terrible tests because we want to know the information and we have been directed by the political powers to determine how students are performing in mathematics. After all, the label on the booklet said "math test" just as the label on the instrument in the doctor's office said "scale." But we cannot evaluate the reliability of the instrument based on its label or our need for information. Rather, we must evaluate the reliability of the instrument based on its demonstrated consistency in providing information to us. With no changes in my food consumption, I should be able to mount the scale three times within a few minutes of each other and get very similar results. Likewise, I should be able to administer the math test to the same individual and, regardless of other influences on that person, get similar results. If I do not, then I do not have a reliable instrument.

If the physician prescribed medicine or surgery based upon an unreliable instrument, it would be unwise. If the physician denied me the opportunity to participate in an activity because of the reading on an unreliable scale, it would be both unwise and unfair. If teachers and school administrators made decisions based upon measurements that are inconsistent, they are as unwise and unfair as this physician is. It happens every day. Students qualify for special programs and activities or are denied opportunities based on grades or tests that are inconsistent and that represent the idiosyncratic judgment of a single teacher or individual test. Reliability is not merely a statistical nicety, but an absolute requirement in any educational system that values fairness.

How Do I Determine if an Assessment Is Reliable?

In the context of multiple-choice tests, there are many measurements of reliability, including the popularly used Cronbach's Alpha. In general, when this statistic exceeds .8, test administrators conclude that the test is not perfectly reliable, but is sufficiently reliable for educators to make reasonable inferences from the tests. If the reliability coefficient were lower than .8, then most educators would be wary of drawing any conclusions from such an inconsistent scale.

In the context of performance assessments, we should adopt the same standard. While perfect reliability never happens, it is reasonable that educators demand a reasonable degree of consistency, or 80%. In practice, this means that when ten teachers look at a particular piece of student work and use the same scoring guide or rubric, eight of them come to the same conclusion about whether the student work is proficient or non-proficient. If the level of agreement is lower than 80%, then we do not chalk it up to academic freedom and call it a day. We call it what it is: an unfair and unreliable assessment that must be improved if educators are to draw any meaning from it. In performance assessments, reliability of lower than 80% means that we must reexamine the scoring guide, make it more specific, discuss how the teachers applying the scoring guide are using it, explore any implicit expectations of the evaluators that are not part of the scoring guide, and reduce these sources of ambiguity until we achieve 80% agreement.

Collaborative Scoring: The Key to Assessment Reliability

Many schools have invested significant time and resources to allow teachers to collaborate. The problem is that they have not carefully defined what "collaboration" means or how this time is to be used. The single most important use of collaborative time is the focus on assessment using real student work. Collaboration is hard work, and few educators will achieve 80% agreement the first time that they sit down to look at the same piece of student work. If fairness is a core value, however, we must persevere in this collaborative exercise until we achieve this standard. Assessments without fairness are worse than no assessments at all. Fairness will not be achieved without reliability. Reliability will not be achieved without collaboration. And collaboration will not happen without a consistent commitment of time and intellectual energy by educators and school administrators. Time for collaboration can be found in faculty meetings, staff development sessions, grade-level meetings, department meetings, and a host of other opportunities that teachers have to meet with one another. These opportunities cannot be wasted on the reading of announcements or other one-way communication; every opportunity for collaboration should be seized and applied to improving the consistency with which educators and school leaders evaluate student work.

Reliability Is Not Enough

Unfortunately, even the most precise scale is insufficient if what I really want to measure is my blood sugar. If I had a scale that scientists assured me was "reliable" to within one millionth of a pound, it would not do my doctor much good if she were attempting to identify problems with my eyesight, my blood sugar, malignant tumors, or any number of other ailments that were not related to my weight.

Our use of reliable (that is, consistent) tests in education is similar to a student getting on a very accurate scale and the teacher saying, "Hmmm – 106 pounds – this student must be very good in social studies." When the shocked parent alleges that the instrument being used has nothing to do with the social studies knowledge of the student, the teacher, supported by a gaggle of salesman, specialists, and administrators in the "Department of Scales" at the school district, might emphatically retort, "But this scale is very reliable! We have tested it, and the consistency is 99.9%!"

The principle is clear: However reliable a scale may be, if we are not measuring the right thing, we will come to faulty conclusions. Often conclusions regarding admissions into special programs, certification of competency, and (perhaps most importantly) first impressions of teachers, are based on instruments having about as much to do with intellectual ability as would a measure of the student's weight. The statistics (which cause the eyes of parents and teachers alike to glaze over, and are frequently associated with multiple choice tests) are almost invariably reliable, but reliability is not enough.

Validity: Are We Telling the Truth With Assessment Results?

Validity means that we are testing what we think we are testing. Academicians have developed a number of other labels to complicate this issue including ecological validity, construct validity, consequential validity, and so forth. Those issues are beyond the scope of this book. Rather, we are focusing on the classic definition of validity as a reflection of the intended measure. In some cases, we can create measures that precisely reflect what we expect. To continue the example of the doctor's scale, if we want to know how much a patient weighs, we can express that in pounds or kilograms. But if we want to know whether or not a patient is obese, then we must use the measurement from the scale as one of several measurements from which we will draw an inference about obesity. We would, at the very least, need to know the patient's height, body mass, and other information in order to come to an accurate conclusion about the issue of obesity. The same is true with regard to blood tests and many other medical procedures. The question being asked is not simply, "What is the white blood cell count?" Rather, the question is, "What does the white blood cell count, along with the results of a number of other measurements, indicate about this patient's general health?"

In the context of education, test results are similar to the white blood cell count: They represent one of many measurements that give the educational physician some insight about the general intellectual health of the student. For example, when a student takes a multiple choice math test, what are we measuring? Is it really a reflection of the student's mathematical ability? Consider the case of the student who is, by the account of a teacher who has observed the student for many years, a brilliant mathematics student. Unfortunately, this teacher is from Moscow and the student's primary language is Russian. The only alphabet the student has ever studied is Cyrillic. We give the student fifty math story problems all in English, all designed to test whether the student is capable of third grade mathematics. The student achieves a score of 25%. This is not a surprising result when the student was guessing randomly among choices a, b, c, or d. We give the student a test again, because the results of this test are at such variance with what the teacher had claimed about the student's great mathematical ability. This time the student scores a 24%. We administer the test yet again, and the student scores a 25%.

The Refuge of Test Experts: Great Reliability, Lousy Validity

What can we conclude about this test? First, some might conclude that this was a very reliable instrument because it provided consistent results every time the student stepped on this particular intellectual scale. However, we also know that this was an invalid instrument to test the student's knowledge of mathematical ability. It might have been somewhat more valid if the purpose of the instrument was to test the student's understanding of English or, for that matter, the student's ability to guess consistently. The choice of instruments that are reliable but not valid, like the example of the Russian student taking a math story problem test, occurs frequently in American schools. Because of students' difficulties in vocabulary and reading on standardized tests and, worse yet, because of students' difficulties with time management, organization, and low grade-point averages, we draw all sorts of inferences about their intelligence and potential. We fail to recognize that the testing instruments involved are tests of neither intelligence nor potential.

How would you have designed the math test for the Russian student differently in order to make it more valid? First, we might have the questions translated into Russian. This would be a good first step, but perhaps would not fully explain all the story problems. Suppose, for example, a math story problem attempting to identify knowledge of ratios and decimals refers to someone as a "0.333 hitter." That has meaning to the American fifth-grade baseball fanatic, but it does not help her Russian counterpart in the least. Our questions that refer to yards and pounds may have meaning to the student in the United States who is used to such concepts, but does not test the mathematical ability of her Latin American counterpart who uses meters and kilograms. In other words, translation is not enough if the questions still contain a cultural context that is alien to the student taking the test.

Cultural Bias in Testing and Assessment

Second, we must address the issue of the cultural environment of the question. This includes a detailed analysis of the examples and settings used in the questions. In addition to considering such issues as measurement and the cultural context of the activities being described in the story problems, we must also consider the language involved. A recent problem from a nationally administered test helps to illustrate the point. Students were asked to distinguish the difference between hatch and hold. As every student from the Midwest knows, hatch is what chickens do and hold is what one does with a new puppy, a friend, or a loved one. The designer of this test, however, having grown up on the east coast and attending summer camps in which yachting was one of the required activities, expected every child across America to understand that hatch and hold were parts of a sailing vessel.

Is this just political correctness? Whenever the question of cultural bias is raised in test questions, the defenders of the test inevitably respond that reform efforts are simply hypersensitive and attempting to be politically correct. If our goal is accurate measurement, rather than political issues, then this is an easy matter to address. The previous examples were clearly not measuring what we intended to measure. This is not an issue of politics, but an issue of accuracy and measurement. If we expect to be able to improve the education of children, then we must first have accurate diagnoses of their successes and weaknesses as learners. That will not happen when we rely exclusively on consistent but irrelevant measures.

How Do I Determine If an Assessment Is Valid?

The following steps may be helpful to provide assurance to teachers, parents, and other constituents that assessments pass the test of validity:

1. **Specify the content area to be assessed.**

   This is more easily said than done. Anyone who has undergone the exercise of establishing content standards for academic areas knows that saying, "a student will learn math," means saying little more than, "the student will go to school." We can only validly assess an area that has been described with some specificity. It is reasonable to test the content area that requires students to "describe the issues for and against the ratification of the constitution." It is irrational simply to expect students to "know American history."

   The description of content requirements is a complex, arduous, and (inevitably) political task. This is because it requires dissecting a subject into its component parts so that teachers and students can understand what is expected of them. It is inevitably political because it involves making choices. Describing anything as political has assumed the negative connotation of arbitrary and capricious choices, as in "he is being very political." The fact is that we must make choices on a political basis in a democracy. For example, it involves deciding whether or not algebra is a higher priority than band. Because a commitment for all students to learn algebra may require the allocation of resources (including books, teachers, and classroom time) to classes that will provide an opportunity to learn algebra, there may not be enough resources for other things which have traditionally been in the curriculum. This is a political choice because it involves allocating resources based upon the wishes of the majority of voters in the school district. If we do not specify content areas and allocate resources accordingly, then our standards are likely to become relatively dull, useless additions to the library.

2. **Use multiple measures to establish the validity of an assessment.**

   Let us return to our medical example, in which we are drawing inferences about a patient's condition based on a variety of different tests. We have not announced the diagnosis of cancer, for example, based upon a count of white blood cells alone, but rather based upon a variety of different instruments, including laboratory results, x-rays, magnetic resonance imaging, physical examination, and so on. When many of these methods of assessment provide similar (but not necessarily identical) information, then we can conclude that we have valid instruments. If, on the other hand, four measures provide consistent results, but the fifth measure indicates otherwise, then over the course of time, we may wish to challenge the validity of that fifth measure.

   In the context of education, validity can be established by using multiple instruments and methods. Standards-based performance assessments, such as those contained in Part Four of this book, would be a good place to start. In addition, classroom observation, group work, peer observations, independent exercises, and even multiple choice tests (if they are not the only assessment method) can also help to provide the multiple methods of assessment necessary to validly describe the content knowledge a student has demonstrated.

   The notion of using multiple assessment methods is a critical one. The greatest danger of the movement towards standards and alternative assessments is that teachers simply replace one set of worksheets with another set. It remains the same "drill and kill" mentality, and classroom teaching practice has not fundamentally changed. One bad test is replaced with another bad test. Teachers who are committed to documenting the performance of their students must be willing to incorporate a variety of assessment techniques into their ultimate evaluation.

3. **Validity can be established by tests administered to random samples of students.**

   The nature of performance assessments is inherently individualized, yet school districts frequently have a legitimate reason for wanting to establish that there is a uniformity of content area, even though there may be a wide diversity of assessment techniques. Rather than invest time and resources on tests for every student in a district, random samples of a standardized instrument can be administered on a district-wide basis. These can help indicate whether the results reported by teachers from their performance assessment are consistent with the results of another instrument.

Assessment and Accountability

The hallmark of an effective assessment system is that it is itself assessed by the end users, including the board of trustees, the public, and other constituencies. Too often, this assessment of assessments has broken down with anecdotal evidence, such as the complaint that "Item number 34 is dumb!" rather than a rigorous and systematic evaluation of validity and reliability. School leaders do not need to become statistical experts to ask these two questions: 1) Are we using assessments that are fair and consistent? 2) Are we using assessments that test what we think we are testing?

If standards-based performance assessments are to change the way we think about student evaluations, then the advocates of these assessments must be willing to subject them to the same thorough evaluation to which they subject multiple-choice tests. This implies that performance assessments are living documents that evolve over time, are modified by teachers, and are based on feedback from students, parents, and other constituents. The scoring guides will become more precise; the directions to students will become clearer; the scenarios will become less culturally biased; and the language will become more inclusive. This is not a threshold that, once crossed, allows the advocates of performance assessments to become complacent. It is rather a continuous process of improvement, reflection, collaboration, and yet more improvement. I cringe every time I hear school leaders and teachers excuse unreliable and invalid assessments because, "After all, these are performance assessments so they are pretty subjective." Such reasoning plays into the hands of performance assessment critics who believe that the only objective test is a nationally standardized multiple-choice instrument. If we want to increase the extent to which performance assessments are used in schools, then we must embrace standards of quality for every assessment, not flee from them.

In short, assessing the assessment is a lot of work. However, if we fail to provide a foundation of validity and reliability for the assessments we create, then everything else in the standards movement will be built upon a foundation of sand. If, on the other hand, this foundation is strong and constantly in the process of becoming stronger, then the advocates of standards-based performance assessments will be able to withstand the inevitable storms that come their way.

CHAPTER ELEVEN

The Role of National and State Standards

The Myth of National Standards

One of the more frequent complaints of those who oppose academic standards is that the standards movement is an effort to remove local control from the schools. Let us put aside the issue of whether local control is a salutary policy. Consider the Tenth Amendment to the U.S. Constitution, which assigns all unspecified powers to the states. Consider also the two hundred years of tradition in which the local pharmacist, businessperson, and farmer have much more to say about what happens in a typical classroom than does any national group (including the U.S. Department of Education). Certainly the national government exercises some authority over school districts on areas such as the prohibitions on racial discrimination and the provision of federal funds. For example, recently enacted legislation requires that school systems must test students in reading and mathematics once each year. For those districts that are already providing reading and math tests at least once a year, this federal requirement will have no impact. On the broad issues of curriculum, instruction, assessment, and standards, however, the authority of the local school district and the various states remain paramount.

Several groups have attempted to promulgate national standards, but these documents are, in fact, little more than national suggestions. Some of these projects, such as those developed for mathematics, have been exceedingly helpful and have guided much of the standards discussions at both state and local levels. Others, such as the proposed history standards, have become the objects of ridicule for opponents of any national educational reform movements. Interestingly, this debate has been focused more on the specific content of these standards than on the fundamental notion of whether or not there should be a national consensus as to what children should learn. As this debate continues, however, the standards established by states and by local school districts are the only binding documents that exist in the field.

The United States is almost alone among industrialized countries in failing to adopt national academic content standards. The nations that routinely score higher than the U.S. in national academic assessments have much more organized national educational systems. Many of these nations have assessments and learning expectations that are published at the beginning of each school year in the nation's leading newspapers. Every parent, teacher, and student in the country knows what is expected in terms of academic performance. The national tests, typically administered in the spring, offer few surprises, as the content is directly related to these well-publicized learning objectives.

Pseudo-Standards: Textbooks and Teacher Preferences

In the absence of clear national standards, two sources have filled the vacuum: textbooks and teacher preferences. Textbook companies, for all practical purposes, define the curriculum in many schools. Teachers presume that if they have covered the book, then they have also covered the subject. To be sure, some textbooks are excellent, with challenging content, engaging illustrations, clear writing, and many suggested classroom activities that make learning the subject interesting for both teacher and student. The best textbooks also include a multidisciplinary approach, integrating social studies, language arts, science, and mathematics. Unfortunately, such excellent textbooks are the exception rather than the rule.

Many textbooks used in the public schools today are dreadful. Teachers who have served on textbook committees will testify to this: Texts omit critical skills, are excruciatingly boring, and (in some cases) are blatantly inaccurate and biased. An example would be the history texts in which the biases of the authors are frequently phrased in a declarative manner, as if their attribution of motives to national leaders were journalism rather than opinion. Independent researchers have discovered an alarming number of factual errors in science texts. These texts, with all their faults and biases, have become the standard in districts that have not adopted content standards. The bias in many textbooks leads to one of the great ironies of the standards debate: The right-wing opposition to national standards leads to a vacuum that is then frequently filled by left-wing textbooks.

Teacher Preferences: The Standard for Districts Without Standards

The second pseudo-standard is the combination of the opinions and preferences of the classroom teacher. To a very large extent, teachers have an extraordinary amount of autonomy with regard to the content and rigor of their classrooms. Thus, some students emerge from the fourth grade with a sound background in mathematics that would meet or exceed most state standards. Other students, whose fourth grade teachers were more comfortable in language arts, emerge from the fourth grade without essential math skills they will need in later grades. Some teachers have frankly admitted to me that they simply "do not like fractions" or "do not like grammar" and thus omit those items from their curriculum, or at best give them only cursory attention. These essentials are frequently replaced with subjects, projects, and activities that the teachers find interesting, regardless of how irrelevant these preferences might be to the learning needs of the students.

One elementary school teacher in a Midwestern state devoted three weeks to teaching his class about the internal combustion engine. Certainly there are wonderful opportunities to use the internal workings of an automobile to teach science, math, English, and social studies. And wonderful standards-based assignments could have been developed around this subject. In this case, however, the teacher simply loved working on cars. The students watched, usually somewhat mystified, as the teacher took apart and reassembled an automobile engine, occasionally drawing on the blackboard notations that might as well have been hieroglyphics. No one challenged the teacher about the content of his class; it was, after all, the teacher's domain. The teacher was popular with students, parents, and administrators because he maintained a well-disciplined classroom. The students were always average or above average on standardized tests, so the illusion of academic progress was added to this stultifying educational environment.

This example is hardly unique. Instances abound in which scores of hours of precious classroom time have been given over to performances, exhibitions, field trips, and the favorite extracurricular activities of the teacher, none of which had a remote relationship to the academic content needs of the students.

From Anarchy to Balance

Many people fear that the implementation of standards will suppress the teaching techniques of creative teachers who have, over the course of many years, developed popular and useful classroom activities. However, standards are not a pedagogical straightjacket. Instead, they create very broad boundaries within which thousands of creative teaching ideas can flourish. Consider the example of the teacher who loved cars. Students could have rotated in small groups to examine parts of the workings of the engine in some detail. In the math/science group, they could have learned about the relationship between air, fuel, and combustion energy, as well as tackled math problems involving acceleration and braking. In the social studies group, the students could have learned about the air pollution control devices attached to cars and what role national legislation played in environmental safety and product liability. In the English group, students (informed by all of their experiences in this project) could have written expository and persuasive essays about the future utility of the automobile and the internal combustion engine.

In the standards-based school, the teacher retains immense autonomy, but not complete autonomy. As in all situations, there are limits. Surely if it is reasonable to ask a teacher not to show an X-rated movie in a classroom, then it is also reasonable to ask the teacher to create assignments which correspond to the district and state standards. One of the most frequent questions I receive from principals and superintendents is, "What do I do with the teacher who just won't implement our standards?" I wonder what the principal would do if a teacher were to engage in other activities that were destructive to children and clearly at odds with district policy. Would these behaviors be regarded as issues of academic freedom? Would a teacher, even with tenure, be permitted the latitude to conduct a class in a way that was hostile or unavailable to minority students, girls, or students who were ill-prepared by their previous classes? Although persuasion, education, and coaching are all preferred ways of dealing with reluctant teachers, experience tells us that some people will constantly test every leadership decision. If the school board will go into paroxysms of anger over the viewing of an inappropriate movie during a class, then surely a similar amount of indignation should be applied to teachers who refuse to engage in the best practices the district has to offer with respect to standards-based teaching and assessment.

Standards as a Filter for the Extraneous

Perhaps the most volatile issue involving standards is the application of standards as a filter for extraneous activities. I am not aware of a single school district in the world with unlimited resources. Virtually every administrator and policy maker with whom I have spoken in the past several years has lamented the need to cut one program or another. Standards can provide a framework in which such resource allocation decisions can be made.

For example, some school districts have academic content standards relating to statistics, and yet there is not a single statistics class in the math curriculum. The traditional math classes in these schools rarely include the statistics content mentioned in the state and district standards. The same district, however, has dozens of classes in psychology and sociology, and yet there are no standards associated with these subjects. A "knee-jerk" response might be to fire the psychology and sociology teachers and hire more math teachers. But a more reflective response might be for an administrator to say this:

> "There is no such thing as a class in this district that does not help students meet our academic content standards. That does not mean we will stop teaching psychology and sociology. Rather, we are going to teach these subjects in such a way that every one of these classes includes several of our academic content areas. In our psychology classes, students are going to learn about the design of psychology experiments and the analysis of their results. Consequently, this class will help our students achieve our standards in statistics. In our sociology classes, students will analyze

demographic trends and their influence on our population. This will help students learn about statistics and will help them achieve many of our social studies standards as well. The more different ways we can find to teach students in a standards-based manner, the better prepared our students will be to demonstrate proficiency in all of our standards."

When standards are seen less as a limitation and more as the external boundaries of a very large and creative environment for teaching and learning, then schools can preserve and encourage the creative energies of teachers. At the same time, these schools can insist on relevance and meaning for every hour in the classroom and every class in the curriculum.

PART TWO

Making Standards Work in the Classroom

CHAPTER TWELVE

Collaboration: The Key to Effective Staff Development

In theory, collaboration is wonderful; some would say it is so obvious it requires little attention. Collaboration sounds warm and cozy, perhaps even a natural practice for professional educators. In practice, however, collaboration is hard work. It requires risk-taking, vulnerability, and the ability to articulate one's point of view in front of potentially critical colleagues. Above all, collaboration in the context of professional development requires a commitment to the principle that no educator is an independent actor and that our students depend upon the commitment of their teachers to be consistent and fair. In brief, we collaborate not because it feels good, but because our commitment to fairness and effectiveness demands it. The collaborative model of staff development is far less common than the prevailing models described in this chapter. While the "Dr. Fox" and "Tai Chi Disco" models that follow may appear to be caricatures, most readers who have been sentenced to vacuous and counterproductive workshops will recognize that crossing the gulf between the promise and reality of effective professional development will require exceptional commitment and effort by all concerned.

Alternative Models of Staff Development

The "Dr. Fox" Model

There are three prevailing models of staff development. The first of these is the Dr. Fox Model, named for a famous series of experiments in educational evaluation studies (Naftulin et al, 1973). A gentleman was introduced to the medical students before him as "Dr. Fox," an eminent expert in his field. His entertaining presentation was utterly without substance, yet it garnered significantly better evaluations than did those hapless presenters who offered substance without entertainment. Most teachers would agree this is the most common staff development model in American schools today. Despite pleas that "we don't need to be entertained," and "we want to be treated as professionals," presentations that offer a subtle mix of the vapid with the humorous, all covered with a heavy dose of patronizing sympathy, seem to be the order of the day in many districts. Administrators seem surprised when their formidable investments in staff development fail to result in changes to classroom practice.

The "Tai Chi Disco" Model

The second type of staff development model I shall label the "Tai Chi Disco" model. At sunrise throughout China, hundreds of people gather in the parks and other public places to go through a series of exercises, collectively known as Tai Chi (formally known as Taijiquan). The exercises involve slow, graceful movements promoting flexibility, coordination, and strength. Even though it may take place in a public setting with hundreds of other people engaging in very similar movements, it is clear to the careful observer that this is an individual exercise. In modern China, however, many young people (accompanied by quite a few Westerners) have attempted to "improve" Tai Chi by engaging in movements to the thumping beat of disco music, transforming the graceful and individualistic movements of their ancestors into lock-step bump-and-grind. Every participant, regardless of individual background, physical capacity, or personal preferences, engages in the same movements to the same music at precisely the same time.

In the Tai Chi Disco model of staff development, the new idea of the day is presented by someone who carries the aura of a Zen Master and presents to true believers the latest version of some insight. I have seen such presentations include comical misquotations of supposed oriental masters, when the correct attribution might have been Shirley MacLaine rather than Lao Tzu. These staff development models focus on adopting a common vocabulary and philosophy, accepting the content of the seminar as the true path of enlightenment. This type of development is particularly divisive, creating a chasm between those who "get it" and those who do not. Worst of all, the research upon which these charlatans rely is frequently nonexistent, and the anecdotes often turn out to be repeated folklore, with a few names and details changed, casually floating from one conference to another.

Both the Dr. Fox and the Tai Chi Disco models of staff development have a common focus on two key points: the performer and the immediate feelings of the participants, rather than results of the instruction. Of course, they rarely need to be concerned with results, because the presenters are long gone when the real work of implementing their philosophies of teaching and learning takes place. There is rarely follow up, and hence there is rarely responsibility. The ink is dry on their paychecks long before anyone asks if these educational emperors are wearing any clothes.

A Better Way: The Collaborative Model

The third model of staff development is the collaborative model. It is certainly not as neat or nearly as entertaining as the two other models we have discussed, but it is the only model offering the opportunity for sustainable systemic change in a school district. There are four distinct characteristics of the collaborative model: First, this model depends to a much smaller degree on the "guru" whose transient presence is the hallmark of the other two methods, and to a much larger degree on teachers teaching teachers. When outside assistance is engaged, it is not for a "one-shot dog and pony show," but to further a continuous and integrated curriculum focused on the needs of the district. The advent of interactive video communications technology has made national experts available at an economical price for many school districts. For less than the cost of a single day of the entertaining but vacuous Dr. Fox, a district can offer an in-depth, integrated, year-long professional development curriculum.

Second, the collaborative model depends upon context. Consider the model Staff Development Curriculum for standards implementation in Figure 6.1. The collaborative model entails not a single idea or skill, but rather an integrated curriculum designed to implement a comprehensive strategy for teachers and administrators throughout a school system. The collaborative model acknowledges that in order for discussions about standards-based performance assessments to make sense, participants must first have an understanding of the educational rationale for standards. Moreover, teachers must not only be exposed to the idea of performance assessments, but they must develop sufficient knowledge and skills in the area that they can actually create complete standards-based performance assessments suitable for classroom use. In addition, administrators must have the ability to lead collaborative faculty meetings and staff development sessions that will focus on teacher-created assessments and real student work.

The third distinguishing feature of the collaborative model of staff development is attention to individual needs. Unlike the Tai Chi Disco model, participants are not marched into a room to listen to the same information, without regard to their professional background and personal objectives. This is particularly important for districts that have effectively used pilot programs (please see Chapter 8). Many teachers and administrators already have a firm grounding in standards and performance assessment practices and can proceed directly to the enrichment portions of the professional development curriculum. This not only conveys professional respect where it is due, but also makes the most economical use of scarce staff development resources.

The fourth and final characteristic of the collaborative model is a staff development system that is, like the standards, distinctively owned by the district. While there is certainly inspiration and information from outside sources (such as state and national standards), as well as researchers and teachers who are familiar with standards and performance assessments, the sustainability of collaborative staff development does not depend upon these outside sources.

It is difficult for most districts to break the Dr. Fox habit. It is fun and, after all, we all need a break now and then. But when schools are confronted with the need to conserve every resource and implement standards in the most effective manner possible, there is no alternative but for a profound change in the manner in which we approach professional development. Only the collaborative model offers hope of sustainable reform.

"But This Is Too Hard!"

The best summation of the collaborative model of professional development is that it requires much more work for the participants than traditional models of staff development. Indeed, I have listened to seminar participants complain, "I didn't expect to have to work today – I just wanted the information." Not only do participants resist the expectation that they produce a written work product, but some of them particularly resent the idea that they must expose their work to the review of colleagues. An integral part of the "Making Standards Work" two-day seminar on which the first edition of this book was based is the collegial review of assessments. Using a "scoring guide for scoring guides," participants compare the work of their colleagues to the criteria for an ideal performance assessment. Invariably, there are opportunities for improvement. After all, if participants produced a perfect performance assessment the first time, they would hardly need any professional development. More to the point, even experienced educators and assessment designers benefit from the constructive feedback of colleagues. Despite the obvious advantages of feedback and revision for both novice and veteran participants, the idea of giving feedback to peers – and even worse, receiving feedback from peers – is an alien notion in many professional development settings. Since the first edition of this book was published, we have provided professional development to tens of thousands of educators, and without question the area of greatest concern to seminar participants has been our insistence that they give and receive constructive feedback.

I persist in the expectation that workshop participants work hard, give feedback, and accept feedback with the conviction that even the most experienced educator is a lifelong learner. My dogged determination, even in the face of some criticism on this point, is based ultimately on the respect that great teachers have for every student. Think of your own best teachers. They never patronized you with pats on the head, bland reassurances, and low expectations. Our best teachers challenged us, prodded us to do our best, and created opportunities for work that seemed impossibly beyond our skill. When we at last succeeded, our spirits soared. Our debts to those challenging educators can never be repaid. We dare not forget such lessons in professional development. It is the ultimate sign of respect for seminar participants to challenge them; it is the ultimate sign of contempt for educators to coddle them, patronize them, tell them funny stories, and define successful staff development as that which provided the maximum entertainment with the minimum work or presumed to make them into clones of the presenter.

But What Do I Do Tomorrow?

Educators are understandably weary of theoretical justifications for education reform. "Sounds great," they reply, "but what do I do on Tuesday morning?" This demand for practical answers to the challenges of standards-based assessments is the foundation for Part II of this book.

The ten steps that follow begin with a recognition of the most common challenge issued by teachers: "Where will I find the time?" The fundamental premise of this book is that standards-based education and assessment is not simply another layer to add to an already overburdened day. The remaining nine steps include an emphasis on creativity, collaboration, and rigor. Together, these steps offer a practical framework for making standards work in the classroom.

CHAPTER THIRTEEN

Step One: Pull the Weeds Before Planting the Flowers

The Toughest Job

Few people would argue with the proposition that teaching is one of the most difficult jobs in the world, particularly when time, energy, and emotion are invested to do it well. Many teachers with whom I come in contact on a daily basis are exhausted and overwhelmed. Those who have significant experience in the profession frequently remark about the changes in their responsibilities in recent years. While they are teachers, counselors, confidants, social workers, and surrogate parents, they are also the most significant adults in the lives of far too many of their students.

Drowning in New Initiatives

In addition to the changing nature of students and their home environments, teachers must cope with increasing levels of administrative burdens. Every year brings new initiatives, many of which sound good in staff development conferences and faculty meetings, but are advocated by people who have not set foot in a classroom in decades. Indeed, many teachers react to standards and standards-based performance assessment in the same way: just one more administrative requirement that does not help them accomplish their daily job. "It just means more paperwork, more hassle, more hoops, but not any more support." This is a typical conclusion reached by many exhausted teachers who are confronted with standards or any other new educational initiative.

Have I Been Doing Everything Wrong?

With a sense of weariness comes a certain level of defensiveness: "I've been doing this for 28 years, and now you are going to tell me that I've been doing it all wrong?" Teachers have assembled their lesson plans, carefully cultivated over the course of years, perhaps decades, and they cannot lightly toss these aside. Tests that were passionately defended for a generation are not easily replaced by new assessment techniques. The suggestion that we "pull the weeds" is challenging to many veteran educators. Indeed, the very notion that there are any weeds at all in teaching practice, curriculum, and popular, time-honored activities may be offensive to some veteran educators.

Nevertheless, we must confront the fact that, despite the hectic pace of teachers' lives and the harried atmosphere of many classrooms, there are some unimportant, non-contributory, irrelevant, and potentially harmful activities taking place in classrooms. This is not caused by malicious intent. It is instead the inevitable result of years of bigger textbooks and more extensive curriculum demands. Indeed, academic standards themselves are part of the problem, with many states appearing to emphasize coverage of more standards than can possibly be addressed in 180 days of classroom instruction. Accumulated political demands for instruction in drug education, health education, safety education, character education, patriotism education, free enterprise education – just to name a few popular and apparently innocuous mandates – is that more is demanded of teachers and students within a fixed amount of curriculum time. Something has to give. At least some of these activities must be stopped or significantly changed. This chapter addresses how to identify the weeds and how to prepare the soil for planting a bountiful educational garden. Simply put, administrators will not have any credibility asking teachers to do more if district and school leaders are not willing to take some things off the table. They must, in brief, pull the weeds before they attempt to plant any new flowers.

Standards and Daily Practice

One of the most thought-provoking exercises a teacher can consider is a careful comparison of every activity in a single day of teaching to the academic standards of the school, district, or state. Dozens of worksheets bearing the imprimatur of national textbook companies have been used for eons and are a permanent fixture in many classrooms. These worksheets fill the weekly parent packet, keep the students busy, and appear to be related to the subjects about which the students are learning. Whether or not these worksheets are weeds or flowers, however, depends not upon their subject matter, but upon the intellectual skills to which the exercises contribute.

Consider this example: A district language arts standard says, "Students must construct a complete sentence, using proper tense and verb forms." Although the standard is explicitly related to sentence construction, does this mean that, on a worksheet, spelling, grammar, context, and meaning are unimportant? Of course not. Some teachers, fixated on the matter of sentence construction, limit their evaluation of student work to a consideration of a subject and verb. This occurs even more frequently when, in evaluating a mathematics answer, teachers will announce that "spelling does not count." Each time we send inconsistent signals to students, they must wonder how serious we are about our academic expectations. One cannot imagine a teacher saying that "for this exercise, our rules against smoking do not count," or the cafeteria supervisor saying that "On Wednesdays, the rules for good hygiene do not count." When important issues, such as health and safety, are at stake, we are consistent. Whenever I have asked veteran teachers, parents, and grandparents about their fundamental principles of classroom management and child discipline, one issue on which they all seem to agree is the need for consistency. Children of all ages must know what we expect and the adults must be consistent in those expectations. Whenever I have asked teachers and other adults to describe their worst experiences in school, the root cause of those bad experiences frequently is associated with a lack of clarity, coherence, and consistency by teachers and leaders.

This is the reason that every assignment, including those in math, science, and social studies, should include a requirement for students to read and write well. Literacy requirements are not the exclusive province of the English class any more than rules of fairness and courtesy are the exclusive domain of the physical education class. Safety, hygiene, spelling, fairness, legibility, courtesy, and mathematical accuracy are all part of the school-wide expectations, and the context of the unit does not alter the imperative for each of these requirements.

The narrow focus on isolated skills rather than academic standards has led to some terrible teaching practices. For example, honors English classes in some middle schools require students to complete reams of worksheets but never have them write paragraphs or essays. Science and math classes in high schools accept lab reports and story problem explanations devoid of the most rudimentary components of grammar and punctuation. Social studies classes accept graphical representations of population data that do not make mathematical sense because "this isn't a math class." When teachers are challenged about these practices, they frequently respond that they do not have the time to deal with all subjects and thus can only focus on one thing at a time. This is true in the same sense that a person who is drowning in shark-infested waters refuses to take a safety rope because he is too busy treading water and fighting sharks.

Break Out of the Curriculum Trap

The only means of escape for teachers and students who are drowning in irrelevant and meaningless assignments is to have an objective means of applying standards to every piece of work in the class. Because the sheer volume of paperwork can be overwhelming, it is usually appropriate to begin with just a single day's work. Consider homework assignments, classroom activities, worksheets, and every other instructional device for a single day. Ask the question, "To what standard and benchmark does this activity relate?" One of two things can be true. Either the assignment is clearly related to a content standard and allows a student to demonstrate proficiency in one or more standards, or it does not. In the latter case, it is possible that there is a grave deficiency in the standards, in which case the standards themselves should be modified so that this important and necessary assignment will, in the future, be clearly related to the content standards. But if the standards have been carefully designed, then it is likely that the activity is a weed. It may be a beautiful weed and one that has been around for so long that people have become used to it. But it is still a weed and it must be pulled.

Fewer Assignments, Richer in Content

Once the weeds are pulled, teachers will find that they can offer fewer assignments, each one of which is richer in content. Rather than a ream of paper consumed with grammar drills, a student can bring home an essay, revised three or four times, that displays flawless grammar, spelling, and punctuation. The content of the essay might include reinforcement of ideas learned in literature, social studies, math, or science class. The parent packet might not be as thick, but the level of student understanding and achievement will be considerably higher as the daily activities of the classroom consistently correspond to the academic standards of the district.

Weeding the Garden

Management consultant Art Waskey encourages people to begin purging their work space with a plastic bag and a box of tissue. The former is used to throw away the piles of papers that have been gathering dust in file cabinets, desk corners, and bookcases for years. The latter is used to wipe away the tears engendered by separation anxiety associated with losing these valued but useless materials. The same approach might be appropriate for pulling the weeds in classroom activities. The most effective teachers are constantly renewing their professional knowledge, their classroom practice, and their classroom activities. They use their experience as a springboard for future growth rather than a defense mechanism for avoiding anything new.

Once the psychological hurdle has been cleared, and the commitment has been made to pull a few weeds, the question becomes, "Where do I begin?" As with cleaning out an old basement or Fibber McGee's closet, the process can seem overwhelming and even dangerous. It is unreasonable to expect a teacher to make a transformation to standards-based instruction in a single year. It must rather be approached in bite-sized pieces. The key to success is doing this in small, measurable portions. The careful gardener will systematically clear the weeds from one square of the garden at a time and will not jump frantically between the radishes and petunias. The teacher who is transforming a class to one based on academic standards must make a similarly deliberate and thoughtful approach.

Assignments Grow in Complexity and Content

An important phenomenon associated with the transformation of a classroom to standards-based instruction is that the vast quantity of individual worksheets associated with incremental instruction is replaced with a smaller number of more complex assignments. These assignments are richer in content, cover several disciplines, and provide a variety of opportunities for basic instruction and educational enrichment. In my view, the best of these assignments are created by teachers. (It is important to note that the examples of standards-based performance assignments and assessments included in Part Four of this book are merely designed to be models for your own creative thought.)

One of the most insidious results of the many half-hearted attempts to implement standards is the distribution of massive workbooks labeled "standards-based assignments" which teachers use in the classroom because, after all, these documents bear the words "standards-based." This is silly. It simply replaces little worksheets with big worksheets, but it does not fundamentally transform a classroom to standards-based instruction. It is somewhat like the teacher who was required to change from a traditional class schedule to a block schedule, theoretically giving the teacher more concentrated time for detailed and complex classroom activities. Upon hearing of this schedule change the teacher said, "Good! Now we can show the whole movie rather than spreading it out over two days." The classroom activities did not change; only the format did. If we truly pull the weeds and plant the flowers, then instruction must be fundamentally different.

The Hallmarks of a Standards-Based Classroom

As you make the transition to standards, ask yourself these questions:

- Are assignments a singularity, or do students have the continuous opportunity to revise and improve their work over the course of several days?

- Are assignments rich in detail and complex in achievement, requiring several days to complete?

- Do assignments dwell on a single set of knowledge in an individual subject, or do they integrate cumulative knowledge on a subject with several other academic disciplines?

- When I evaluate student work, am I only considering a particular subject, or am I demanding student proficiency in every academic subject?

- Is the purpose of this activity to build a skill that will be tested in a different form at the end of the semester, or is the activity an opportunity for a student to demonstrate proficiency so that the assignment itself can become an assessment?

For each of these questions, the contrast between traditional worksheets and standards-based assignments is stark. All of us who have spent time in the classroom will recognize many instances in which our classroom practice has fallen short of the ideals described in these questions. This is the essence of the weeds metaphor. The most meticulous gardeners, with many years of experience, still regularly get down on their hands and knees and pull the weeds. If we are committed to making standards work, then we must be willing to do the same in our classrooms.

CHAPTER FOURTEEN

Step Two: Identify the Primary Standard

In the creation of standards-based assignments and assessments, it is sometimes too easy to overlook the obvious: We must begin at the beginning. The identification of a primary standard is a place to begin, but it certainly does not limit the creation of an interesting multidisciplinary assignment. Rather, it forces the creator of the assignment to address the central question, "If I were to place this completed assignment in a student's portfolio, for which standards would it demonstrate proficiency?" This chapter addresses this first creative step.

Where Do I Begin?

A frequent temptation in the creation of any new assignment is to begin with the lowest level standard. Unfortunately, this is a prescription for the "drill and kill" strategy at the heart of most workbooks. The assignment must instead strike a balance between being challenging enough to engage student interest and reasonable enough to allow the student to at least envision its successful completion. Thus, a middle school mathematics assignment need not begin, as a textbook might, with the rudiments of reviewing elementary school math. Neither should it begin with the algebra completed at the end of eighth grade. A reasonable rule of thumb is this: At the beginning of the year, start with a standard in the middle range of difficulty. This technique challenges the students who are thoroughly proficient at the beginning of the year, but does not overwhelm students who still need review. This is particularly important for subjects such as mathematics, in which knowledge is cumulative. Such a strategy will allow students to refine and reinforce continually their previous skills in that subject. As the year progresses and the class gains proficiency, this middle point can become more advanced. Finally, students are not only demonstrating proficiency in the current year's standards, but they have an opportunity, at the exemplary level, to demonstrate proficiency in content they would not ordinarily learn until years later in school. Therefore, an effective assignment begins with several different benchmarks within one standard.

Power Standards: Adding Value to Your State Standards

Most states have adopted a cumulative approach to standards, with their tentative beginnings in the standards movement of the early 1990's augmented over the succeeding years by additional layers of content and specificity. Unfortunately, the allocation of additional resources or the creation of more time in the school year did not accompany this augmentation. Thus, educators and curriculum leaders are faced with the state's daunting expectation that they accomplish more learning in a fixed amount of time. Some districts have created pacing charts and curriculum maps, hoping that the right combination of time management and exceedingly rapid speech will provide the necessary coverage of standards and curriculum. A more thoughtful approach is addressed by the concept of power standards. By applying some criteria to each state standard, educators can add the important dimensions of prioritization and discernment to their state standards, giving classroom teachers and students the opportunity to focus their attention on the standards that are most important for academic success.

There are three criteria that can be applied to develop power standards: endurance, leverage, and necessity for the next level of instruction. The property of endurance implies that the standard has lasting value. Some standards, such as those relating to reading comprehension, writing skill, and understanding of mathematical relationships, provide students knowledge and skills that will endure throughout their academic careers and beyond. Other standards, by contrast, have limited endurance and provide limited utility after a single grade in school.

The principle of leverage is related to the application of a standard to multiple academic disciplines. For example, student proficiency in non-fiction writing is directly related to student success in reading, mathematics, social studies and science. Student success in the creation and interpretation of tables, charts, and graphs is related to student success in mathematics, social studies, and science. Thus, these skills with the property of leverage deserve far greater emphasis than many other standards with limited relevance to other subjects.

The third criterion for a power standard is the degree to which the standard is necessary for the next level of instruction. A wonderful exercise for a faculty meeting is for the leader to ask this question: "What advice would each of you give to a new teacher in the next lower grade with regard to the knowledge and skills that he or she must impart to students so that these students will enter your class with confidence and success?" I have conducted this exercise with hundreds of teachers around the nation, and not once has a participant responded, "In order to enter my class with confidence and success, the previous teacher must have covered every single academic standard." Rather the teachers uniformly provide a list that is brief and focused on literacy, academic content, and student behavior. In so doing, these teachers resolve the "standards paradox" in which states simultaneously provide too many and too few standards. When teachers have only a day or two to address each standard for many classes, there are too many standards. At the same time, there are too few standards when state policy makers have omitted standards for time management, organization, and deportment of students. When teachers respond to the question, "What should a teacher in the earlier grade provide so that students can enter my class with confidence and success?" there is a remarkable degree of focus. Science and social studies teachers, for example, routinely put reading and writing at the top of their lists. Math teachers include not only computational skills, but also the ability to work in teams, submit work on time, and work independently as part of their list. In other words, literacy, behavior, and academic skills are balanced in a way that make the power standards a powerful tool for planning curriculum and instruction.

Assignment, Activity, or Assessment?

Readers will notice that the words "assignment," "activity," and "assessment" have been used interchangeably with respect to the creation of standards-based learning activities. This is intentional. Some learning activities can be used to develop student knowledge, performed in a group setting, and accompanied by significant coaching from the teacher. Other similar activities can be used by the teacher as assessments for individual students. From the student's point of view, assessment, learning activities, and assignments are indistinguishable. All are clearly based on standards, require tasks to be performed proficiently, and have explicitly stated expectations for each task. The test is neither secret nor withheld until the end of the semester, but is an integral part of the learning activities that have taken place throughout the semester. Each of these assignments, activities, and assessments give the students an opportunity to demonstrate proficiency in meeting a standard or, in the alternative, to make progress toward meeting the standard. In fact, in a standards-based classroom, *assessment is instruction*.

Identify Complementary Standards

A major contrast between the standards-based assignment and workbooks is the fact that the standards-based assignment will include a variety of different activities and hence a variety of different standards. For example, students studying geometry will reinforce their knowledge of algebra and arithmetic. Students studying American history may have the opportunity to reinforce their knowledge of government, politics, and geography. Students studying economics, psychology, and other social sciences will have the opportunity to reinforce their knowledge of mathematics and science.

Once the decision is made with respect to the primary standard on which the assignment will focus, then the complementary standards in similar academic areas will begin to suggest themselves. As a rule of thumb, a successful assignment will identify at least two or three complementary standards in addition to the primary standard. Remember, the fundamental rationale for the replacement of old worksheets with new standards-based performance assignments and assessments is that there will be fewer assignments, but each assignment will be richer in content. This is done not only for the sake of efficiency, but also because multidisciplinary assignments are more interesting for both teacher and student.

Now that you have selected the primary standard and some complementary standards, you are ready to proceed to Step Three: Develop an Engaging Scenario.

CHAPTER FIFTEEN

Step Three: Develop an Engaging Scenario

Perhaps the most critical element of an effective standards-based performance assessment is the development of an engaging scenario. The opportunities are limitless, and students are usually the best judges of this. Students have provided rave reviews of the following effective scenarios:

- Running the Iditarod dog sled race from Anchorage to Nome, Alaska

- Searching for ocean treasure

- On the case with Sherlock Holmes

- Opening an import-export business

- Is the water safe to drink?

- Competing in the Olympics

What Do All of These Scenarios Have in Common?

1. **Engaging scenarios allow students to play a role in a real-world challenge.**

    It is amusing to listen to students, even in primary grades, express contempt for the way parents, teachers, and textbooks treat them. We can smile listening to a third grade student complain, "Who do they think we are – kids?" Students can tell if they are intellectually respected by the role-playing assignments created by teachers and textbook authors. When students perceive something as a fairy tale or an inconsequential game, they respond accordingly. On the other hand, when they perceive that they are being taken seriously and much is expected of them, they respond intellectually, emotionally, and behaviorally in an entirely different manner.

    This becomes even more important as students grow older. At the secondary school level, it is less effective for children to engage in a mock government than it is for them to identify a public issue and participate in a genuine public policy dialogue. If they wish to investigate issues involving public health as part of a science and social studies assignment, then they need not "play doctor," but can visit the local health department, measure impurities in real food and water, calculate statistics on real public health issues, and report their findings to real public officials. In brief, engaging scenarios are realistic and respectful. These scenarios motivate students because the consequences of their work are real.

2. **Engaging scenarios require reinforcement of many academic standards.**

At the heart of every standards-based performance assessment is the reinforcement of reading and writing standards. Every standards-based performance assignment should create an opportunity for a final written product that has undergone several drafts. Although the primary standard may be selected from social studies, science, or mathematics, the written product should adhere to the writing standards with respect to spelling, grammar, handwriting, punctuation, clarity, and expression. A note of caution: The multidisciplinary approach must be used only by teachers with a relatively thick skin. One student, whose faulty grammar and spelling were noted in my comments on his math paper, reacted in his complaint to the principal, "Doesn't this fool [yours truly] know this isn't an English class?" My response was unequivocal: Mathematics is about describing the universe using numbers, symbols, and words. Thus, communication is an integral part of mathematics, and effective communication includes organization, expression, and the conventions of the English language.

The imperative for multidisciplinary work has important implications for cooperative learning and group work. Although many processes in a performance assessment may be completed in a cooperative manner by a group of students, it is essential that teachers provide every individual student with the opportunity to express in writing a personal contribution to the completed assessment. Individual accountability is an important part of effective collaboration, group work, and cooperative learning.

3. **Engaging scenarios frequently include the arts.**

Music, dance, poetry, literature, drama, painting, sculpture, and the other arts can engage student attention in a manner which academic subjects alone cannot. A student who might roll his eyes skyward at the prospect of a mathematics or science assignment might find such an assignment more engaging if part of his responsibility is to communicate about that assignment using one of the visual arts, or if part of her exploration of scientific or mathematical phenomenon falls within the realm of the arts. In fact, the more different ways that students represent knowledge, the more likely they are to achieve a deep understanding of the concept they are studying.

The inclusion of the arts in academic standards makes an important point, particularly for those who have expressed the concern that the application of academic standards diminishes the arts. Only when art and music teachers have the opportunity to contribute in a meaningful way to math and social studies assignments, will the full interdisciplinary value of their disciplines be realized. The integration of the arts into academic standards is hardly an educational fad or a method of conducting an avant-garde classroom. Instead, it is a mechanism for effective communication with students. Moreover, the integration of the arts with academic standards is a deliberate means for creating both academic and political constituencies for the arts and other subjects that have typically been regarded as "non-academic."

In fact, we know that students will learn mathematics better on an interdisciplinary basis. Students who have difficulty with fractions can clap complex rhythms including quarter notes, eighth notes, triplets, and other fractional relationships to a single beat. Students who are challenged by geometry can recognize the relationships between angles and sides when they are working on two- and three-dimensional models of buildings or analyzing one of the wonderful geometrical works of art by Kandinsky. Hence art, music, home economics, metalwork, and other "non-academic" subjects are not frills, but can make essential contributions to the achievement of academic standards.

The development of engaging scenarios is at the heart of effective standards-based performance assignments. Before students are attracted to a subject, they are attracted to a role. Moreover, scenarios create an association between academic work and the world of actual employment, and thus students gain skills that can improve business and community perceptions of public education.

4. **Engaging scenarios promote student understanding.**

I have frequently heard that, "some subjects are just abstract. You can't teach them in a real-world scenario." I usually meet such a challenge by establishing engaging scenarios on the spot, often with the assistance of students, parents, and teachers in the room. Rather than filling a worksheet with quadratic equations, students can apply their knowledge of quadratics and other algebraic methods to descriptions of the behavior of people, animals, and organizations. Instead of answering multiple-choice questions about characters in a Shakespearean play, students can conduct psychological evaluations of those characters, or adapt those characters for a British tourism advertisement. Rather than complete a tedious homework assignment involving ratios, students can identify the challenges faced by an import-export company when it evaluates the impact of daily currency fluctuations. While this process may not necessarily make every enterprise fun, the use of real-world engaging scenarios certainly can make schoolwork more interesting, challenging, and worthwhile.

The Role of Parents in Creating Engaging Scenarios

The clarion call for parental involvement in education has met with mixed response from educators. Some welcome any adult assistance they can get in a classroom, while others wonder what contribution non-educators can make to the complex enterprise of working with students.

In fact, some of the things we do, such as the construction of scoring guides and the evaluation of student work, are tasks that may not be appropriate for many non-educators. However, the development of engaging scenarios is something on which parents can provide invaluable assistance. Some of the best scenarios for standards-based assignments and assessments have come from non-educators. These interesting and compelling scenarios come from the real vocational and home experiences of parents. Their contributions are meaningful and can be highlighted in the titles and scenarios of the assignments. But the critical work of translating standards into tasks and describing levels of proficiency for each task remains the province of the teacher. Thus parents make meaningful contributions without supplanting the essential role of the teacher.

CHAPTER SIXTEEN

Step Four: Develop Requirements for Students to Apply, Analyze, and Demonstrate Knowledge

One of the key distinctions between standards-based performance assessments and traditional tests is the higher thinking skills required by performance assessments. It is the difference, for example, between a teacher-education student who is required to respond to a multiple choice question such as, "Who invented Bloom's taxonomy?" and the teacher who is required to create a series of classroom activities that illustrate each level of the taxonomy.

Far too many answers that pass for "knowledge" in the classroom are, in fact, rather elementary memory games requiring only the lowest levels of thought and analysis. Moreover, the real world of work does not require the regurgitation of facts that are irrelevant to the technological workplace. Instead, the workplace requires the ability to constantly take into account new facts, which emerge in virtually every discipline after a student has completed formal schooling. The most crucial skill a school can impart to students is the ability to apply and analyze new information with respect to a given situation, not simply the ability to memorize a fixed body of facts.

The inadequacy of fact-based education does not mean that memorization and basic skills are irrelevant. Students need to know the alphabet, math facts, and the uses of multiple learning tools. There is a wide chasm, however, between knowing the letters of the alphabet and writing a persuasive essay. Similarly, an understanding of math facts is necessary, but not sufficient, for a student to perform complex equations. Unfortunately, the debate about factual knowledge and analytical applications has been over-simplified, with one side on the argument decrying the use of "mere facts" and "drill and kill" with a sneer, while the other side derides the pretense of pseudo-analysis without a factual foundation. The former school of thought denies to students fundamental knowledge that helps form a common foundation for learning; the latter elevates recitation over understanding. Surely thoughtful educators can stop the argument long enough to find an appropriate middle ground.

Most scientists, attorneys, engineers, physicians, and teachers will agree that the developments in their fields since they received their "final" degree are far more important than the information they acquired during their formal schooling. Similarly, there are skills and concepts they use daily that, while they cannot be taught in school, these professionals must learn in the "real world" in order to survive in it. Therefore, the critical part of training is learning how to learn, so that as new information emerges, students are successfully able to apply it to their discipline. Yet the typical assessments these professionals received in the course of their studies were usually tests that required them to recall a limited set of facts without the use of reference books. In the course of their work, however, they routinely encounter new situations not contemplated in school, that frequently require the use of reference books. In fact, one attorney recently remarked to me that the failure to use references to double-check one's recollection of the facts and law by deliberate use of reference material could be regarded as malpractice. Diligence, resourcefulness, and the use of all available resources – not encyclopedic recall – is the hallmark of professionalism. To reiterate, I am not making the case that memorization and factual understanding are irrelevant, but only that they are insufficient.

Educators must avoid professional malpractice by creating performance assessments that emulate the tasks students will face in the real world. This means that a premium is placed not on rote memorization, but on the ability to apply, analyze, and demonstrate mastery of a subject.

The "Core Knowledge" Dilemma

The debate surrounding the need for "core knowledge," or the facts that allow students to create a meaningful frame of reference for their ideas and evaluations, has created a false dichotomy between knowledge and thinking. The proponents of core knowledge include most notably E. D. Hirsch, Jr., the author of such volumes as, *Cultural Literacy; The Schools We Need: And Why We Don't Have Them;* and the popular series *What Your First Grader Needs to Know*. Professor Hirsch is quite correct when he asserts that students cannot apply, evaluate, and synthesize what they do not know. In other words, facts are an essential part of the equation for higher order thinking skills, and factual knowledge should not be disparaged by teachers. This is reasonable and appropriate. The best standards-based performance assessments require both content knowledge and analysis.

Unfortunately, many partisans on both sides of the core knowledge debate have extended the argument to the point of a false dichotomy. They claim that an emphasis on analysis, evaluation, and synthesis excludes a commitment to core knowledge; and an emphasis on core knowledge excludes a commitment to high order thinking skills. These extreme positions are often espoused when the focus of the debate is the type of assessment that is appropriate for schools. Some core knowledge adherents, including

Professor Hirsch, correctly criticize performance assessments that are lacking in rigor and that expect too little of students. Their conclusion, however, that all performance assessments are inferior to standardized multiple-choice tests does not logically follow.

High Standards Require Both Content Knowledge and Advanced Analysis

Most of the academic content standards of states and districts require an effective combination of content and analysis. It is impossible discuss with any insight the Civil War, for example, if one does not know that it occurred between 1861 and 1865. Meaningful academic standards demand more than knowledge of dates, names, and places. Students must have the ability to integrate their knowledge of history, literature, economics, and other fields. Academic standards further require that students coherently explain their analyses in written and oral forms. A testing system that required essays but avoided content would be silly; but a testing system that relies exclusively on multiple-choice items and required facts, but excludes written expression, analysis, and synthesis, would be incomplete and lacking in the very rigor that core knowledge advocates espouse.

The two sides in the core knowledge debate have many essential views in common: Students can succeed academically when presented with high expectations and rigorous challenges. If the advocates of each side can apply these areas of common agreement to educational assessment, students will be better served by their cooperation rather than by their arguments.

Tasks That Require Application of Knowledge: The Key to Effective Assessments

The key element of this requirement is that the student must be able to use the information acquired and apply it to different sets of facts and circumstances. For example, a math student may have learned to calculate the statistical mean, median, and mode. But the requirement for a student to analyze data would take one more step. Why are these terms – mean, median, and mode – important? Because different sets of data – family income, student grades, baseball scores – might be best represented by different measurements of central tendency.

To continue this example, a good assessment would begin with a set of real-world data, perhaps the income distribution of several different areas of a city in which only one area will receive income-based government assistance. The student would then not only calculate the statistics, but also explain which measure of central tendency is more meaningful for policy makers. Using written and oral reports, illustrations, and appropriate graphics, the students could make a final recommendation as to which of the neighborhoods should receive the government assistance.

There are many students who can calculate the arithmetic mean but who cannot successfully complete this assignment at the proficient or exemplary level. This makes the critical point that *performance assignments are more challenging than traditional assignments. They require more work by the teacher to create and far more work by the student to complete. Nevertheless, students frequently prefer these assignments because they are realistic, engaging, and, most importantly, do not involve the one-shot terrorism of the traditional test.*

This example of measurements of central tendency provides an ironic twist in the context of a discussion of student assessment. The mathematics standards of every state require students to understand the differences between the mean, median, and mode. Every middle school student in the nation is expected to understand the fact that the arithmetic average is often *not* the best measurement of central tendency. Yet classroom teachers, school systems, and state education departments almost invariably rely on the average – the arithmetic mean – to describe student achievement and thus ignore the important policy implications that the use of other measurements of central tendency might offer. This is particularly true in bimodal distributions of test scores, in which a plurality of students receives high scores and another group of students receives low scores. The use of the average masks the needs of two strikingly different groups of students.

Continuous Improvement of Student Work

When students can take risks, make mistakes, and gain essential information by coaching, they transform their work method from the one-shot approach to which we have conditioned students for generations to an approach based on *continuous improvement*. In performance assessments, students have the opportunity to improve their work. This emphasis on continuous improvement is an essential characteristic of the real world of work. Few employees have a promising future in a career when they shove a piece of hastily done work toward their boss and say, "That's my best shot. Take it or leave it!" Yet this is precisely how the prototypical final exam or final paper prepares students to perform. Most employers, by contrast, expect people to work in a team to create a product that will undergo several drafts and, over the course of time, will be edited and improved. The best performance assessments will encourage this process. Feedback from the teacher must be respected and applied and subsequent iterations of each assignment will reflect a higher level of student achievement.

The Impact of Continuous Improvement on Deadline Planning and Assessment

If we believe in the ethic and realism of continuous improvement, then there are some practical implications for teachers and administrators. First, deadlines for student projects must be moved up to several days prior to the end of a grading period. There must be sufficient time for teachers to provide feedback to students and for students to have the opportunity to improve their work. In fact, teachers should schedule multiple drafts of projects and papers so that students are conditioned to the principle of improvement and the one-shot habit is broken.

Secondly, assessments must mirror our expectations of student work. In a few district- and state-level writing assessments, students engage in pre-writing activities, including at least one rough draft. In far too many writing assessments, however, states and districts provide a single writing prompt and then evaluate the immediate student response. No matter what teachers may say about the value of editing and re-writing, this assessment practice screams to teachers and students this message: *"All we want is a one-shot response; editing and rewriting don't really matter when it comes to the test. If you want to teach about editing and rewriting, that's fine, but we're not going to evaluate these skills when it comes time for our assessments."* Students of any age place far more emphasis on the actions than the words of their educational leaders. Assessments must mirror our values about what is important. If continuous improvement is important, it must be part of the assessment process.

Tasks That Require Analysis of Knowledge

A major element in designing a successful performance assessment is the understanding that students must apply the knowledge they have acquired. This requirement alone makes performance assessment more challenging, rigorous, and meaningful than the traditional multiple choice test. Yet another significant improvement in the quality of assessment will occur when students are required to analyze the results of their own work.

Consider the example used earlier, in which students not only had to understand the differences between the mean, median, and mode, but they also had to apply that understanding to a realistic scenario. The next step, analysis, requires students to draw inferences about their work. For what sort of distribution is the mean the best measure of central tendency? When is the median a better reflection of the center of a distribution? What are the implications of these inferences when averages are used in public policy, physical science, biology, and education?

Students who can answer these questions have done far more than learn three mathematical terms; they have mastered the concepts behind the terminology. They have done far more than memorize facts. They have demonstrated the ability to apply the information to different contexts, analyze the results, and use their knowledge in the real-world situation. This is the result to which educators should aspire for every performance assignment we create.

Tasks That Require a Demonstration of Knowledge

Though application and analysis are important, a standards-based performance assessment is not complete without the requirement to demonstrate the results of the work. Demonstrations usually entail both written and oral presentations. If a team is formed to create the demonstration, care should be taken to ensure that all team members have an equal opportunity during the school year to participate in the oral presentations and the physical creation of the written products. Teachers who allow the most gregarious students to dominate the oral presentations do no favors for either the outgoing students or their quieter classmates. All students must master the art of presenting their views in a cogent and persuasive manner.

There is an important point here with regard to the proper implementation of teamwork and cooperative learning techniques. While teamwork is important and cooperative learning is demonstrably effective, neither of these practices eliminates the essential nature of individual accountability. Four students might conduct a science lab together, but each student should submit a lab report. While a group may share research on a social studies project, each student must play a role in the oral and written reports and bear individual accountability for their contribution to the final product.

Individual student accountability requires careful classroom management. The classroom environment must offer safety and reassurance to reticent students who may never have received respect and attention for their ideas. The effective classroom will also convey to the loquacious students that the power of their ideas is not necessarily proportional to their willingness to express them, and that they have much to learn from listening to the students who have usually been unwilling to speak.

Demonstrations and performance assessments offer an exceptional opportunity to improve communication with parents by making testing and evaluation a much more meaningful enterprise. Instead of attempting to reduce student performance to a letter or number, the teacher is able to show in three dimensions what proficient performance looks like. Students need a model of successful performance, a clear scoring guide, and the relentless persistence of a teacher who expects nothing less than proficiency. Students and their parents can compare their work to the model of proficiency, notice the differences, make appropriate adjustments, and eventually achieve proficiency.

In sum, this step in the assessment development process is far more than the creation of a test. It is the essence of teaching and learning. By asking the right questions, combining factual knowledge with deep understanding, and providing multiple opportunities for success after detailed feedback and coaching, assessments can be transformed from fearful evaluations into constructive learning experiences.

CHAPTER SEVENTEEN

Step Five: Develop Scoring Guides (Rubrics)

We should begin with a note about terminology. Some authors have used the term "scoring guide" while others have used the term "rubric" to describe the method of evaluating student performance and its relationship to a standard. While each school system may have its own preference when it comes to these terms, I would like to encourage clear and direct use of language wherever possible and to avoid anything that smacks of educational jargon. The term "scoring guide" is used interchangeably with the term "rubric" in this book. Since the publication of the first edition, I have endured a few lectures from those who wish to insist on a distinction without a difference between these terms. I remain unrepentant. If educators are to build the necessary bridges with the parents and communities we serve, we must supplant jargon with clarity of language wherever possible. Hence, this book uses the following definition for both terms.

> A **Scoring Guide** is a document that describes student performance on a specific task. The descriptions in the scoring guide clearly differentiate levels of performance, such as exemplary, proficient, progressing toward the standard, or not yet meeting the standard.

The Qualities of a Meaningful Scoring Guide

Justice Lewis Powell famously described pornography in an opinion of the United States Supreme Court when he wrote, "I cannot say what it is, but I know it when I see it." Unfortunately, this "pornography" definition of student proficiency prevails in far too many classrooms where the teacher in effect says, "Students must submit their work to me and then I will tell them if it is satisfactory." Proficiency in this context is a mystery, resolved only by the judgment of the teacher.

Scoring guides and standards-based performance assessments take a strikingly different approach by identifying the precise definition of proficiency before students begin their work. Success is not a mystery, but the result of hard work by the student and clear guidance by feedback from the teacher. Thus, the development of scoring guides, the clear descriptions of proficient student work, is a challenging and complex task. The effort is worthwhile, however, because scoring guides not only help the teacher evaluate student work but, properly written, they also help the student know how to achieve and exceed the performance standard.

Models of Scoring Guides

The literature surrounding authentic assessment provides two general models of rubrics or scoring guides. One common model is the "holistic" rubric. The sound is appealing, somewhat like a description of a healthy breakfast cereal or exercise regimen. Unfortunately, holistic rubrics have become less useful to classroom teachers as the documents have grown in size and complexity. In their most extreme forms, they consume a page or more, in solid text, of descriptions. Moreover, their comprehensive nature forces the teacher to apply the rubric to an entire project rather than engaging in incremental corrections that would encourage improvement in student work. The holistic model is difficult for the teacher to apply and even more difficult for the student to understand. A holistic rating of "2" might be the result of any number of deficiencies, and the language of these rubrics can sometimes be impenetrable for both educators and students.

A better model is the one used in Part Four of this book and in other large-scale performance assessments, such as those of the International Performance Assessment System. These scoring guides are brief descriptions of student performance for each task within an assessment. This model can be applied incrementally by students and teachers so that frequent corrections and improvements can be made. With task-specific scoring guides, student work can be evaluated on a task-by-task basis by teachers and peers. This makes the final work product submitted to the teacher far more reflective of proficient performance and sends the unambiguous message to the students that they must take responsibility for frequent evaluation, changes, and improvements to their work before submitting it to the teacher.

The following five characteristics of a good scoring guide are also summarized as a reproducible handout in Part Four.

1. **Scoring Guides Must Be Specific**

   Here is an example of an insufficiently specific scoring guide: "The paper must communicate a variety of ideas in a coherent manner." A clearer and more specific scoring guide might include wording such as the following:

   > "To achieve a rating of Exemplary (4), the paper will be completely free of spelling errors; to achieve a rating of Proficient (3), the paper will not have more than two spelling errors; to achieve a rating of Progressing (2), the paper may have two to four spelling errors; and to achieve a rating of Not Meeting Standards (1), the paper will have five or more spelling errors."

A similarly specific scoring guide should deal with grammar, and yet another scoring guide should deal with legibility. In this way, students clearly understand what is necessary to become proficient in all standards for which they are responsible.

Many readers will recoil at this degree of specificity. Before rejecting the need for specific feedback, let us consider the model of our best educators in music and physical education . The orchestra teacher will not tell me to "Play the concerto well," but will probably say, "Play the F-sharp again – it's not in tune." The basketball coach will not say, "Fly like Michael Jordan," but rather give me specific instructions on the elements of a jump shot. Student response to feedback depends upon specificity and clarity.

Students are not the only beneficiaries of our clear specification of success. The more clear and specific we are in identifying the qualities of proficient student work, the more consistent, reliable, and fair we will be in evaluating student work. Teacher credibility and assessment practice is enhanced through the clear and consistent description of proficiency.

2. **Scoring Guides Should Be Expressed in the Student's Own Words**

Contrast the scoring guide, "The student will demonstrate mastery in decoding and articulation," to the requirement, "To get a 4, I have to read and say all the words in the story." An excellent way to determine if scoring guides are sufficiently clear is to have students express them in their own language. If their interpretations are remarkably different from what the teacher intended, it should be no surprise if student performance is also different from what the teacher had anticipated. The student who wrote, "If I can read the letters, but my words are squished up like a worm, I only get a 2," understands the value of legibility better than the student who thinks that legibility is a mysterious ideal that rests upon the subjective judgment of the teacher.

3. **Scoring Guides Should Be Accompanied by an Exemplary Assignment**

Despite our best efforts to express scoring guides clearly, students usually do their best if they have a model of effective and exemplary work. This is not done to provide the students with something to copy, but rather so that students understand visually, as well as verbally, what constitutes exemplary performance. At the secondary level, the creation of an exemplary assignment is also an excellent way for teachers to think through the clarity of instructions and to refine and improve their own level of content knowledge.

4. **Scoring Guides Should Be Created Through Numerous Drafts**

The acid test for any scoring guide is the degree to which different teachers can apply it with consistency in the classroom. Even for experienced teachers, it is an extraordinary rarity when the first draft of a scoring guide is as good as a final draft. The initial draft, when submitted to several colleagues and students, can almost always be improved. If we wish to ask students to engage in the process of continuous improvement by editing and rewriting, then we must be willing to do the same and model that behavior in our professional work. I have designed more than a few scoring guides, and have been astonished and embarrassed to find that, when my colleagues use them to assess real student work, their level of agreement is around thirty percent. Only with multiple revisions and the reduction of ambiguity can we reach the necessary level of consistency and reliability to the point that four out of five teachers agree on what the word "proficient" really means.

5. **Scoring Guides Must Be Clearly Linked to Standards**

Although this should be obvious, it can never be reiterated too frequently. In schools today there are simply too many brilliantly executed assignments based on requirements not even remotely related to standards. Almost every school has its time-honored activities in which the tradition has become more important than academic achievement. The most magnificent replicas of Spanish missions, Greek amphitheaters, and Inca temples do not demonstrate a mastery of academic standards unless those activities reflect specific academic requirements.

CHAPTER EIGHTEEN

Step Six: Create a Model of Exemplary Student Work

Since the first edition of this book was published, many books and articles have been devoted to the establishment of academic standards and the creation of performance assessments. School systems have invested significant amounts of time and resources to these subjects. Nevertheless, the results of this effort have been inconsistent. Some districts have radically transformed their approach to teaching and learning, supplanting the Bell Curve with standards-based instruction. In those districts, success is not a mystery because teachers, students, and parents all know precisely what it means to be academically successful. In these high-performing districts, it is clear that teaching strategies, not student demographic characteristics, are the most important variables affecting student achievement. In other districts, however, there is only the superficial implementation of standards. Colorful charts of state standards adorn the walls and every teacher professes to have endured some variety of training in standards, yet they fail to provide a clear and convincing response to this question: How are teaching and learning different today than they were a few years ago?

One of the most important techniques that differentiates the superficial implementation of standards from the realization of the potential of excellence and equity offered by effective academic standards is the creation of models of exemplary student work by the teachers. In all schools, educators and administrators must grapple with the very question that students must face: What does "proficiency" mean and how will I know when I have achieved it? The ineffective schools continue the search for a pre-packaged program with all the answers, while the effective schools understand that there is no substitute for the time and effort devoted to deep understanding of standards by the educators who must teach those standards to real students.

While the state, district, or vendor may provide sample performance assessments and rubrics, there is simply no substitute for the classroom teacher completing a series of performance assessment tasks.

The immediate rejoinder to the request that teachers not only create assessments but also create model responses is the lack of time. If school leaders are to request that teachers do more work, then those leaders have the obligation to create time for this work to be done. Because assessment design and refinement is an inherently collaborative activity, the two best sources of time for the creation of model student responses are the faculty meeting and the professional development seminar. Having conducted seminars in which this request has been made of the participants, I can attest that some educators and administrators respond to this request with a distinct lack of enthusiasm. They remain stuck in the tradition in which students provide responses and teachers grade them. Moreover, if they were to provide model responses, then students would simply copy those responses and learn nothing. These are reasonable concerns and deserve a thoughtful discussion.

Why Should I Do the Same Work my Students Do?

First, why should teachers bother to perform a task when their fundamental job is to evaluate student performance on that task? When teachers – particularly a group of teachers – take the time to create an exemplary student response, they are frequently surprised to find out how widely varying their respective definitions of superior work might be. The conversation might include such difficult, challenging, and necessary statements as the following:

- "What you called 'exemplary' would be only 'proficient' in my classroom."

- "Where did that response come from? It's not in the scoring rubric."

- "I can't give it an 'exemplary' rating unless it is more than proficient – but I can't figure out if that's just a little bit better than 'proficient' work or a great deal more. If it is a great deal more, then how much more? If it's this unclear to me, then it must be really unclear for my students."

- "If they meet my expectations and are proficient, then they get an A. So what's the incentive to do any extra or 'exemplary' work? I'm just trying to get people to do basic quality work and get it in on time. It's not reasonable to expect kids these days to do any more than that."

- "I can see that every teacher is interpreting this standard in a very different way. I wonder if students and parents have this much difference in their approach to this task?"

These conversations and many like them help us to understand that even with the presence of standards and scoring rubrics, inconsistency and subjectivity rule the day. It takes more than a notebook full of standards and rubrics for effective standards implementation and clarity of expectations to become a reality in a classroom. When these discussions take place among colleagues, our responses generally will be tolerant, polite, and open-minded. We might change the way that we teach and will certainly see the value of reducing the ambiguity of our instructions and expectations. Without these conversations, we are left with the teacher as expert and the student as novice, and the teacher to whom everything is crystal clear too frequently resolves disagreements and misunderstandings. The student, meanwhile, remains lost in a murky sea of ambiguity.

It is therefore essential that the teachers creating assignments complete the activity, ask colleagues to score the work, and collaboratively create an exemplary assignment that can be shared with students. Over the course of time, teachers will collect further examples of both proficient and exemplary assignments from students, and this body of work, along with the assessment tasks, scoring guides, and curriculum materials, will form a comprehensive guide to teaching and learning in each class.

In order to achieve the objectives of this chapter, teachers must have confidence that the quality of their work is superior to that provided by the professional writers who work for textbook publishers. Too frequently, we have been conditioned that the only right answer is the one found in a teacher's guide or at the back of a textbook. But the act of the teacher completing the assignment himself is one that cannot be substituted with the provision of a publisher's *Teacher's Guide*. Thus, it is not merely the evolving work product that is important in the creation of the model of exemplary work, but the process of creating and scoring the work that provides educational value far greater than the sterile answers in the typical text.

Won't Some Students Copy the Exemplary Responses?

The second major concern teachers voice when asked to create their own exemplary work is that some students may simply copy it without doing any work of their own. The creation of exemplary work by the teacher does, in fact, carry with it the risk of copying. The answer to this potential risk is not the avoidance of model work, but rather the careful definition of what "exemplary" really means. If there is only a single student work product that can earn this designation, then copying is inevitable. But if, on the other hand, the tasks are sufficiently creative in scope that there are numerous possible responses, all of which can be proficient or exemplary in quality, then the danger of copying is minimized.

One of the best ways for teachers to reduce the risk of copying is to include the requirements for prediction, analysis, and comparison for students. Purely mechanical requirements — computation in mathematics or recollection of the plot in literature — will not vary from one student to another. But the higher order skills entailed in prediction based on past events, comparison of this experiment, algorithm, or literary character to other experiences of the student will offer a great deal of potential for variation from one student to another. Therefore, the student can emulate the quality of the model response without emulating the details of that response.

An Extra Benefit: Enhancing Teacher Content Knowledge

In some districts, the move to higher standards has out-paced the ability of the personnel office to provide certified teachers in every subject. In one major metropolitan area, more than 40% of the math and science teachers in middle schools are not certified to teach in those areas. Moreover, the national distribution of subject-matter certified teachers disproportionately favors students who are economically advantaged. Finally, even when teachers are certified, it is possible that the content knowledge required by some performance assessments differs from the academic background of the teachers. In science, technology, and social studies particularly, new knowledge and information is continually evolving, and teachers have a continuous need for supplementing the knowledge and skills learned in college.

By taking the step outlined in this chapter and completing the tasks of a performance assessment, we will acquire new knowledge and skills and also be able to evaluate our own level of proficiency. When such an exercise shows that more content knowledge and training is necessary, it is not a cause for embarrassment, but rather a cause for focusing professional development efforts on academic content, not merely pedagogical process. In one particularly progressive district, elementary and secondary school math teachers acknowledged that to teach more effectively, they needed to increase their own level of math proficiency. These teachers engaged in a three-week summer "math camp" in which they focused on improving their own math skills and knowledge. They understood what too few professional development programs acknowledge: All the pedagogical techniques in the world are of little value if the teacher does not first become a master of the subject matter at hand.

The Value of Empathy

Finally, the completion of the tasks in a performance assessment gives the teacher a realistic assessment of the challenge, interest, boredom, engagement, repetitiveness, or other intangible elements of a performance activity. Rather than criticizing an assessment in the abstract, teachers can say, "I've walked a mile in the shoes of my students, and I understand their frustrations. Now here's how we can fix this."

CHAPTER NINETEEN

Step Seven: Get Feedback

Excellent performance assignments are never developed in a vacuum. They are the result of a collaborative process between teacher, students, and colleagues. In order to gain systematic feedback on the creation of standards-based performance assessments, the following are four specific areas of feedback teachers should pursue: student performance, student engagement, clarity of instructions, and clarity of evaluation.

Student Performance

Feedback from student performance is clearly the start of the process of evaluating a performance assignment. When a teacher is asked, "How did the assignment work?" the typical response has to do with an increase in student learning. While this is surely an important outcome of every assignment, it is important to understand that simply because a student has successfully completed all of the teacher's instructions does not necessarily mean she has learned something. A good starting point for an estimation of student learning is the traditional pre-test/post-test analysis in which the teacher compares student knowledge before the lesson to student performance on a similar test after the instruction.

Such pre-assessment not only provides a baseline of student knowledge so that the effectiveness of the lesson can be measured, but it can save the teacher many hours of valuable classroom time if the pre-assessment reveals that student knowledge and skills before the assessment are not what the teacher had assumed them to be. As valuable as pre-test/post-test analysis is, however, it is not sufficient for a comprehensive understanding of student performance. Such an analysis might reveal that the average score before instruction was 55% correct and the average score after instruction was 80% correct – an impressive achievement by students and teacher. But there is more to the story.

One can easily envision two sets of test scores that provided averages of 55% and 80%, with the second number indicating that the "average" student in the class was proficient, having achieved a score of 80%. A much better measurement, however, is the "percentage of students proficient or better" on the performance assessment. It is a common experience for many teachers to observe a class that has two distinct groups of students, with a few performing at a very high level and a larger number performing below the level of proficiency. In measurement terms, this is a "bi-modal" distribution and is very common in schools. An average score of 80% might indicate that a significant number of students are proficient. It is much more likely that as few as 30% of the students are proficient. Consider this distribution of scores, with a few high-performing students interspersed among a much larger number who submit work that is "good enough" to pass, but not close to meeting the standards:

99
75
77
76
100
74
75
45
76
100

In such a class, we should take scant comfort in the results of a pre-test/post-test analysis that show an improvement in the average score, and must instead return to the concept of proficiency. More than two-thirds of these students are not proficient, and there will be an educational train-wreck in the months ahead if the teacher does not address the issue now by requiring that students submit work that is proficient. By increasing the time spent on this assignment and emphasizing a demand for proficient work, the teacher will save countless hours in the future by ceasing to conduct lessons for which the students are fundamentally unprepared.

Student Engagement

Assessments that are engaging to students have been given a bad name by those who are firm in the conviction that real learning, perhaps like real medicine, must be unpleasant. If students are enjoying it too much, then clearly something must be amiss. In fact, the consideration of student engagement in a classroom activity is not merely a focus on student enjoyment (although I would hardly apologize for that). It is, rather, an acknowledgment that some of the most important learning takes place outside of the classroom. Moreover, if the ultimate purpose of school is to prepare students to become lifelong learners, then it is critically important that they find learning activities worthy of pursuit, even when an authority figure is not insisting that they do so. It must be noted that student engagement does not imply a lack of rigor. On the contrary, students are not engaged by assignments that are easy to the point of being insulting. They are, rather, engaged by assignments that have value, intellectual challenge, and real-world application.

Student engagement can be assessed in a number of ways. With older students, anonymous questionnaires are useful. Students should be encouraged to provide regular feedback on the quality and usefulness of a lesson, as well as the sheer fun a learning activity engenders. A large number of research studies have confirmed the validity of such student feedback. A substantial body of research by Professor Herbert Marsh of the University of New South Wales in Sydney, Australia, has demonstrated that student evaluations are closely related to other indicators of educational quality and often are more reliable than evaluations by peers and administrators. Marsh's instrument, the Student Evaluation of Educational Quality (SEEQ), has been administered to more than one million students in the U.S. at various levels in secondary and college classes.

With younger students, teachers may find that students are reluctant to articulate their satisfaction or dissatisfaction with an assignment. Nevertheless, teachers are able to gather very important feedback by observing students in unstructured time. If they choose to continue a learning activity, even when they have the choice of other "fun" activities, the teacher has powerful confirmation that the engagement level of the students is very high. In the case of some of the performance assessments in the appendix of this book, I have personally observed students devoting time during recess, as well as time before and after school, to those engaging tasks.

Clarity of Instructions

Colleagues and students are particularly helpful in the evaluation of the clarity of instructions. A delicate balance is necessary here. On one hand, teachers want to be sufficiently clear to ensure that the objectives of the learning activity are met. But the creator of an assignment should avoid being so pedantic that students have no opportunity to respond to the assignment in a manner that complies with the instructions yet is individually creative. As the examples in the previous chapters illustrate, there may be multiple ways students can respond to instructions and achieve the learning objectives the teacher had in mind, combining diligence in following directions with creativity and individual expression.

At the very least, the creator of a new assignment should ask one or two colleagues to review it and then ask a couple of students to read the instructions and then explain in their own words what the instructions mean. This process will usually allow the teacher to weed out unclear wording and replace it with more precise language where appropriate.

Clarity of Evaluation

The acid test of performance assessments is the extent to which two different evaluators can consider the same piece of student work and arrive at the same conclusion with regard to the essential question, "Does the work meet a specified performance standard?" To assess the clarity of your scoring guides, start with the reproducible handout entitled "Effective Scoring Guides" at the end of this book. Next, apply the rubric to five pieces of actual student work, recording your evaluation on a separate piece of paper so that other scorers will not see how you marked the student work. Then ask three or four colleagues to evaluate the same pieces of student work. If you agree on four out of five ratings, it is a good bet that your scoring guide is clear, consistent, and precise. But if the agreement is any less frequent than four out of five, then some additional clarity is necessary. Ambiguity in scoring guides is the enemy of clarity, consistency, and fairness. The improvement of performance assessments depends upon the relentless pursuit of clarity, so that students, parents, and potential critics of performance assessment know that your evaluations are objective, consistent, and fair.

Once you have made the language of the scoring guide as clear as possible with the help of a colleague, it is time for the real critics, the students, to help make the assignment the best it can be. Ask the students to rephrase the scoring guide in their own words. Sentences should begin, "To get a 1, I have to . . ." or "To meet the standard for this task, I must. . ." These descriptions may be more detailed and, on the surface, less elegant than those created by the teacher. The key criterion, however, is whether or not they are clear and meaningful to the students. If everyone in the class can agree on the relationship between various types of student work and the resulting evaluation, then a huge degree of subjectivity has been removed from the teacher's evaluation of student work.

Finally, a note must be added about the sources of the feedback you seek. These must be people who understand and believe in the concept of standards-based education. Unfortunately, this does not include all of your colleagues and administrators, some of whom are emotionally attached to a system of grading that is steeped in mystery and the presumption of subjective expertise. A personal example illustrates the point. Some years ago, while I was teaching graduate students about assessment, the dean of education criticized me for being "too objective." My syllabus outlined a menu of student assignments and specified the standards students were required to achieve in order to be proficient. If the students did not complete an assignment satisfactorily, they were required to submit it again. There was no such thing as a "C" for poor work. Either the assignment met the standards or it did not. This troubled the dean. After all, she reasoned, professors were supposed to be experts, and by definition, were to be subjective in their evaluations, drawing subtle distinctions between "A" and "B" work based on their superior knowledge of the subject matter. When I attempted to explain that rigor should have nothing to do with mystery and subjectivity, the dean replied that if the evaluation system were completely objective, "Then the students would simply be able to identify what they needed to do for an A and then achieve those objectives. There's nothing more to it! Why, in that system, everyone could get an A!" She did not say this with an expression of happiness or approval.

"Right," I responded, not understanding why there should be anything "more to it." The job of a teacher, whether in kindergarten or in graduate school, is not to sort and select, to award grades based on superior knowledge and mysterious insight. The job of the teacher is to establish clear standards and then give students the knowledge and skills to meet those standards. In a classroom dominated by the ethic of intellectual rigor, fairness, and transparency in evaluation systems, it is quite possible for all students to receive an "A" and, of course, it is possible that none of the students achieve this mark. In either case, however, there is absolutely no mystery about the matter. The dean and I were, and remain, galaxies apart in our understanding of the role of a teacher, but the incident gave me a valuable insight into why one cannot assume that everyone agrees with the standards-based approach to education.

Fortunately, the standards movement has suggested alternatives to those who see teachers as Confucian masters and students as helpless pawns. To create an educated populace while retaining a commitment to equity, we must use a process of standards-based assignments and assessments. These assessments must include careful evaluation and feedback, and will allow students and teachers to come to similar conclusions when comparing student work with an objective standard. The achievement of a standard does not require specialized knowledge, but rather should be as clear to the learner as it is to the teacher.

CHAPTER TWENTY

Step Eight: Clarify and Enrich the Assignment

The feedback you received in Step Seven (Chapter 19) will help the process of clarification. The two key elements to ensure sufficient clarity in a standards-based performance assignment are: 1) directions that students can follow with some consistency, and 2) scoring guides applied by teachers with the same results at least eighty percent of the time. Enrichment of the assignment is limited by the practical problem of time. The use of more complex and interesting activities means that there are, of necessity, fewer assignments in the course of a school year. Thus, it is essential that each assignment be as rich as possible in content, covering the most important standards. Some standards, particularly those involving reading comprehension and written expression, will be addressed in almost every assignment.

Augmentation for Diverse Abilities

The process of enrichment involves not only a consideration of the inclusion of other standards in the assignment, but also the augmentation of the assignment so that students with a wide range of abilities and backgrounds will find the activity challenging and engaging.

An example of this process is provided in the Ideal School exercise (you can find it among the sample performance assessments at the end of this book), which originated in a very diverse middle school mathematics class. A third of the students were recent immigrants with minimal English skills and another third had lost an entire year of middle school mathematics instruction due to changes in the school staff.

Thus, in one class there were students who knew trigonometry alongside students for whom number operations and elementary decimal problems were a significant challenge. In the past, the class had been divided into separate groups, with very little interaction between the "fast" students and the "slow" students. It did not take long for those labeled "slow" to understand that the worse their performance, the lower the expectations were for them. They were, in essence, being rewarded for playing dumb. They earned sympathy, early recess, and minimal work as rewards.

When this class became a standards-based classroom, all students were expected to demonstrate proficiency in number operations and elementary geometry. Those who were ready were expected to have the opportunity to demonstrate proficiency in more advanced subjects. To avoid the insidious "fast" and "slow" grouping with its negative academic and social consequences, the students were randomly divided into groups of three and were asked to create the plans for the Ideal School.

Architectural drawings offer a good illustration of the potential for the enrichment of an assignment because they can begin with problems as simple as the calculation of linear measures and scales: If one square equals three feet, how many squares will be used to represent 30 feet? But on the same problem, and in the same group, students can also calculate the areas of irregular geometric shapes, the angles of rooflines, the weight of materials, and even the load-bearing capacity of walls.

Every student in the group, regardless of his mathematical background, could make a meaningful contribution to the project and learn directly from the others. Because they were all working on the same project and had the same reference point, the mathematical relationships made sense to every member of the group. Moreover, the project was just plain fun. Students designed a luxurious student lounge overlooking major-league-size athletic fields and beautiful tennis courts (all drawn to scale and according to authentic dimensions they found from appropriate reference materials), while teachers and administrators were relegated to tiny rooms in the main building. Each classroom was designed with an abundance of windows, as the school was built around a courtyard and permitted light to enter each classroom from at least two sides. The students went beyond the requirements of the Americans with Disabilities Act (ADA) to provide practical help for a wheelchair-bound classmate. They included creative gym equipment within easy reach, ramps to the copy machine in the library so that all the buttons were accessible, and an elevator to the student lounge and to the athletic field.

As important as group work and collaborative learning are for the educational and social dynamics of a classroom, it is important to note that cooperative learning and individual accountability go hand in hand. The assignment of students to groups does not relieve them of the responsibility to submit individual work and to be individually accountable for the quality, timeliness, and proficiency of their work.

Extension Beyond the Grade Level

While there remains room for improvement in this assignment (every standards-based performance assignment is a work in progress), the Ideal School assignment illustrates the possibilities of a single enterprise capturing the attention of a very diverse group of students. When I am told, "You just can't have every student working on the same thing when their abilities are so different," my mind turns to the Ideal School assignment and the number of students who, in ten classroom days, learned more math than some of them had in the previous semester.

The opportunities for enrichment are there for every academic field, and the standards provide the key guidelines for this enrichment. A good rule of thumb is that students should have the opportunity to demonstrate proficiency in their own grade level as well as beyond it. Hence in a fourth grade classroom, teachers should consider not only the Kindergarten through fourth grade standards, but also several fifth through eighth grade standards as well. This is even more important at the high school level, where standards remain appallingly low in many districts. The dropout rate, which many people have attributed to inadequate academic abilities, is in many cases due to the sheer boredom faced by bright and capable students who see little point in devoting three years to a demonstration of the obvious. Secondary schools have a particularly challenging task to create performance assignments that will not only allow students to demonstrate proficiency in high school standards, but will also challenge and engage students who are otherwise bored and disinterested.

Engagement Through Motivation and Realism

Particularly at the secondary school level, the best enrichment is realism. Students need to come to school every day with the conviction that their presence makes a difference, not only to themselves but also to others. An enterprising middle school principal in one urban district inherited a terrible attendance problem. Students would get off the bus and simply walk away from school. In the afternoon they would wander back to the school grounds, board the bus, and head home to parents who were none the wiser. While some administrators may have hired truant officers, threatened expulsions, or sought other punitive measures to motivate students, this principal was aware of research establishing a positive relationship between the number of team activities and attendance rates. He tripled the number of team activities, starting several groups such as a debate team and sports teams normally available only at the high school level. A concerted effort was made to get every student in the school, not just the traditional athlete, involved in at least one of these activities. Teams were small and relationships were tight. Competitions and appropriate celebrations were held frequently, and students quickly learned that without their attendance, their team was in trouble. As student participation in teams increased, absenteeism decreased. By the end of the first year, truancy had declined an astonishing 35%. Why? Students, like most members of the human race, need to be needed. This principal created multiple opportunities for every student in school to feel that their presence was necessary and that their teammates depended on them. These students responded to neither pleas nor threats. They responded to the real need for their presence.

At the high school level, realism need not depend on team competitions, but can include the needs of the neighborhood and community. Students can understand that their participation in a social studies or mathematics class can make a difference in public works, pollution levels, governmental assistance, or any number of areas that can be analyzed in the context of a standards-based performance assignment.

Technology

The final means of enrichment available to teachers is the Internet. Students throughout the world are communicating directly with their counterparts in other countries, sharing information, and building bridges. For many students both here and abroad, this may be their only opportunity to change the stereotypes they have held of other cultures. The interdisciplinary possibilities are endless. A few examples include the creation of Internet newspapers (which can be distributed to classes in other countries) or a multi-national dialogue on an issue of public policy, such as the disposal of toxic wastes or international arms sales. These activities include student work in science, math, language, and social studies, and present an unlimited degree of complexity and challenge.

CHAPTER TWENTY-ONE

Step Nine: The Acid Test — Student Understanding and Use

At last we are ready to use the standards-based performance assessment with our students. If this is the first time students have approached such an assignment, it will be as different for them as it is for the teacher. Students who are used to a large number of short, self-contained assignments might be uncomfortable, because for years they have been trained to work quickly and alone so that upon the completion of the assignment, they can turn their attention to activities they enjoy. The rewards associated with classroom assignments have always been for haste and independence, rather than on revision, improvement, and cooperation. To smooth the transition during your first standards-based assignments, three elements are essential: parental involvement, modeling, and feedback.

Parental Involvement

Some initial communication with students and parents can be particularly helpful to avoid misunderstandings and possible confrontations. (See Chapter 25, Communicating About Standards With Parents and the Public.) Some students and their parents may challenge the new method of doing things. The parent packet, normally bulging with worksheets, will seem light to many parents after the first week of standards-based performance assessments. They are used to seeing many different assignments done once, rather than a single assignment with many revisions and improvements.

These issues should be addressed directly. Parents can be encouraged to become active participants in the development, improvement, and enrichment of standards-based assignments. Invite parents to school to discuss the assignment. Show them the standards and make it clear how the assignment is related to these essential learning expectations. Demonstrate how much more challenging the standards-based performance assessment is when compared to the worksheets used in the past. Enlist the help of parents, perhaps by asking them to develop an exemplary assignment or to clarify the scoring guide. Many teachers have shared with me excellent results when asking parents to use a scoring guide to practice evaluating student work. The anti-standards conversations surrounding effort and intentions, such as, "She tried so hard" and, "But he meant to do it differently," are replaced with, "This is what the student work is, and this is what the scoring guide required. Now I see how she can improve her work the next time."

Parents particularly welcome the use of scoring guides as an opportunity to improve the quality and accuracy of parent-child discussions surrounding school and homework. In standards-based schools, parents have moved far beyond the typical daily dialog:

"What did you do in school today?" *Nothin'.*

"Is your homework done?" *Sure.*

"Did you do your homework correctly?" *I dunno. I'll have to see what the teacher says tomorrow.*

When parents know that there are clear guidelines for student work, they ask to see the scoring guide or rubric. In a growing number of schools, teachers provide commonly used rubrics to parents at the beginning of the year. For task-specific rubrics, teachers routinely send them home and require parents to sign a statement to the effect that both the parent and student have read and understood the rubric. While this process represents a little more work at the beginning of an assignment, it saves many hours of complaints, aimless searching, and pointless excuses. In these standards-based classrooms, the rules for success are clear, and the opportunity for every student to achieve success rests with the students themselves. Rather than accept the contention that "the teacher didn't like me," parents are empowered to compare the student work to the requirements of the scoring guide.

Not every parent will respond to the introduction of standards-based performance assessments with enthusiasm. Nevertheless, I ask that teachers and school leaders persist.

Although the first foray into standards-based assignments may occasionally be uncomfortable, the policy must be implemented because it is the right thing to do. It is not only the right thing to do for academically gifted children who need additional challenge and rigor in the classroom, but it is emphatically the right thing to do for children who have traditionally been passed along without any expectation that they can or should meet the same standards other children are expected to meet.

Modeling

Step Six (Chapter 18) has already discussed the importance of developing an exemplary assignment. In addition, teachers should take advantage of the resources that are available to demonstrate vividly to students successful standards-based performance assignments. Teachers should also attempt to document each step of this process, including the use of videotapes (another opportunity for parental help). This will help students review their own performance against the scoring guide, provide documentation of proficient and exemplary performances for groups in the future, and also allow the teacher and district to monitor their progress toward standards achievement.

Some teachers maintain a "wall of fame" in which exemplary student work is displayed. In the most compelling examples of such displays, the scoring guide for each task is in the center of the "wall of fame" and an arrow or piece of yarn extends from the scoring guide text to the specific part of the displayed student work that marks it as exemplary. Success in these classes is not a mystery to be unraveled, but the result of persistence, hard work, and diligent pursuit of excellence. The path to success is not through popularity, but through matching student work to the standard.

Feedback

Because each standards-based assignment is a living document, constantly undergoing revision and improvement, a heavy emphasis should be placed on feedback from students and parents. The feedback must be focused on how the process can be improved. Parents can be particularly helpful with suggestions for scenarios involving their workplaces, personal activities, and community issues. As you shift classroom activities to a greater emphasis on realism, parents, as well as students, will become more interested in the real-world impact of their contributions to the classroom.

If you use cooperative learning groups as part of your teaching strategies, you can expect some comments such as, "Why does my child have to work in a group with the dumb kids?" and, "Why did that kid get the same grade as my child, when my child got it right the first time and that kid only got it right after getting feedback from the teacher and revising his work? That's not fair!"

Instead of reacting to such challenges with anger and defensiveness, it is best to think rationally through the process of learning with the parent. Most parents would agree that there have been times when they have learned a skill best by teaching others, and this is one opportunity created by randomly assigned groups. In addition, you can point out the enrichment opportunities available to students when they have demonstrated complete proficiency in a standard. Most importantly, standards present the opportunity for parents to identify the gap between what their children can do and what they are expected to do. Even the students with years of "A" and "B" grades on report cards will probably fall short on several standards and, thus, cannot afford to become complacent simply because they have performed at higher levels than other students in the same class.

One of the most significant changes in a standards-based classroom is the concept of revision and improvement. Because many of the assignments are done in groups, the notion that the student (and parents) should stay up late the night before a due date to finish work in a hasty and sloppy manner should become a relic of the past. Several intermediate evaluations must be provided so students can check their work against the scoring guide and determine what modifications are required. Parents can also assist the student in understanding the requirements, removing most of the ambiguity, which typically surrounds evaluation. Continuous effort with work clearly compared to a standard will replace last-minute frantic attempts to meet a deadline.

At the conclusion of the assignment, take some time to celebrate. Ask students to brainstorm ways the assignment can be made more challenging and fun for students in classes that follow. Invite parents and community members to observe the finished products, including the videotapes of some of the oral presentations. Give students the opportunity to express the sense of accomplishment they feel and ask them to write how the project has changed their view of learning and their view of themselves as learners. When the days are long and the profession seems more stressful than you can bear, take a moment to read those student comments. You will be reminded of the reasons why you put the extraordinary and worthwhile effort into becoming a standards-based educator.

CHAPTER TWENTY-TWO

Step Ten: Collaborate With Colleagues

If you have faithfully completed the first nine steps, you know that the development and implementation of standards-based performance assignments is hard work. In fact, it is impossible to do alone, and that is why the Tenth Step is so important. This step involves taking the time to share the results of your work with colleagues and to learn from their recent experiences in the creation of new performance assignments. Effective schools will do more than encourage teachers to share their work. They will foster an environment of professional collaboration by ensuring four elements are present: complete documentation, intensive and uninterrupted time, systematic distribution of information, and a program of recognition and rewards for teachers who create and share standards-based performance assignments.

Complete Documentation

Although the opportunities for creativity are almost unlimited, there should be some consistency in the format of standards-based performance assignments. In addition, teachers should include the following when creating a complete documentation package to share with their colleagues:

- Standard(s) on which the assignment is based

- Assignment instructions and detailed descriptions

- Scoring guide

- Results of actual student work

- Student comments

- Parent comments

- Personal reflections and suggestions for improvement

This complete documentation package will make it clear that collaboration with colleagues is not a cookbook of how to do performance assessments in three easy steps. Instead, it is a frank acknowledgment that your creative work involved an extraordinary effort and remains a work in progress. You fully expect the assignment to change, improve, and evolve over time.

Intensive and Uninterrupted Time

Because school faculties inevitably change from year to year, it is essential that administrators provide more than casual opportunities for the sharing of new performance assignments. A few minutes at a faculty meeting is not enough. The common practice of copying the documentation list and placing it in the mail boxes of other teachers without a word of explanation is insufficient. An administrator who is intent on making standards work will provide at least two uninterrupted hours every week for teachers to present, discuss, and improve upon the performance assignments they have created. I routinely work in schools where 45 minutes, an hour, and even 90 minutes of collaboration time are provided every day for educators. These are not in isolated, wealthy schools, but common practices among many public schools throughout the nation.

Although budgets are tight in virtually every district, clever administrators have found a number of ways to create time for teacher collaboration. Some of these methods include:

1. **Media Center Workshops**

   Most media center coordinators are woefully under-used. These professionals have a number of important skills, well beyond keeping the media center organized, and they have essential information they can readily share with students. The systematic use of media center workshops allows the classroom teachers time for collaboration.

2. **Volunteer Monitors for Study Groups**

   The teacher need not be present during every minute of every class. A number of volunteer sources (including parents, Americorps, Foster Grandparents, Service Corps of Retired Executives (SCORE), and community service groups) can all be tapped to provide a half-day per week of small group supervision.

3. **Administrator Classroom Activities**

   Principals who put their day-timers where their priorities are will spend time in the classroom so teachers can spend time developing and improving standards-based performance assignments. Some administrators spend a full day every week, usually in two-hour blocks, in one or two classes, working on subjects ranging from physical education to science or music. This expenditure of time sends an important message to teachers, parents, students, and central office administrators that standards are important.

Systematic Distribution of Information

To ensure information is shared with colleagues, there must be an ethic of consistent distribution of information, including works in progress. I have observed a problem in the early stages of standards implementation: Teachers are reluctant to share assignments they have created because these creations are less than perfect. Months, even years, can pass as nothing happens when everyone is reluctant to share work. Therefore, sharing must be systematic, with all teachers expected to share their results (even for works in progress) on at least a monthly basis. It will soon become clear that these preliminary results have the opportunity to become significant successes as teachers collaborate and work through the Steps in Part Two of this book. It will also become clear if some teachers are unwilling to participate in the standards movement. In this case, administrators will have to make some important decisions about the role that these people will play in a standards-based school district. In some schools, a "staff journalist" is appointed with the responsibility of identifying and codifying the best practices in teaching, assessment, parent communication, and other key components of educational effectiveness. These strategies are gathered in a booklet that is distributed at two important times. At the end of the year, the booklet is used to celebrate and recognize those who took the risk of contributing their work to the best practices booklet. At the beginning of the following school year, the booklet is used to set a standard of professional behavior for new faculty members. It sends an unmistakable message: "We expect you to share information and we need you to share your success stories. By the way, we don't expect you to say that student achievement can't happen here or that standards-based assessments will not work here, because this booklet is full of evidence of our success stories."

Recognition and Rewards

Teachers who create effective standards-based performance assignments are the real heroes of the standards movement. Their status should be celebrated and recognized on a continuous basis. Examples of effective means of recognition and rewards include the following:

- Publication credit in books of best practices in standards-based education.

- Professional development opportunities, including conference presentations and attendance at national and regional conferences.

- Cash bonuses for contributions to standards implementation. (Although employment agreements may inhibit some forms of additional payments, districts can purchase the rights to use the creative efforts of a teacher, as they would from private contractors.)

- Publication of success stories in local newspapers and magazines.

- Provision of recognition and rewards by business groups. (For example, some local business education committees have provided cash awards and vacation trips for teachers who have created and shared standards-based assignments. These businesses are particularly impressed with the realism, rigor, and high expectations of these assignments.)

Part Two of this book can be almost overwhelming. The Ten Steps to the creation of standards-based performance assignments require an enormous commitment of time, energy, and resources. In addition, they require the willingness of teachers to try new ideas, sometimes abandoning classroom activities that have been used for decades. These new techniques may also require occasional confrontations with parents and political forces opposed to the implementation of standards. The results are worth these efforts because every student, and ultimately the community, will reap enormous benefits as well.

The costs of delay or, worse yet, the price of failure in the implementation of standards can be enormous. These costs are measured in lifetimes of lost opportunities by those students who are stuck in a system that expects too little in the way of academic performance and demands too much in the way of mindless conformity. The ultimate costs for society are even greater.

Teachers cannot make standards work in a vacuum. We now turn our attention to the challenges faced by administrators and policy makers who must address standards implementation on district, state, and national levels.

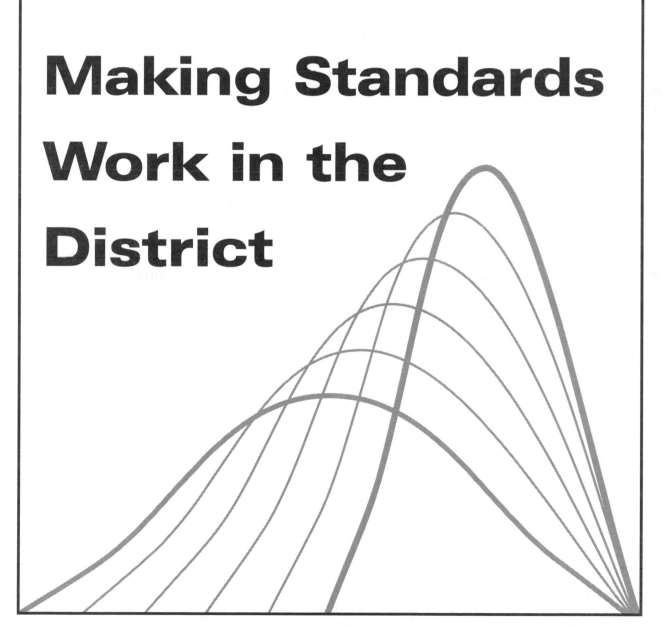

PART THREE

Making Standards Work in the District

CHAPTER TWENTY-THREE

Accountability: The Key to Public Acceptance

Schools at every level must be accountable. Whether it is the one-room private school reporting to the parents who pay the teacher's salary or the school systems of a nation reporting to political leaders, schools must do more than hold classes and discipline students. In the United States and throughout the world, the dominant theme in discussions of educational policy makers is accountability. From Nantucket to Nanjing, the questions are the same:

- How do we know if schools are making progress?

- How do we know if our students are learning what they should?

- How do we know if our children can be competitive in the global economy?

- How do we know if the resources we are investing in education are worthwhile?

Accountability is More Than Test Scores

The traditional response to these questions has been a litany of test scores. It is clear that the amount of testing is increasing; more than half the states have a high-stakes high school graduation examination and all states test students in the elementary and middle school years in reading and mathematics. These examinations, however, cannot provide a comprehensive answer to the questions posed by parents and policy makers. The difficulty of exclusive reliance on annual testing programs results from both methodological and political problems.

Some critics complain that tests lack validity. In order for a test to be valid, it must provide information on the quality that it purports to assess. Thus a driving test might be a perfectly fine assessment instrument, but the results from that test are not a valid representation of the mathematical ability of the student. If a test purports to reflect both the academic achievement of a student and the quality of a school, then it stands to reason that such a test is based on the standards and curriculum learned by those students in those schools. If, by contrast, the test assesses the general knowledge and skills of students but is not linked to the specific academic content learned by the student, then such a test cannot meet the essential requirement for validity. Like the driving test, the test of general knowledge and skills may be a fine test, but it is not a valid representation of student learning and teaching quality, because the test is not based on what was taught and learned. This is a problem in an astonishing number of states where the demand for a quick and easy test led to the selection of an "off the shelf" product rather than an assessment based on the academic standards that are in use in classrooms throughout the state. The problem becomes even worse when policy makers use data from national tests, such as the SAT I, to measure "progress" because such a test addresses neither the curriculum of the schools nor the degree to which students meet academic content standards.

Another common complaint directed at the use of test data is that the results appear to be contrived to make all children appear to be "above average," a phenomenon known as the Lake Woebegone Syndrome. As silly as this may sound, it is unfortunately true. In recent reports, all fifty states have claimed to be above average in educational performance. Derived from public radio personality Garrison Keillor's mythical community in which "all the children are above average," this phenomenon is a result of the comparison of test scores with a national comparison group. This comparison group, whose relationship to the national average may be as fictional as Lake Woebegone, creates the benchmark against which districts measure themselves. Hence, all of these districts can claim to be above average.

More troubling to policy makers is the chasm between many assessments and the academic content for which the schools are theoretically responsible. Academic content standards are complex documents, and it is a rare assessment that can possibly encompass all of the standards. But if accountability is to be reduced to a test score, then which standards are important? Is reading comprehension important, but written expression irrelevant? Is mathematical computation essential, but analysis and application of mathematical ideas unimportant? Any single answer to these questions is inherently unsatisfactory. Therefore, a number of districts are turning away from the use of test scores as they have traditionally been used. This chapter suggests some alternative methods of accountability that school systems may wish to consider as they seek to implement standards.

Between the Extremes: A Balanced View of Testing and Accountability

It is important to maintain a balanced view of testing. The national debate tends to two extremes, with one side excoriating all tests as wasteful and dangerous, with the very existence of testing leading teachers to transforms their classes into mindless boot camps devoted to test preparation. The other side, equally strident, declares that the only way to measure a school's effectiveness is annual test scores. Neither extreme offers clear answers to the reasonable questions raised at the beginning of this chapter. The reasonable middle ground includes two fundamental propositions. First, no single data point provides sufficient evidence to address student learning and school quality. Rather, a body of evidence that includes, but is not limited to, test scores should be considered. Second, data on student achievement is an important part of the equation, but it is an insufficient basis for evaluating school quality. A comprehensive approach requires both an analysis of effects (student achievement information) and causes (data on teaching, leadership, and curriculum).

Principles of Effective Accountability

Although accountability systems may vary from one school system to the next, the following four principles have universal application for the standards-based school system: 1) The accountability plan must be built on the foundation of standards; 2) The accountability measures must reflect both academic achievement and instructional variables; 3) Accountability measures must be clearly and immediately communicated; 4) The accountability system must itself be accountable.

1. **The accountability plan must be built on the foundation of academic standards.**

   If a board of education wishes to transform the process of standards administration into one more "Dead on Arrival" bureaucratic initiative, it need only create accountability measures based on the latest political fad, rather than the academic content standards of the district. The principle measurement of success in a standards-based district is the extent to which students are meeting the academic standards of the district and state. This is a subtle but important distinction. The most important measurement is not the average test score, the rank in the state, the average percentile, or any other comparative number. Rather, the critical measurement is the percentage of students who meet or exceed academic standards.

   • Measuring Student Progress

   The most important comparison is the same number for a previous time period. While most districts make year-to-year comparisons, they are almost always flawed because different students are being compared. The "gold standard" of accountability is a comparison of the same student group, so that the achievement of a group of students is followed over the course of years. Only in this way can policy makers address the question, "Are students improving their academic performance as a result of their experiences in our schools?" In a growing number of schools that are resolved to transform educational accountability into a constructive force, the flawed use of annual comparisons has been replaced with monthly indicators that show how the same group of students is progressing on a few key indicators. Rather than attempting to measure hundreds of standards once a year, these schools provide parents, teachers, and the public with the percentage of students who are proficient or higher in a few key areas, such as reading, writing, and mathematical problem-solving.

- The Comprehensive Student Achievement Record: The Foundation of Accountability Data

In order to create an effective accountability system, a school system must make a commitment to the technology needed to create a student-based data record. This student-based record includes the most important academic content standards (from kindergarten through high school graduation) and the dates the student was assessed on proficiency in these standards. Note that this is not a record of every academic standard, but only the most important ones that are essential for the student to proceed to the next level of instruction with success and confidence. Few teachers would insist that for a student to proceed to the 5th grade every single 4th grade standard must be met, but most teachers would agree that there are a few standards – perhaps only a dozen or so – that are absolutely vital if the student completing 4th grade is to experience success in the 5th grade. This snapshot of student performance is far more helpful in planning instruction and assistance for the student than the typical report card or the results of a single test. The student data record is ideally maintained in an Internet or Intranet accessible format, so that when the student moves from school to school, the frantic search for the traditional "cumulative folder" does not take place. Rather, the administrators, counselors, and teachers in each school have immediate access to the prior performance of this student. Middle school counselors need not wait to see a failure report before knowing that the 7th grader that entered school unable to perform number operations will require some assistance in mathematics before being successful in a pre-algebra class, or that the student who is reading on a 4th grade level should not be expected to comprehend a social studies textbook that presumes a 6th grade reading level. The student data record should be made available to parents at periodic intervals throughout each academic year. The accumulated data allow district policy makers to determine the extent to which students (and groups of students) are meeting standards. Thus the parents can ask, "How is my child doing?" and the policy makers and curriculum planners can ask, "How is our school system doing in preparing students for success in high school English?" Most importantly, the continuous nature of these records allows parents and policy makers to address these questions in a timely manner so that appropriate, corrective action can be taken.

- Practical Considerations in Creating Student Data Records

The creation of a single student-based data record will also accomplish another important objective most districts have failed to achieve: uniformity in computer hardware and software. In many districts, the computer system can best be described as creative anarchy, with students and teachers rigidly adhering to whatever brand name was in vogue years ago when they first learned to use a computer. As a consequence, when students and teachers move from one building to another, they must constantly relearn new software commands, keyboard layouts, and hardware schemes. The least sophisticated machines and the most stubborn building-level computer gurus determine this archaic connectivity of computers. Once a determination is made that every building will use a common student-based data record, then everything else, including databases, software, and hardware, will fall into place. The nation managed to agree that pencils with a "Number Two" lead would best meet the requirements of mechanical scoring machines, and I have never heard the advocates of number three or number one lead pencils complain that our common use of the number two lead infringed on their freedom. It is time that school systems come to a similar agreement about computer hardware and software.

2. **The accountability measures must reflect both academic achievement and instructional variables.**

Policies that announce an emphasis on math or reading, but provide no changes in curriculum, will create only cynicism and distrust. In order to create the opportunity to learn, a school system must acknowledge that the task is not accomplished simply by offering one more section of Algebra I because the school board has decided that more students should study algebra. Creating the opportunity to learn requires that the school system acknowledge that the academic expectations are fixed, but the time it takes students to achieve those standards will be variable. Hence, it is necessary to offer a curriculum that permits students to take longer than has traditionally been the case to achieve math standards, instead of simply recycling students through the same math classes again and again.

There are three models of the relationship between courses, student achievement, and curriculum change. In the first model, the system responds to student failure with repetition of the same strategy. You fail Algebra I, so you retake Algebra I. Perhaps, the old joke goes, if we "do algebra louder" the second time around it will be more effective.

The second model anticipates failure and avoids it by allowing students to choose to avoid challenging academic standards. Thus the student in danger of failing Algebra I is channeled into a basic mathematics course, with a title that is clever enough to meet accreditation requirements from the state but transparent to the students and teachers who are part of the model. In these classes, expectations are lower, students are not prepared for future success in math class, and, in fact, the low expectations that students have of themselves are confirmed. They call it "dummy math" not only because of the low level of challenge, but because of the students' images of themselves.

In the third model of instruction, time is the variable, but the expectations of students are consistent. To continue the example of the 9th grade student facing failure in Algebra I, this model recognizes the truth (the student is unable to succeed in the traditional Algebra I class) but employs a strikingly different strategy than the second model. Rather than channel the student away from challenge and rigor, the third model identifies the steps necessary for success in Algebra I, and provides those steps. If the 9th grade student cannot add, subtract, multiply, and divide, it does not logically follow that the student cannot learn algebra, but it does imply that the student will need more than one 42-minute per day traditional algebra class. The inevitable but mythical challenge to the implementation of the third model is that assessment and intervention requires more resources than most schools have. This is not logical, since the same schools have the resources to repeat courses after a failure in the first model and to add new courses after a failure in the second model. Surely the same resources could be used in a proactive manner to stop the cycle of failure.

- Cross-Curricular Opportunities for Achievement

    A district shows it has created the opportunity to learn when students can demonstrate mathematics proficiency in their home economics and woodshop classes and when they can demonstrate their statistics proficiency in a psychology class. In other words, the opportunities are widely varied, but the standards and expectations are consistent. A commitment to the principle of measuring instructional variables will reveal whether such mantras as "writing across the curriculum" and "cross-curricular mathematics" are illusions or realities. A quick examination of the student data records that are the core of the accountability system will reveal the extent to which writing has been assessed outside of the confines of an English Language Arts class and the degree to which mathematics has been assessed outside of a traditional math class. If every teacher is committed to making a clear and measurable contribution to the academics of students, then every teacher in every subject will have the opportunity to provide a meaningful contribution to the accountability system.

    The comprehensive nature of accountability addresses an important morale issue that plagues many schools in which only some teachers in some grades feel accountable. In other districts, by contrast, every teacher in every subject at every grade level provides monthly or quarterly information on the performance of students in the most important academic content standards. Case studies of several such school systems reveal that the faculty has better morale, greater levels of teamwork, and higher levels of student achievement than when they are fragmented and the burden of accountability falls on only a few teachers and is measured with only a few tests. For more elaboration on successful models of educational accountability, readers may wish to consult two books on this subject: *Holistic Accountability: Helping Students, Schools, and Communities* (Reeves, 2001) and *Accountability in Action: A Blueprint for Learning Organizations* (Reeves, 2000).

3. **Accountability measures must be clearly and immediately communicated.**

Delays in the dissemination of information spark public distrust about any accountability system, and this prevents administrators from making meaningful data-driven decisions. Once a district has established the student-based data record, within days of every reporting period it should be clear the extent to which standards are being met for every student, classroom, building, and area within a district. This collection of information from the accountability system must be immediately and directly shared with principals, teachers, students, parents, leaders, policy makers, and other key constituencies.

Accountability, properly done, is not a nasty surprise from a higher authority, but a strategic tool designed to affect directly the educational environment in the classroom. In creative districts such as Wayne Township near Indianapolis, Indiana; Riverview Gardens near St. Louis, Missouri; Columbus, Ohio; Orange County, California; Milwaukee, Wisconsin; and a growing number of other schools, the goals that principals and site-based decision-making teams establish in their annual educational plans are directly related to a district-wide accountability system.

4. **The accountability system must itself be accountable.**

The validity and reliability of accountability measures cannot be assumed, but must be constantly measured and subjected to challenge, improvement, and revision. This emphatically does not mean that every student must take the same test in order for the achievement of standards to be demonstrated. Instead, districts should consider the concept of concurrent validity tests, in which teacher-created assessments are the primary determinant of standards achievement, and district-wide assessments are performed to obtain random samples of students. Samples of students can take a district-wide assessment (also based on the same standards), and the results of these assessments can be compared to the data from the standards achievement reports. While some disparities may occur due to differences in the forms of the assessments, the results should be consistent in a very high percentage of cases. If a teacher is reporting that 95% of her students are meeting standards, but a district-wide assessment performed with a sample of students from that class indicates that only 50% of students are meeting standards, then such a disparity should be investigated. The converse may be the case in some schools, and it is possible that classroom teachers will be more rigorous in determining whether or not students meet standards. Well-crafted, teacher-created, classroom-level assessments are more likely to indicate a student does not meet the academic content standards than are the results of a standardized test. Traditional assessments might label that student as "average" and hence give him the false sense of security that he is "satisfactory," while the standards-based performance assessment will clearly label student performance as "progressing" or "not meeting standards," even if a comparison to other students might indicate that such work is above average.

The use of this concurrent validity system saves enormous resources for the district. In most cases it will increase public confidence when the district-wide test results show a higher level of achievement than had been reported by the teachers.

Accountability is a complex issue. Readers desiring to learn more about this subject should consult the web site of the International Center for Educational Accountability, www.edaccountability.org and the Center for Performance Assessment, www.makingstandardswork.com. Both of these sites provide free articles and access to other resources to help teachers, school leaders, and educational policy makers make accountability a constructive force for improving teaching, learning, and leadership.

Organizing the District for Standards Implementation

Just as the creation of standards is a team effort, the successful implementation of standards at the district level requires a masterful job of coordination by the superintendent and other educational leaders. It is not enough to issue decrees, pass resolutions, and appoint a standards coordinator in order for a district to achieve the equity and academic success that are the hallmarks of effective standards implementation. A network of implementing entities must be created and continually fine-tuned to meet the individual needs of the schools within the system. To achieve this purpose, I favor the use of task forces instead of committees.

Task Forces Replace Committees

The task force, as its name implies, is assembled by the superintendent for a specific purpose. It has a clear mandate for action. Unlike a committee, a task force does not have perpetual existence. The task force does not exist to hear reports, but to analyze and synthesize information, make recommendations, and take action. The task force exists for the sole purpose of implementing standards and reporting directly to the superintendent on its successes and challenges. The task force also provides tremendous flexibility. The composition and direction of the task force can be changed whenever it is necessary.

Task Force Structure

It is essential that standards task forces not be lost in the bureaucracy. If you expect to attract the best teachers and administrators, as well as busy parents, community activists, business leaders, and students to serve on these bodies, then it must be clear to all concerned that the task forces have clout. In the educational system, that means direct access to and attention from the superintendent. A group of ten to twelve people for each of the three task forces discussed below will provide a large enough group for community representation, but a small enough group so that every individual can make a significant contribution.

Operations of the Task Forces

The task forces should meet quarterly. My experience is that a monthly meeting is too great a commitment for many busy people and the absentee rate becomes excessive. By contrast, quarterly meetings offer the promise of fewer meetings that are longer in duration. If all four meetings are scheduled a year in advance (most busy people keep their calendar at least that far in advance), then it will be clear at the time members are recruited whether or not they will be able to attend every meeting. It should be clearly understood that missing more than one meeting will automatically result in the superintendent appointing a replacement.

Each meeting entails a substantial commitment of time, perhaps as much as four hours. Initially, two hours are devoted to the agenda of the task force, and then another two hours should be devoted to public input. Public participation is essential during the implementation phase of standards. Therefore, task force members must be good listeners as well as people who can articulate their own ideas thoughtfully.

Many administrators have become frustrated with what seems to be an unending discussion of standards. "Can't we just get to it?" they ask. The frustration is understandable, and therefore some boundaries must be placed on the discussion. The purpose of public input is to decide how best to improve student achievement and improve equity. It is not about whether to pursue these goals. In brief, the conversation is about how to make standards work, not whether we should abandon standards and return to the Bell Curve. That may be a conversation that some people in your community want to have, and they are free to lobby their legislators for the repeal of academic standards. But that is not the purpose of the public input to the task forces. This is a focused and constructive conversation about the best way to make progress, not whether progress is a good idea.

Although the needs of each district will vary, and the composition, titles, and missions of task forces can be changed to meet local needs, you may wish to consider the following three key task forces for standards implementation: Standards Development, Assessment, and Curriculum.

1. **Standards Development Task Force**

   Wait a minute! Forty-nine states have already developed standards and the fiftieth, Iowa, has developed standards at the district level. So isn't this job already done? In fact, the states have established standards, but the job of developing the standards is far from complete. The Standards Development Task Force exists for the purpose of increasing the value of state standards by adding focus, prioritization, and discernment to the standards implementation process. The principal purpose of this task force is to review, revise, and improve standards. The very existence of such a task force makes it clear that the district's standards are a living document, and that standards will change with advances in technology and the needs of the community. Although state standards may appear to be non-negotiable demands that are not subject to revision and discussion, the role of the Standards Development Task Force is essential. By prioritizing standards, the task force can help the superintendent and board to say what every teacher knows: There are too many standards and some standards are more important than others.

Organizations as diverse as the American Association of School Administrators, the National Education Association, and the National Association of Secondary School Principals have all agreed that there is a critical need for focus and prioritization in state standards. Because the state departments of education are committed to the principle of listening to different points of view and accumulating various ideas for academic standards, the national trend has been the creation of standards documents that grow in size and specificity with each revision. Because the number of school days and the hours has remained constant, the unintended consequence of the growing number of standards has been a reduction in emphasis on each academic requirement. The only way out of this conundrum is for the Standards Development Task Force to identify with clarity and authority those few standards that are essential.

By having a single group look at all of the standards in a holistic manner, it will be clear that some key skills appear in multiple disciplines and thus offer great opportunities for focus and cross-disciplinary instruction. The omission of a state standard from the "essential" list does not mean that the district is rejecting it. On the contrary, the district is embracing the state standards by adding value to them and not dealing with them in a superficial manner. Finally, this process gives clear guidance to teachers, curriculum planners, and assessment designers so that all participants in the instructional and leadership system are focusing on the most important areas.

2. **Assessment Task Force**

This group should include teachers who have developed successful, standards-based performance assessments as well as parents and business community members. It is essential that the superintendent help to prevent this group from becoming dominated by the assessment bureaucracy that exists in many districts. Although the expertise of people in testing and assessment departments can be useful, they frequently have a vested interest in the use of standardized tests as the sole measurement of student achievement. They may even be threatened by the idea that the primary focus of standards-based assessment is on teacher-created instruments rather than on nationally standardized multiple-choice tests.

The Assessment Task Force should scour the district for the best practices in assessment and help to provide the systematic documentation essential to sharing these assessments throughout the district. The business representatives in the group can be of enormous assistance in the continuous improvement of assessments so that they contain realistic scenarios. This Task Force can also serve as the strategic impetus to the district-wide accountability system and mobilize support for the implementation of the student-based record of standards achievement.

In order for the Assessment Task Force to focus on the most important standards, it is imperative that communication between this group and the Standards Development Task Force is frequent and clear. Even the best assessment is of limited value if it focuses on a nonessential standard. In the most successful Assessment Task Forces I have observed, the ultimate results include common end-of-course assessments and, ultimately, common end-of-unit assessments. While teachers retain a great deal of creativity and independence with respect to when and how to teach certain subjects, at the end of the year each student is expected to meet the standards and to be assessed using a common testing instrument. This assures consistent expectations and allows teachers and instructional leaders to find strengths and challenges, a process essential to the continuing improvement of teaching and learning.

3. **Curriculum Task Force**

The purpose of this task force is to review and monitor school curricula and ensure that every child in every school has the opportunity to meet the district's standards. While this need not imply a "curriculum of the day" approach to instruction, it certainly indicates that there are clear objectives each year and perhaps at more frequent intervals so that the opportunities students have for learning are governed by the standards and not by a neighborhood.

This can be a very threatening prospect to those who have operated independently in the creation of curricula in individual schools. In the name of site-based decision making, many districts have dismantled a large part of the curriculum development capabilities of the district, and principals, parents, and teachers have filled the vacuum. Although site-based decision-making has provided some excellent opportunities for creativity in individual schools, it has also led to some grave omissions from a standards-based curriculum. In my discussions with some principals and teachers about the need to implement a standards-based curriculum, some have responded indignantly, "We have site-based decision-making, so we do our own curriculum." Well, not exactly. When the state and district have established academic content standards, then students must have the opportunity to meet those standards at every school in the district. Site councils notwithstanding, a school does not have the prerogative to decide that it need not offer an algebra class. Schools have the flexibility to decide *how* to meet standards, but they do not have the flexibility to decide *whether* to meet standards.

Consider a couple of examples taken from discussions with teachers in the past few years.

"In my 7th grade English class, we just focus on literature. They will get composition next year and they should have learned to write before they came here." If the state standards include writing for middle school students, and this is the case in every state, then the omission of writing is not an option. Of course the requirement for writing can be integrated with literature, but it is a requirement, not an option. It should be noted in passing that one of the best ways for teachers to assess a student's understanding of literature is to require the student to write summaries, analyses, and comparisons.

"This is a math class, not an English class. I just want the right answer; I don't care if they can write about it." State standards routinely require students to explain their mathematical reasoning, and a growing number of state math tests include the requirements for students to explain their answers in writing. In these circumstances, the decision to deny students the opportunity to learn about writing in a math class is not a matter of personal choice. It is unfair and wrong. Few math teachers (and I am one) would regard it as an acceptable strategy to omit the Pythagorean Theorem from a geometry class. It is equally unacceptable to omit writing from a math class when written communication about mathematical reasoning is part of the state academic standards.

"In my social studies class, the kids just aren't interested in history, so we spend most of our time on current events." There are many times in the life of a teacher when we are called to distinguish between popularity and effectiveness. If ever there was a time for students to learn history, the nature of democracy, and the sacrifices made by generations that preceded us, it is now. An essential part of the critical thinking that should accompany a productive discussion of current events is a grounding in the facts of history, geography, economics, and culture. While many current-events discussions in schools create the opportunity for a "fact-free" discussion of opinions, an approach rooted in academic standards requires that facts precede opinions. Thus current events are not irrelevant, but are rigorously placed in historical context.

These are just a few of the examples of how a Curriculum Task Force can help educators and school leaders implement academic standards with fairness, rigor, and equity. Ultimately, the rationale for this task force is not the reduction of academic freedom, but the increase of educational opportunities for all students throughout the school system.

Task Force Results

Each of these task forces should have staff support, including a senior administrator and secretary. The history of education reform is littered with ineffective committees that spoke eloquently about the need to change, while the central office, principals, and teachers proceeded without noticing their existence. Task forces associated with standards implementation must be different. Their composition and operation, as well as the personal involvement of the superintendent in the recruiting and appointment of members, will signal this striking difference. Some other strategies that will make standards task forces more effective include the following:

1. **Public Reporting**

   At least once each year the task forces should provide a detailed public report to the school board. Particular attention should be paid to the public hearings the task force has held and the emphasis the group has placed on public participation. The performance of the task force on its specific goals for the past year should be reviewed and the goals for the coming year should be announced. There is great power in allowing the task force, rather than the media department of the school district or the superintendent, to make this report. The news media may be unimpressed with one more unsolicited news release, but they may be willing to cover a press conference held by a major community or business leader who is discussing educational issues.

2. **Data Collection and Reporting**

   Every effective task force must be data-driven. This means that their goals are established in quantitative terms and reported graphically. In particular, the Assessment Task Force should examine far more than the score reports from standardized tests. They must dig into the results of Standards Achievement Reports and other quantitative and qualitative indicators of student performance. Reports of teacher and leadership performance are equally important. The number of teacher-created performance assessments based on academic standards is a quantifiable indicator, and it should be clear whether the district is providing more assessments of higher quality this year than last year.

3. **Leadership**

   The superintendent, who ultimately bears the responsibility for implementing standards, should identify task force leadership. The superintendent should not hesitate to replace leaders who cannot or will not achieve the objectives of the task force. Leaders should not necessarily be drawn from the ranks of senior central office administrators. In fact, it would send an important message if one of the task force leaders were a classroom teacher and if another leader was a business or community leader. The community must own standards, and the role of administrators is to support and implement this jointly held vision.

CHAPTER TWENTY-FIVE

Communicating About Standards with Parents and the Public

In the politically charged atmosphere surrounding most educational discussions, rarely do emotional convictions give way to facts and logic. Certainly this is the case when it comes to debates about standards and performance assessments.

This chapter seeks to identify some myths both sides have used in this particularly muddled debate in the hope that, regardless of predisposition, we can place in the forefront our belief in integrity and intellectual discourse, which are best served by facts rather than myths.

This chapter also offers some observations about the use of a Standards Achievement Report as a means of effectively and consistently communicating to parents and other constituencies about the progress of students in your schools. (The Standards Achievement Report is covered in more detail in Chapter 9.) The chapter concludes with some comments about the frequently heard allegation that educational standards lead to the presumably evil practice of "teaching the test."

Defending Performance Assessments Without Being Defensive

The chasm between the two sides of the standards issue is rendered wider because of the rancorous tone of the rhetoric both sides employ. When the debate should be focused on the issues of rigor, validity, and reliability, it appears all too frequently to be focused instead on an exchange of angry words that generate more heat than light. Defenders of standards-based performance assessments are castigated as "politically correct" or "educational sentimentalists." Defenders of multiple choice tests are, in turn, described in such terms as "old fashioned" and "inflexible," or are dismissed as people who just do not understand the problem. Neither set of labels is particularly constructive for those whose genuine concern is the development of a rational educational assessment system.

Myth Number 1: Multiple Choice Tests are Inherently Objective, While Performance-Based Tests Are Inherently Subjective.

The adherents to this particular myth begin with the premise that there is one true answer to every question. Only an educational assessment specialist or an economist, they joke, could believe that mathematical questions have more than a single answer. Apparently such people are unacquainted with some of the mathematics worksheets common in elementary schools today.

The history of multiple choice testing is replete with predisposition, bias, and outright bigotry. In the 1920's, the precursors to the modern college admission tests were used to demonstrate not only that people with white skin were superior to those with black and brown skin, but also that northern Europeans were superior to southern Europeans.

Clearly, the notion that a limited answer-set conveys the status of objectivity is unsupported by the evidence. The objectivity of a test does not depend on a limited number of responses, but rather upon the extent to which a response to a question fairly and accurately indicates the degree of the student's knowledge of a subject. It is possible for a multiple-choice test to achieve this standard. It is also possible for a performance-based test to achieve this same standard. Both test formats can fail the test of objectivity. Thus it is not format, but consistency and fairness that is the appropriate test of objectivity.

Myth Number 2: Multiple Choice Tests Are More Rigorous Than Performance-Based Tests.

This is another popular notion surrounding the debate about performance assessments. Educators who have administered multiple-choice tests know that a certain number of the correct answers are simply the result of random selection. These answers are not associated with the student's knowledge, but with guessing, rightly termed "error," as educational measurement specialists use the word. With four or five possible responses in most multiple-choice tests, the possibility for random choices being labeled as correct is between 20% and 25%. Contrast this to a performance-based examination in which a student is required to demonstrate mastery of a task, such as an algebraic proof, an elaboration of the causes of the American Civil War, or the dissection of a frog. There is not a 25% likelihood that a student will guess right in any of these instances. Indeed, virtually any performance assessment is clearly more rigorous than its multiple-choice counterpart.

Myth Number 3: Performance-Based Tests Yield Inconsistent Results.

As is the case with many myths, there is an element of truth in this. Indeed, performance-based tests do yield inconsistent results, but that is true of every single test of any type that has a reliability coefficient of less than 1.00. A reliability coefficient is a measure of how two judges score the same exam. A reliability coefficient of 1.00 means they are in complete 100% agreement. Multiple-choice tests also yield inconsistent results that can be studied and measured. Most of the literature surrounding performance-based tests indicates that poor levels of consistency, frequently measured by inter-rater reliability, is a direct function of the amount of training the raters have received. **Inter-rater reliability** is a term used to describe the relationship of the scores (ratings) among two or more judges (raters). It can be computed in a variety of ways from simple correlation to percentage of agreement. A larger number indicates a greater degree of agreement. When teachers rely on a two-hour workshop and a cursory review of instructions, they are likely to provide inconsistent ratings to student work. Extensive training, combined with clear and specific rating rules, provides for much higher degrees of consistency. This requirement for clear rating rules not only leads to statistical soundness, but also leads to a greater fairness for the students. After all, they are the ones who have taken the examination. It does not seem to be an excessive requirement for any teacher or any school district to state in simple and clear language exactly what the requirements are for student success and for the vast majority of teachers to agree on the meaning of those requirements.

Myth Number 4: Performance-Based Assessments Are Inherently Virtuous.

The exaggerations by the defenders of performance-based assessments are just as damaging as the myths of those who attack them. Successful education reform does not depend on the mere implementation of something labeled a "performance assessment," but rather upon excellent, rigorous, valid, and reliable performance assessments. Unfortunately, many school districts and states have fallen into the trap of taking a traditional multiple-choice test, adding a quick essay or short answer response to it, and labeling the whole affair a "performance assessment." Merely labeling it as a performance assessment does not make it so.

Performance-based assessments, meeting the criteria discussed throughout this book, must be clearly linked to an objective standard. These standards must be described in specific terms that students, not merely the committees that distribute them, clearly understand. They must also be supported with significant amounts of professional development time and energy, so that the results of the assessments are similar, regardless of which teacher is doing the rating. If students are to be held to higher standards, and this surely is the core of most educational reform efforts, then the assessment of those standards must be the best we can devise.

In making the case for performance-based assessments, educators and policy makers alike should focus on the essentials of rigor, validity, and reliability rather than engage in polemics on the evils of multiple-choice testing. Indeed, the political price to be paid for the introduction of performance testing may well be the concurrent use of some multiple-choice tests, at least on a random basis. The result that thoughtful people must seek is not a debating victory, but improved educational achievement for the students to whom we are ultimately accountable.

Myth Number 5: Teaching to the Test Corrupts the Process of Learning.

Some people believe the practice of teaching to the test is inherently limiting. Such a practice, they argue, prevents the exposure of students to a broad range of subjects, and sends the message that acquisition of knowledge is merely for the purpose of achieving the short-range goal of regurgitating information on a test, rather than integrating and synthesizing knowledge over a lifetime.

Other participants in this debate respond with equal vigor that assessment should have a direct impact on curriculum, and that teaching to the test is precisely what teachers ought to be doing. If this is limiting, it is only because the test itself is too narrowly constructed or because the teacher has chosen to limit curriculum inappropriately. Such an argument, unfortunately, misses the essential point. It is clearly of little ethical or educational value to teach specific answers to specifically anticipated test questions at the exclusion of broad and deep knowledge of an academic subject. However, it can be entirely appropriate to teach to the test when the test is not a single assessment, but a yearlong series of complex and comprehensive performance assessments. In this context, "teaching to the test" implies a coherent, relevant, and fair series of instructional practices that are clearly linked to assessment. Students are accountable for knowledge and analytical techniques that they have studied. Assessments help students demonstrate proficiency in these areas, and teachers can plan instruction to help promote these areas of proficiency.

Teaching Test-Taking Skills

In addition to the essential role of aligning assessment with curriculum, the correct method of teaching to the test can help students learn test-taking skills. In every other school endeavor, we expect students to learn the rules of the game. This is evidenced most clearly in physical education classes, in which students must learn the boundaries of the athletic field, the method of passing a soccer ball, football, baseball, or volleyball, and a host of other rules. We know that an understanding of the rules will help lead to success in that particular endeavor. In academic classes, students also learn rules of behavior, discourse, written expression, and other skills that will help them achieve success in those arenas.

Why, then, should we be at all reluctant to acknowledge that there are rules of the game in the common practice of taking tests? Given the increasing propensity in all areas to test employees on a repeated basis, a strong argument can be made that test-taking is a skill, as essential to the successful student as excellent communication, mathematical ability, and other skills upon which there would be common agreement about their essential nature.

What constitutes test-taking skills? Contrary to the frequent allegations of test critics, it is not mindless drills with practice test questions. Test-taking skills, properly developed, have nothing to do with the memorization of specific answers to specific questions, but rather involve the development of mechanisms for analyzing test questions and responding efficiently and effectively to them. The first principle of successful development of test-taking skills is the recognition that it is a skill and not a natural result of innate intellectual ability.

None of us would expect to pass an examination dependent upon our ability to shoot 10 consecutive basketball shots from a free throw line by reading books by Dr. Naismith (the originator of basketball) or attending lectures by Michael Jordan. Instead, the development of this skill depends on picking up the basketball and practicing the skill of shooting free throws. The same principle applies to the development of the skill of test taking. For example, instead of just reading history, students should prepare for a history test by writing responses to possible essay questions, short answer questions, and multiple choice questions. Effective practice, however, is not merely an endless repetition of practice questions. Rather, students and teachers analyze the question, explaining not only the correct responses, but why the wrong answers are wrong.

If We Do Not Have Multiple Choice Test Scores, What Do We Report?

Parents and students naturally want to have a straight answer to the question, "How is the student doing?" In the past, this question was answered with a letter or a number. A student with an 81 average or a "C" was presumed to be satisfactory, whether or not that student had met the expectations of teachers and the community at large. On the other hand, some schools have implemented standards, leaving parents and the community with a vague sense of unease. When parents are told only that students are "in progress" on the path toward proficiency, they are left without a clear sense of how the student can improve. One creative response to this dilemma is the Standards Achievement Report, or SAR. (Please see Chapter 9 for more information, including a sample SAR.)

Effective communication about standards depends on a discussion that is, above all, committed to the principles of truth and mutual respect. Moreover, when parents, students, and teachers discuss academic performance, effective communication depends on the use of a consistent vocabulary about standards. The SAR is a good first step in initiating these discussions.

Why Before What

A final rule for educators and school leaders to consider when communicating about standards to parents, the public, and to professionals within our schools is "why before what." Almost a decade after academic standards became the dominant movement in American education, there remains a mountain of misunderstanding and mistrust. The only way to break through the fog that hangs over many educational discussions is a relentless pursuit of clarity and truth. Before presenting information about what the standards are or how students are performing on standards-based tests, we must first remind ourselves and our stakeholders about why we have standards in the first place. The two compelling justifications for standards – fairness and effectiveness – are not self-evident. In a recent conversation with public television officials who arranged a forum to discuss academic standards, they noted that it was easy to assemble a panel dominated by those who opposed standards, but difficult to find advocates. If that is true of sophisticated students of public policy at our television stations, how much more likely is it to be true of parents and community members? They receive a steady diet of allegations that standards are linked to tests and those tests are bad for children, and that therefore standards are an evil to be rooted out of the schools.

As a reader who has persisted to the penultimate chapter of this book, the case for standards may be clear to you. But that case is not clear to your community or to the nation. You must persist in making it on a regular basis by communicating the "why" of standards each time the opportunity presents itself. Every standards-based report card, every accountability report, and every release of standards-based performance data should include a brief reminder to readers, listeners, and viewers that fairness and effectiveness are at the heart of the rationale for academic standards.

CHAPTER TWENTY-SIX

Responding to Constituent Challenges

School superintendents and board of education members live in an environment of almost constant challenge. Political and religious groups, union leaders, business owners, and a host of other administrators and board candidates all believe that they can do the job better. Every initiative, particularly a sweeping one such as standards implementation, provides an opportunity for public criticism. In a democracy, such dissent is an inevitable part of public life. Our fervent wish that political discourse at the beginning of the 21st century would become a bit more civil than it was in the closing years of the last century does not appear to have much hope of coming to fruition.

Even consultants get to be on the receiving end of this vituperation. I have been excoriated by the religious right for advocating too much national and state involvement in education, criticized by union leaders for encouraging unrealistic expectations of school employees, and chastised by district officials for being insufficiently critical of teachers and principals. If a commitment to the truth entails making all sides equally angry, then these accusations are probably best described as a good day's work.

As most superintendents, policy makers, and other educational leaders must admit, we do make mistakes, and make them with a high degree of regularity. In a "Skunk Camp" (an intensive workshop for senior managers) I attended fifteen years ago, management theorist Tom Peters remarked that as the pace of society increases in the 21st century, we cannot count on making fewer mistakes. Rather, Peters concluded, it is necessary that we make our mistakes more quickly and recover from them faster. Effective leaders are willing to follow Martin Luther's dictum to "sin boldly," and there are no doubt elements of this book that fall into that category.

This chapter suggests four fundamental strategies for effective leaders who face inevitable challenges in their quest to make standards work: personal responsibility, focus, networking, and, as a final but necessary alternative, confrontation.

Personal Responsibility

There are few things more disarming to a critic than simply saying, "You're right. We goofed, and it's my fault." If I had any advice for a superintendent (whether new on the job or a twenty-year incumbent) it would be this: The way to establish credibility with parents, students, teachers, board members, and the public is not to try to be perfect. Admit to making a colossal mistake the moment you recognize it and immediately take personal responsibility for it, assuring your stunned critics that they can count on many more mistakes as you move decisively to improve the educational quality of schools in your district. Most leaders will not have to wait too long before making such a grand faux pas, particularly in the complex enterprise of implementing standards. There will be terrible textbooks, bad teachers, inappropriate assignments, invalid assessments, incompetent administrators, and task forces that never get off the ground. Each of these offers the opportunity for the leader to take personal responsibility and, without missing a beat, continue the steady implementation of standards. It will soon become apparent that neither political challenges nor administrative snafus will stop you from your mission. And each admission of personal responsibility will earn genuine (if grudging) respect from those who are used to the administrative tap dance of circumlocution and a search for culprits on whom blame can be assigned.

Focus

Just as the effective teacher must pull the weeds before planting the flowers, the leader of a district must also make standards implementation the focus for the next several years, which means that some of the other issues in which the leader may have traditionally played a personal role must give way. It is not reasonable for the superintendent to become personally involved in budget formation, union negotiations, and capital construction while creating 25 direct reports and reviewing several hundred performance evaluations every year. Yet this is the norm, not the exception, for the organization of many school districts. Best-selling author Jim Collins has documented the leadership practices behind the success of some of the world's most flourishing and enduring organizations. Collins suggests that anyone can make a "to do" list; it is the creation of a "not to do" list that is far more challenging. The discipline of focus is a characteristic of the best organizations and the most successful leaders, and focus comes not only from deciding what to do, but what to avoid.

Focus Requires Delegation to a Senior Leader

If the leader is to focus on standards implementation—the initiative that can have the greatest long-term impact on the quality of education and the success of the leader's administration—then other responsibilities must be delegated to a capable senior leader. A senior leader is not the same as a high-level administrator. The senior leader is a senior executive comparable to a chief operating officer in the corporate sphere. The chief operating officer does not replace the chief executive officer (the superintendent), but instead assumes responsibility for many of the day-to-day issues that formerly consumed large amounts of the superintendent's day. Decisions on school closings, weather delays, discipline, and even a good number of central office staff meetings can be handled by the chief operating officer. Only with this assistance can the district's leader focus on standards. When constituent objections occur the leader can address these objections personally and immediately. If a lack of focus prevents the leader from such a response, then objections can become a public and media issue before the leader has the opportunity to respond effectively.

Networking: Cutting Through the Bureaucracy of Complex Organizations

School districts have traditionally been hierarchical organizations. As is the case with most complex entities, school systems cannot avoid a certain amount of bureaucracy. Anyone who has spent some time in the command center of a large ocean-going vessel knows that it takes some time after the captain's order of "thirty degrees starboard" for the ship to be actually heading on that course.

The decisions of superintendents in a bureaucratic structure can make the ship appear to be a formula-one race car by comparison. In many instances, even emphatic instructions from the superintendent are simply ignored. This rarely happens with deliberate contempt (though that happens in an astonishing number of cases). More commonly, the directive is studied, delegated, referred to a committee, and when all else fails, tabled for further clarification.

Each of these delays provides opportunities for a leader to use a network as an effective supplement to the traditional chain of command. The starting point for this network should be the task forces discussed in Chapter 24. In addition, superintendents can effectively use town meetings held at various schools. This helps to communicate the message about standards and affords an opportunity to hear directly from teachers, students, and parents about how things are going. Even when the participants are the same, the dynamics of communication change markedly when a meeting is not held in the inner sanctum of the central office conference room. Most effective leaders develop an informal network of key constituents. Those who have effective organization and focus also have the time to spend a few minutes every day on telephone calls to cultivate and maintain this network. With an effective network in place, the superintendent is not alone when inevitable challenges to standards arise. Moreover, with a network in place, the standards initiative is not viewed as a creation (and illusion) of a small group of central office administrators.

Confrontation

In some cases, the opposition to standards is based on misunderstanding and misinformation. That opposition can be dealt with by effective communication and patient dialog. But there are also times when the differences between the advocates and opponents of standards cannot be dealt with by explanation, persuasion, or compromise. The differences are deep, personal, and sometimes bitter. Examples of these objections include:

> "What do you mean 'all children can learn'? That's a bunch of malarkey. I've been around kids for 30 years, and some of 'em just can't do it. Why can't you just admit that?"

> "Standards are just another way for the feds to get their hands in education. They are taking away local control and anything to do with standards is simply one more denial of my rights as a parent."

> "Standards, schmandards. It's just one more piece of paper on the principal's desk, and I'm doing twelve hours a day of paperwork for the district already."

> "Standards are just a politically correct method of bringing every kid down to the lowest common denominator because educational bureaucrats won't admit that some kids are always going to do better than other kids. My kids have always been above average, and you just can't stand the idea that white kids have higher math scores, so you invented standards to prove that everybody's 'equal' even when common sense tells you that's not true."

> "Just leave me alone and let me teach. I didn't get into this profession to have some state legislator trying to tell me what to do in my classroom."

I could go on, but you get the idea. These are comments reflecting a fundamentally different value system than that held by the leaders of districts that are committed to standards. However sincerely held, deeply felt, and articulately presented, these comments are emphatically wrong. There are times when leaders need to confront the advocates of such positions and make the case for standards.

When faced with comments such as those above, the effective leader (who already has made many other attempts at communication and persuasion) does not say, "Gee, Mr. Jones, maybe you have a point there. Let's study the matter some more." The effective leader confronts the issue directly. This confrontation does not take place with the oratorical flair of a Daniel Webster or the plaintive plea of a James Stewart. A better model for the delivery of a proper response is Barbara Jordan, the member of Congress who first came to national attention as a member of the House Judiciary Committee during the impeachment hearings of President Nixon. Unlike many of her colleagues, Jordan did not engage in hyperbole or appeals to emotionalism. She spoke in even, measured tones that said, with every syllable, "This is serious business, and these words are not rhetoric but fact." Were Barbara Jordan a school superintendent faced with challenges such as those above, she would have first tried reason and discussion. When that failed, however, I think she would say something like this:

"There are times when both sides of an issue have merit. This is not one of them. This district has some fundamental beliefs that are bone deep. If this were thirty years ago, and the comment was made that black and white children just can't learn together in the same school, I would not temporize, but I would say that such a comment was wrong and was contrary to my beliefs and the beliefs of this district. That is the case now.

"You say, 'Not all children can learn.' You are wrong. Our jobs as educators have never been simply to help the students who are the best and brightest, but to reach out to every single child in the school and ensure they have the chance to prove to themselves they can do things that, a short while ago, they would have sworn they could not do.

"You say that standards are the result of intrusion from the federal government. You are wrong. These standards were developed by people in our community, including your neighbors, colleagues, and friends. The standards are the expectations of our community about what our children must know and be able to do to be productive citizens and to participate fully in our democratic society.

"You say that you have too much to do to implement standards. You are wrong. You have too much to do because you have not defined what the primary focus of your school should be, and standards will help you to do that. If you cannot manage your priorities in order to start implementing standards, then I will find someone who will.

"You dismiss the belief that all children can achieve as a politically correct idea and suggest that only certain students, usually the white upper class, are the only ones who can really compete. You are wrong. Any district of which I am the leader is committed to the principle that every child can excel, and that those who have done well in the past can do even better. The test scores your children have achieved in the past, or the scores their parents and grandparents achieved, don't cut much ice with me. In fact, we have had too many children with good test scores who cannot meet our standards, but their test scores have confirmed in their mind and yours that they are doing well. I am here to tell you that they are not doing well. If they cannot meet our standards, then they are not satisfactory. And if I were you, I would go home and tell your 'above average' child to get busy.

"You say, 'Just leave me alone and let me teach.' You are wrong. Ours is an inherently collaborative profession. We need each other. When you close the door on our requirements for academic standards, you close the door on fairness, opportunity, and achievement. I will not allow those doors to be closed in this district."

I do not know if a superintendent or board president will ever deliver this speech, but I have dreamed it at least a hundred times. At the dawn of every great educational reform, the discussion eventually moved from conception to reality, and that is when the trouble started. Leaders of standards-driven districts are willing to tolerate a certain amount of this discomfort. When every attempt at conciliation and dialog has failed and you deliver your version of this speech, I will be cheering for you.

PART FOUR

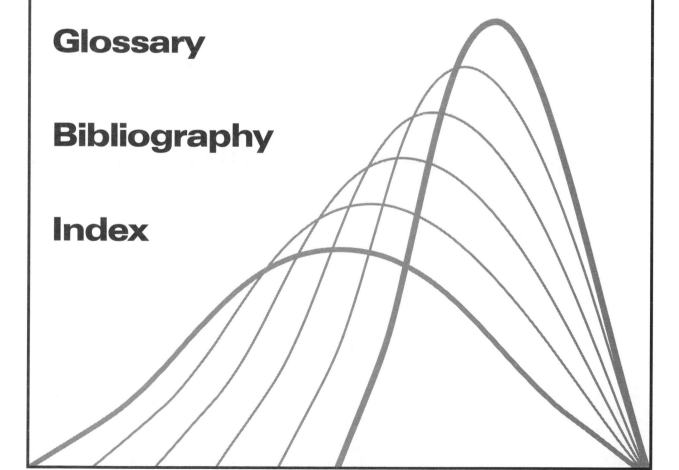

Reproducible Handouts

Appendices

Glossary

Bibliography

Index

Reproducible Handouts

Comparison of Assessment Methods

Standards-Based	Norms-Based
1. Standards are fixed.	1. Norms move.
2. Standards are cooperative.	2. Norms are competitive.
3. Standards measure proficiency.	3. Norms (and their counterparts, grades) measure behavior.
4. Standards promote mixed ability grouping.	4. Norms promote segregation of students by ability.
5. Standards are challenging.	5. Norms provide excuses for a "dumbed down" curriculum.
6. Standards are complicated.	6. Norms are simple.
7. Standards address causes, intermediate effects, and achievement.	7. Norms reflect only test scores.

Effective Assessments

1. Standards-based assessments are open, not secret.

2. Standards-based assessments are designed so that a large number of students—ideally every student—can achieve proficiency.

3. Standards-based assessments involve a demonstration of proficiency, not a guess on a multiple-choice test.

4. Performance assessments recognize the fact that there is not a single "right" answer on a number of test items.

5. Standards-based performance assessments force educators to come to grips with the central question: "What do we expect of our students?"

The Role of the Principal

1.   Understand the standards.

2.   Identify faculty leaders.

3.   Create professional development opportunities.

4.   Assess student progress.

5.   Analyze classroom activity.

6.   Recognize outstanding performance.

7.   Reflect, revise, and improve.

The Role of the District

1. Ownership—assure broad ownership of standards.

2. Congruence—does the initiative conform with our commitment to standards?

3. Experimentation—develop pilot programs.

4. Support—with time, money, and protection.

5. Focus—consider a one-year moratorium on any new initiatives.

Advantages of Pilot Programs

1. Pilot programs create enthusiasm among the key faculty leaders and principals.

2. Pilot programs allow the initial bugs to be worked out of a system with lower costs of errors.

3. The justification for pilot programs is leverage.

4. Pilot schools provide an ideal long-term source of mentors for student teachers.

5. The use of pilot programs gives the district leadership the opportunity to provide public recognition and rewards for those who are leaders in the standards movement.

Standards-Based Classroom

1. Are assignments a "one-shot" affair, or do students have the opportunity to continuously revise and improve their work over the course of several days?

2. Are assignments rich in detail and complex in achievement, requiring several days to complete?

3. Do assignments dwell on a single set of knowledge in an individual subject, or do they integrate cumulative knowledge within a subject with several other academic disciplines?

4. When I evaluate student work, am I looking only for a particular subject, or am I demanding proficiency in all the academic subjects?

5. Is the purpose of the activity to build a skill that will be tested in a different form at the end of the semester, or is the activity an opportunity for a student to demonstrate proficiency so that the assignment itself can become an assessment?

Effective Scoring Guides (Rubrics)

1. Scoring Guides must be specific.

2. Scoring Guides should be expressed in a student's own words.

3. Scoring Guides should be accompanied by an exemplary assignment.

4. Scoring Guides should be created through numerous drafts.

5. Scoring Guides must be clearly linked to standards.

Accountability—The Key to Public Acceptance

1.   The accountability plan must be built on the foundation of standards.

2.   The accountability measures must reflect both academic achievement and the opportunity to learn.

3.   Accountability measures must be clearly and immediately communicated.

4.   Any accountability system must itself be accountable.

Myths

1. Multiple choice tests are inherently objective, while performance-based tests are inherently subjective.

2. Multiple choice tests are more rigorous than performance-based tests.

3. Performance-based tests yield inconsistent results.

4. Performance-based assessments are inherently virtuous.

5. Teaching the test corrupts the process of learning.

Appendices

APPENDIX A

Performance Assessments

The International Performance Assessment System (IPAS)
Improved Accountability Through Cost-Effective, Standards-Based Performance Assessments

The Need

School systems are under increasing demands to be accountable for student performance. Teachers need classroom assessment and instructional material to help them improve student achievement in a standards-based system. Unfortunately, traditional multiple-choice tests fail to reflect student achievement accurately and comprehensively, and many of the performance assessments are prohibitively expensive. Students, teachers, and school leaders need timely feedback so that appropriate mid-course corrections can be made in teaching and learning strategies.

A Solution

The International Performance Assessment System (IPAS) is a set of 192 performance assessments available for purchase by school systems that are working toward improving accountability and student performance. The purpose is to provide rigorous, multi-disciplinary, high quality, reasonably priced assessments and scoring guides for school systems throughout the world. These schools share a commitment to high academic standards and equity of educational opportunity.

The Commitment

Our fundamental belief in achievement and equity demands that we have assessments that are rigorous, fair, and relevant. Using the best international and domestic models, we create assessments and scoring guides that can become integral parts of the learning process, not part of a week of "test terror" for a tiny fraction of the school year. School systems are supported in the use of IPAS assessments through professional development workshops and continuous communication with qualified consultants at the Center.

The Cost

The fee for the International Performance Assessment System (IPAS) is based on the number of students in a school or district. When a school system purchases IPAS, the system obtains a license for unlimited modification, reproduction, and use of all performance assessments for that school system. The schools have complete access to the 192 assessments and are able to reproduce the assessments without charge or copyright violation. Additional services, such as staff development for standards-based performance assessments, are also available at an additional cost.

Delivery Commitments

All 192 performance assessments are available now. Delivery can be expected approximately three weeks after the assessments are ordered. Clients receive the assessments in paper and electronic format (CD-Rom or disks) so that the assessments can be easily distributed to schools, placed on a district's password-protected web site, or otherwise shared with teachers and students.

IPAS performance assessments are also available through **Learning Connection Online**, a web-based subscription service developed by Educational Consulting Services. Learning Connection Online provides teachers, students, and parents IPAS performance assessments linked to your state standards, plus fun quizzes, challenging puzzles, your state's department of education information, and web search functions. Visit www.learningconnectiononline.com for more information.

Assessment Format

All assessments are linked to YOUR state or district standards. Each performance assessment includes a cover page that indicates the academic content standards that are addressed by that assessment. Each assessment contains a minimum of four tasks and the scoring guide (or rubric) for each task. The scoring guides are uniform for all assessments: 4=exemplary; 3=proficient; 2=progressing; 1=not meeting the standard(s).

192 Assessments	Lower Elementary	Elementary	Middle School	High School
Language Arts	24	12	12	12
Mathematics	24	12	12	12
Science		12	12	12
Social Studies		12	12	12

IPAS Benefits

- Teachers save time on assessment development

- Databank of assessments in four core subject areas

- Electronic and hard copies available

- Download from disk or your intranet for easy modification

- Send to each school in district for consistent assessment and scoring systems across district

- Four tasks in each assessment; scoring guides for *each* task

- Cost-effective resource for individual schools and entire school districts

Contact the Center for Performance Assessment for additional information.

Phone: 800-844-6599 (800-THINK-99) • (303) 504-9312

Website: www.makingstandardswork.com

E-mail: resources@makingstandardswork.com

Fax: (303) 504-9417

Mail: 1660 South Albion Street, Suite 1110, Denver, CO 80222

IPAS Assumptions About Assessment

- Assessments are part of the curriculum: they are tools for reaching proficiency. It is tempting to think of an assessment as a replacement for some other type of test. On the contrary, the IPAS assessments are intended to go along with, support, and reinforce the other things you do to prepare students to become proficient at standards. Educators should use more than one measure to make determinations about student performance. If, however, a student is proficient on an assessment, along with other measures of his or her performance, it is safe to assume that proficiency has been reached for the standard being addressed by the assessment.

- Multiple assessments are the ideal. Performance-based assessments can be an important part of a unit in the curriculum and are an excellent way for the student to self-assess his or her knowledge. In performing the tasks on the assessment, the student works through the material and has a chance to show often and in more than one way that the material has been mastered. Frequent and repeated assessment throughout the school year is recommended.

- Multiple attempts at an assessment are important. The IPAS assessments are designed so that large numbers of students — ideally every student — can achieve proficiency. Multiple tasks and scoring guides on an assessment encourage the use of teacher feedback as the student builds on his or her skills throughout the assessment. Students who do not achieve a proficient score on a task should be encouraged to revise their work and resubmit it, or to redo the task until they reach proficiency. Students who achieve a proficient score the first time around can be challenged to achieve an exemplary score. And those who achieve an exemplary score on the first attempt can be offered enrichment activities.

- IPAS assessments are open, not secret. It is recommended that the assessments and scoring guides be known by and discussed among students. Rather than locking up the assessments until test day, freely distribute them to students, teachers, and parents so that the expectations about performance are clearly understood by all.

- Frequently, there is not a single "right way" to respond to the tasks on the assessments. The scoring guides that accompany each task provide sample criteria for each level of performance. This follows the philosophy that there are myriad ways that a student can show exemplary, proficient, or progressing performance.

- IPAS assessments require the students to "show what they know." Using standards-based performance assessments enables students to demonstrate proficiency when they have truly mastered the subject.

Banned Books: Where Do You Stand?

Benchmark Grades

Middle School

Content Areas Addressed

Social Studies; Language Arts

Essential Questions

1. What are the best ways to communicate my ideas about a controversial issue?

2. What is the balance between freedom of speech and protection of essential public interests?

3. Are there ever any circumstances in which the distribution of books, ideas, or information should be limited?

Assessment Summary

This assessment will examine the area of censorship, freedom of speech and the press, the rights of people to express themselves, and the role of government in governing for the common good.

Concepts

Constitutional guidelines
Freedom of expression
Freedom of speech
Government regulation
Legal rulings

Keywords

Amendments   Prohibition
Censorship   Regulations
Constitution   Restriction
Expression
Freedom
Government

Standards Addressed

National Council for Teachers of English Standards

Standard 1: Students read a wide range of print and non-print texts to build an understanding of texts, of themselves, and of the cultures of the United States and the world; to acquire new information; to respond to the needs and demands of society and the workplace; and for personal fulfillment. Among these texts are fiction and nonfiction, classic and contemporary works.

Standard 3: Students apply a wide range of strategies to comprehend, interpret, evaluate, and appreciate texts. They draw on their prior experience, their interactions with other readers and writers, their knowledge of word meaning and of other texts, their word identification strategies, and their understanding of textual features (e.g., sound-letter correspondence, sentence structure, context, graphics).

Standard 4: Students adjust their use of spoken, written, and visual language (e.g., conventions, style, vocabulary) to communicate effectively with a variety of audiences and for different purposes.

Standard 5: Students employ a wide range of strategies as they write and use different writing process elements appropriately to communicate with different audiences for a variety of purposes.

Standard 7: Students conduct research on issues and interests by generating ideas and questions, and by posing problems. They gather, evaluate, and synthesize data from a variety of sources (e.g., print and non-print texts, artifacts, people) to communicate their discoveries in ways that suit their purpose and audience.

Standard 10: Students whose first language is not English make use of their first language to develop competency in the English language arts and to develop understanding of content across the curriculum.

Social Studies Standards
(National Assessment of Educational Progress, 8th grade "Proficient" level)

Standard 4: Identify discrepancies between the ideals expressed in the nation's core documents and reality and ways in which those discrepancies have been addressed in the past.

Standard 6: Identify, describe, and explain fundamental ideas in the nation's core documents of the founding era and core documents of subsequent periods in U.S. history.

Standard 16: Explain how citizens can interact with one another and how they can monitor and influence their government.

Subject	Standard(s)

Overview for the Teacher

This assessment will require approximately 8-10 instructional hours. Although this is a substantial investment of time, the assignment has a great deal of depth and rigor. Moreover, the assessment can be a joint project of language arts and social studies classes, gaining credit in both classes. If both teachers agree on the scoring guides and apply them consistently, then the grading and evaluation duties can be divided between the language arts and social studies teachers. The library/media center specialist in your school, your community libraries, and booksellers will be important collaborators. Some of the posters in Task #4 may be appropriate for posting in and around the libraries in your area. In addition, these specialists, librarians, and booksellers may be enlisted to respond to the letters written by your students in Task #3.

Adaptations and Accommodations:

The reading list for Task #2 includes a broad range of reading materials, from elementary level reading (such as the Goosebumps series) to post-secondary reading levels. For inclusion students who are emerging readers or non-readers, the teacher may wish to consider a variety of oral stories and discuss the critical thinking skills of comparing and contrasting different stories and the reasoning skill of categorization. Examples of concepts that can be applied to oral stories include: appropriate and inappropriate stories for younger children; scary and funny stories; grownup stories and children's stories; and so on. For non-writing students, pictures that represent scenes of characters may be substituted for the written requirements. For exceptionally advanced students, please see the "enrichment" task at the conclusion of the assessment.

Overview for the Student

This is an exciting project. Some people may even call it "dangerous." For much of our history, books that were critical of the government or that included topics that were regarded as unsupportive of dominant points of view were called "dangerous" and were subject to prohibition. You will be considering one of the most controversial issues in literary and American history: Should books be banned, and if so, how do we decide what books to ban and what to allow? There are no clear or easy answers. You might find some books that, indeed, should be either banned or should be the subject of limited distribution. You might find other books that have been banned that you believe should be easily available in a middle school library. *You will not be evaluated on your point of view or whether it agrees or disagrees with the teacher. You will not be asked to read anything that you find offensive or that contradicts your values or those of your family. In fact, you should share this assessment with your parents and ask their views on the subject of censorship and ask why they feel as they do. You will be evaluated on your ability to follow the directions of this assessment, express yourself in writing, and support your point of view with logic and evidence.*

Since the existence of governments and nations, authorities have sought to limit information available to the people. Our nation is no exception. Sometimes authorities seek to limit information for reasons that society has accepted as good and valid, such as limits on the disclosure of important national secrets or the limits on the distribution of pornography. Other times, however, the reasons for controlling information are more difficult to understand. This assessment is not about whether the various opinions in American history or in your own classroom are right or wrong. Rather, this assessment is about our ability to identify differing points of view, gather information, develop a personal point of view, and express it in different formats.

Each task in this assessment is important. Please submit your completed work on each task to your teacher for review and feedback. Before you submit your work to the teacher, compare your work to the scoring guides in this assessment. How would you evaluate your own work? If you believe that your work is "exemplary" or "proficient" based on the scoring guide, then submit your work to the teacher for review and feedback. *If you think that your work is "progressing" or "not meeting the standard," then go back and make the necessary revisions before you submit the work to the teacher.*

After you have received the teacher's feedback and made any necessary changes so that your work is "proficient" or better, then you can proceed to the next task. If you receive feedback from your teacher that your work is "progressing" or "not meeting standards," then you must re-submit your work, using the teacher's feedback as your guide for improving the quality of your work to "proficient" or better.

Summary of Tasks

First, you will do some research about freedom of expression and the roots of that freedom in the Bill of Rights. You will also consider the limits that have been placed on that freedom by the U.S. Supreme Court, and you will consider other limitations on our freedom of expression that may or may not be appropriate. You will be required to write a summary of the main ideas in the historical documents that you read.

Second, you will select a book (with the approval of your teacher and parents) from the list of books that have been banned or limited. You will read this book and write a report that includes not only a review of the book, but also your conclusion about why it might have been banned or limited, and your own opinion about the appropriateness of that book today.

Third, you will write a letter to your school media center specialists, public librarian, or local bookseller expressing your point of view about banning or limiting books. You may advocate any point of view you wish, but you must express yourself in appropriate "business letter" form.

Fourth, you will work with one or more of your classmates to create a "point-counterpoint" poster that will identify arguments for and against banning or limiting books. Regardless of your own point of view, you must consider arguments both for and against banning or limiting books.

Scoring Guides

After every task, you will find a scoring guide. You must read and understand this scoring guide because it tells you how you will be evaluated. Your grade on this assessment will not be a mystery; the scoring guide tells you exactly what you must do to achieve the required rating of "proficient" or the highest rating of "exemplary."

If English is Not Your Home Language:

(Note: Please follow the policy for your own school system. The following is suggested language for use if appropriate for the student and if it confirms to the policies of your school.) If you and your family do not speak English at home, *your participation is very important in this assessment.* You will have the opportunity to read and write in English, and you will also have the opportunity to read or listen to information in your home language. The teacher will work with you so that you can read to or listen to articles and books for Task Two that are in your home language. This will not only help you to participate in the assignment, but will also help everyone else in the class understand the point of view of a different culture and language. Because it is very important that you write English very well, the teacher will work with you to create a final draft of Tasks Three and Four in English. You will also read the information in Task One in English and write your report in English.

Task #1 - Explore the Roots of Freedom - and Limits on Freedom

Note: Read this information carefully. You will need this information to complete Task #1.

What are the roots of freedom of expression? Although historians can find many examples in which people have expressed the need for free speech, assembly, and expression, the fundamental right in American culture is expressed in the first amendment to the Constitution:

> "Congress shall make no law respecting an establishment or religion, or prohibiting the free exercise thereof; of abridging the freedom of speech, or of the press, or the right of the people peaceably to assemble, and to petition the government for a redress of grievances."

If we stop there, it might appear that the freedoms of speech, assembly, and expression are unlimited. But for every freedom, there is a limitation. In the United States, the Constitution does not stand alone as the statement of our law. The Constitution is interpreted and applied by the United States Supreme Court. Here are two famous cases in which the Supreme Court considered the rights of the first amendment. In one case, the Court limited the first amendment. In the other case, the Court concluded that a law passed by Congress was unconstitutional because it violated the first amendment. Read the following passages from both cases, then complete Task #1.

Schenck v. United States, Case No. 249 U.S. 47 (1919), decided March 3, 1919

Background of the case: During the First World War, Congress pass the Espionage Act of 1917. This law attempted to prevent people from interfering with the military recruiting and enlistment activities. When Mr. Schenck printed and circulated a document that encouraged people to avoid military service, he was charged with violating this law. The Supreme Court held that the right of free speech is not absolute, but has limits placed on it.

The majority opinion of the Court was delivered by Chief Justice Holmes:

> The document in question upon its first printed side recited the first section of the Thirteenth Amendment [prohibiting slavery], said that the idea embodied in it was violated by the conscription act and that a conscript is little better than a convict. In impassioned language it intimated that conscription was despotism in its worst form and a monstrous wrong against humanity in the interest of Wall Street's chosen few. It said, "Do not submit to intimidation," but in form at least confined itself to peaceful measures such as a petition for the repeal of the act. The other and later printed side of the sheet was headed "Assert Your Rights." It stated reasons for alleging that any one violated the Constitution when he refused to recognize "your right to assert your opposition to the draft," and went on, "If you do not assert and support your rights, you are helping to deny or disparage rights which it is the

---

solemn duty of all citizens and residents of the United States to retain." It described the arguments on the other side as coming from cunning politicians and a mercenary capitalist press, and even silent consent to the conscription law as helping to support an infamous conspiracy. It denied the power to send our citizens away to foreign shores to shoot up the people of other lands, and added that words could not express the condemnation of such cold-blooded ruthlessness deserves, winding up, "You must do your share to maintain, support and uphold the rights of the people of this country."

The most stringent protection of free speech would not protect a man in falsely shouting fire in a theatre and causing a panic. It does not even protect a man from an injunction against uttering words that may have all the effect of force. The question in every case is whether the words used are in such circumstances and are of such a nature as to create a clear and present danger that they will bring about the substantive evils that Congress has a right to prevent... When a nation is at war many things that might be said in time of peace are such a hindrance to its effort that their utterance will not be endured so long as men fight and that no Court could regard them as protected by any constitutional right. It seems to be admitted that if an actual obstruction of the recruiting service were proved, liability for words that produced that effect might be enforced.

Reno vs. American Civil Liberties Union, Case no. 96-511, decided June 26, 1997

Background of the case: Two provisions of the Communications Decency Act of 1996 (CDA) seek to protect minors from harmful material on the Internet. The American Civil Liberties Union challenged the law as an unconstitutional limit on free speech.

The majority opinion of the Court was delivered by Justice Stevens:

"We are persuaded that the CDA lacks the precision that the First Amendment requires when a statute regulates the content of speech. In order to deny minors access to potentially harmful speech, the CDA effectively suppresses a large amount of speech that adults have a constitutional right to receive and to address to one another. That burden on adult speech is unacceptable if less restrictive alternatives would be at least as effective in achieving the legitimate purpose that the statute was enacted to serve.

[In previous Supreme Court cases we have found that] "the fact that society may find speech offensive is not a sufficient reason for suppressing it."

It is true that we have repeatedly recognized the governmental interest in protecting children from harmful materials. But that interest does not justify an unnecessarily broad suppression of speech addressed to adults.

As a matter of constitutional tradition, in the absence of evidence to the contrary, we presume that governmental regulation of the content of speech is more likely to interfere with the free exchange of ideas than to encourage it. The interest in encouraging freedom of expression in a democratic society outweighs any theoretical but unproven benefit of censorship."

Directions:

1. Create an outline that describes the reasons for limiting free speech, the reasons for protecting free speech, and your conclusions. Your outline will include three major sections (I, II, and III) and appropriate substructure (A, B, C, etc.) for each section. Use the Supreme Court cases as well as your own reasoning to complete your outline.

2. Based on your outline, write a descriptive essay that explains the free speech provisions of the First Amendment to the Constitution, including limits on free speech.

Your outline must be no longer than one page. Your essay must be at least three pages and not longer than five pages. If you use a word processor, your work must be double-spaced. If you write, use a pen and double-space your writing on college-ruled paper.

Task #1 Scoring Guide

Exemplary

I met all of the requirements for "proficient" work and also included more advanced work, such as the following:

❑ In my explanation of the First Amendment, I included other portions of the Constitution, my state's constitution, federal laws, or state laws that support my point of view.

❑ In my essay, I considered different points of view, including views that disagreed with me. Then I compared those views to my own and I explained the reasons my opinion was better.

❑ I have no errors in spelling, grammar, and punctuation.

Proficient

❑ My outline and essay are legible. If my report is handwritten, another person can read the report out loud without stopping to ask me to help them identify the letters.

❑ My outline is complete and correctly labeled. There are at least three levels of substructure (A, B, and C) for each roman numeral.

❑ My essay includes at least three quotations from the Supreme Court cases that support my reasoning.

❑ My outline and essay are submitted on or before the date specified by my teacher.

❑ My outline and essay are my own individual work. If I used any quotations, I identified the source of those quotations and gave credit to the source. Although I may have asked parents or others for help, I wrote the report myself.

❑ I made a few errors in spelling, grammar, or punctuation, but none of them prevent the reader from understanding my intended meaning. There are no more than five errors in the report.

❑ If my first submission of this report resulted in an evaluation of "progressing" or "not meeting standards" I reviewed the feedback from my teacher, implemented all of the suggestions, and made all necessary corrections.

❑ I followed the required format.

Progressing

❑ My outline has the major sections, but does not have complete substructure.

❑ I am missing a part of the essay: limits on free speech, reasons for protected speech, quotations to support my point of view, or my personal evaluation.

❑ I did not follow the required format.

❑ I submitted the report late.

❑ I have more than five errors in spelling, grammar, or punctuation, or my errors were so significant that the reader could not understand my intended meaning.

Not Meeting Standards

❑ I did not submit the outline and essay.

❑ My outline and essay are not readable.

Task #2 – Read a "Banned Book"

The following list of books includes those that have been banned, limited, or challenged in American libraries. Please note that this list does not represent all of the books that have been limited or banned. Some publications containing dangerous information (such as how to create dangerous chemicals or weapons) have been limited for good reasons. But there are many other books that are banned mainly because some people disagree with their contents or find the contents offensive. In fact, you or your family may disagree with some of these books, and that is your right. This list doesn't mean that all of these books are great any more than it means that all of these books are terrible. The list simply identifies books that have been banned.

You will select one of these books, with the approval of your parents and teacher. If you cannot find a book that is acceptable to you and your parents, then your parents will suggest books and your teacher and parents will agree on the book that will be assigned. Your report on the book that you read must be at least three pages and not longer than five pages. If you use a word processor, your work must be double-spaced. If you write, use a pen and double-space your writing on college-ruled paper.

> **Part 1** – Summary. Describe the setting, main characters, and most important events of the books.

> **Part 2** – Reasons the book might have been banned. Explain in your own words the reasons that the book might have been banned. Consider the political, social, and ethical points of view in the book. Provides examples (including the page number of your example) of potentially offensive passages and explain why someone might object to them.

> **Part 3** – Your evaluation of the book. Explain why the book should or should not be limited or banned. If you believe that the book should be limited (for example, available to middle school students but not available to elementary school students) then explain your reasoning.

Selected List of Books
That Have Been Banned, Censored, Restricted, or Limited

(Source: American Library Association news release, January 18, 2000)

A Farewell to Arms, Ernest Hemingway

A Wrinkle in Time, Madeleine L'Engle

Black Beauty, Anna Sewell

Blubber, Judy Blume

Can Such Things Be?, Ambrose Bierce

Christine, Stephen King

Did Six Million Really Die?, Ernst Zundel

Essay Concerning Human Understanding, John Locke

Frankenstein, Mary Shelley

Goosebumps series, R.L. Stine

Harry Potter series, J.K. Rowling

I Know Why the Caged Bird Sings, Maya Angelou

James and the Giant Peach, Roald Dahl

Leaves of Grass, Walt Whitman

Little Red Riding Hood, Jacob and Wilhelm Grimm

Native Son, Richard Wight

Of Mice and Men, John Steinbeck

Origin of Species, Charles Darwin

Revolting Rhymes, Roald Dahl

Schindler's List, Thomas Keneally

Slaughterhouse-Five, Kurt Vonnegut

Snow Falling on Cedars, David Guterson

The Adventures of Huckleberry Finn, Samuel Clemens

The Grapes of Wrath, John Steinbeck

The Learning Tree, Gordon Parks

The Merchant of Venice, William Shakespeare

The Rights of Man, Thomas Paine

The Witches, Roald Dahl

Tom Sawyer, Samuel Clemens

Twelfth Night, William Shakespeare

Ulyssess, James Joyce

Uncle Tom's Cabin, Harriet Beecher Stowe

Book Selection Form

Students: Complete this form and have it signed by your parents and your teacher. Before you ask to read a book, make sure that it is available from the school library or other appropriate source.

Student Name: _____

Teacher Name: _____

For the assessment "Banned Books: Where Do You Stand?" I would like to read the following book:

Book Name: _____

Author: _____

Source: __ School Library ___ Public Library ___Personal Book

__ Classroom Collection ___Other (please specify) _____

Parent Approval:

_____ I give my permission for my child, _____, to read this "banned book" and I agree that this book is appropriate and reasonable for my child to read as part of this class project.

_____ I do NOT give permission for my child, _____, to read this "banned book" and I would prefer that my child read one of the following books. Parents: Please provide the names of three books that you would approve. If you would like to discuss this matter with the teacher, please call the school and I will be happy to discuss this matter with you.

Alternative 1: _____

Alternative 2: _____

Alternative 3: _____

Signed: _____

Date: _____

Teacher Approval:

_____ I approve this book for this project.

_____ I do NOT approve this book, but the parents and I agree that the following book will be assigned for this project:

Signed: _____

Date: _____

Task #2 Scoring Guide

Exemplary

I met all of the requirements for "proficient" work and also included more advanced work, such as the following:

❑ In my explanation of why the book might have been banned, I identified actual historical instances in which this book was banned and I identified the research sources I used to learn about those incidents.

❑ In my evaluation of the book, I considered different points of view, including views that disagreed with me. Then I compared those views to my own and I explained the reasons my opinion was better.

❑ I have no errors in spelling, grammar or punctuation.

Proficient

❑ My report is legible. If my report is handwritten, another person can read the report out loud without stopping to ask me to help them identify the letters.

❑ My report has a summary, with setting, main characters, and most important events of the book.

❑ My report includes reasons the book might have been banned, with examples and identification of the page number for each example.

❑ My report has an evaluation and my recommendation as to whether the book should be limited or banned.

❑ My report is on a book that has been approved by my parents and teacher.

❑ My report is submitted on or before the date specified by my teacher.

❑ If I used any quotations, I identified the source of those quotations and gave credit to the source.

❑ My report is my own individual work. Although I may have asked parents or others for help, I wrote the report myself.

❑ I made a few errors in spelling, grammar, or punctuation, but none of them prevent the reader from understanding my intended meaning. There are no more than five errors in the report.

❑ If my first submission of this report resulted in an evaluation of "progressing" or "not meeting standards," I reviewed the feedback from my teacher, implemented all of the suggestions, and made all necessary corrections.

Progressing

❑ My report is on a book that has been approved by my parents and teacher.

❑ I am missing a part of the report: summary, reason the book might been banned, or evaluation.

❑ I did not follow the required format.

❑ I submitted the report late.

❑ I have more than five errors in spelling, grammar, or punctuation, or my errors were so significant that the reader could not understand my intended meaning.

Not Meeting Standards

❑ I did not submit the report.

❑ I did not receive appropriate permission from parents and teacher for the book.

❑ My report is not readable.

Task #3 – Advocate Your Point of View

Librarians, media center specialists, and booksellers receive letters on a frequent basis that encourage them to ban or limit access to certain books. You have a right to advocate your point of view as well. In this task, you will exercise that right by sending a letter to the school or public librarian, media center specialist, or bookseller of your choice. Your letter will be in "business letter" format and will be based on the reasoning you have learned in the first two tasks. *You may advocate any point of view you wish, including support for the limiting or banning of a book, or support for the abolition of bans or limits on books. You will be evaluated based on your written expression, not whether your opinion agrees or disagrees with your teacher or library/media center specialist.*

Directions: Write a letter in business letter format to your school media center specialist, community librarian, bookseller, or other government or private organization that is involved in the distribution of information. In your letter, express your support or opposition for bans or limits on a specific book or group of books. Use the logic, reasoning, and understanding of Constitutional law that you learned in Task #1. Use the analysis about the book that you learned in Task #2. Your letter must begin with a clear statement of your point of view. Then your letter must include support for that point of view with examples and evidence from your readings. Your letter must conclude with a clear statement of your opinion and a direct request to the addressee of the action you would like them to take. Your letter must be at least two pages and not longer than four pages. If you use a word processor, your work must be double-spaced. If you write, use a pen and double-space your writing on college-ruled paper.

Task #3 Scoring Guide

Exemplary

I met all of the requirements for "proficient" work and also included more advanced work, such as the following:

- ❏ I included examples of banned books other than the book about which I am writing.
- ❏ I proposed more than one solution for the addressee to consider.
- ❏ In my letter, I considered different points of view, including views that disagreed with me. Then I compared those views to my own and I explained the reasons my opinion was better.
- ❏ I have no errors in spelling, grammar or punctuation.

Proficient

- ❏ My letter is legible. If my letter is handwritten, another person can read the letter out loud without stopping to ask me to help them identify the letters.
- ❏ My letter includes all the elements listed in the directions, including an opening, separate paragraphs to support my point of view, and a conclusion with a direct request for action by the addressee.
- ❏ My letter is submitted on or before the date specified by my teacher.
- ❏ My letter is my own individual work. If I used any quotations, I identified the source of those quotations and gave credit to the source. Although I may have asked parents or others for help, I wrote the letter myself.
- ❏ I made a few errors in spelling, grammar, or punctuation, but none of them prevent the reader from understanding my intended meaning. There are no more than five errors in the letter.
- ❏ If my first submission of this letter resulted in an evaluation of "progressing" or "not meeting standards" I reviewed the feedback from my teacher, implemented all of the suggestions, and made all necessary corrections.

Progressing

- ❏ I am missing a part of the letter.
- ❏ I did not follow the required format.
- ❏ I submitted the letter late.
- ❏ I have more than five errors in spelling, grammar, or punctuation or my errors were so significant that the reader could not understand my intended meaning.

Not Meeting Standards

- ❏ I did not submit the letter.
- ❏ My letter is not readable.

Task #4 – Point – Counterpoint

Create a poster that includes arguments in favor of banning and limiting books on the left-hand side, and arguments against banning and limiting books on the right-hand side. You must consider points of view other than your own in order to complete this task. You may work in groups assigned by your teacher, although your teacher may determine that it is better if you work on this task individually. The teacher and library/media center specialist may select some posters for display in the school and community library.

Directions: Using standard poster-board, create a "Point-Counterpoint" poster that includes arguments for and against the banning or limiting of books. Include at least one quotation from the Constitution or court cases we have studied. Include at least four examples of books that have been banned or limited.

Task #4 Scoring Guide:

Exemplary

I met all of the requirements for "proficient" work and also included more advanced work, such as the following:

- ❑ The poster includes quotations from banned or limited books to illustrate each point of the chart.
- ❑ The poster is visually compelling, with pictures and other images that are interesting and that involve the reader.
- ❑ There are no errors in spelling, grammar, or punctuation.

Proficient

- ❑ My poster is legible.
- ❑ My poster includes all the elements listed in the directions, including persuasive arguments for each side of the issue.
- ❑ My poster is submitted on or before the date specified by my teacher.
- ❑ My poster is the individual and collaborative work of the group. If there are any quotations on the poster, the source of those quotations has been identified.
- ❑ There are a few errors in spelling, grammar, or punctuation, but none of them prevent the reader from understanding my intended meaning. There are no more than three errors in the poster.
- ❑ If my first submission of this poster resulted in an evaluation of "progressing" or "not meeting standards," I reviewed the feedback from my teacher, implemented all of the suggestions, and made all necessary corrections.

Progressing

- ❑ I am missing a part of the poster.
- ❑ I did not follow the required format.
- ❑ I submitted the poster late.
- ❑ I have more than three errors in spelling, grammar, or punctuation, or my errors were so significant that the reader could not understand my intended meaning.

Not Meeting Standards

- ❑ I did not submit the poster.
- ❑ My poster is not readable.

Enrichment Task – Before the Supreme Court

Note to the Teacher: This enrichment task is appropriate for students for whom special adaptations and accommodations are required because of their exceptionally rapid learning or need for additional challenge. In addition, this task is appropriate for any students who successfully complete the first four tasks prior to the time that the teacher is ready to complete the assessment for the entire class. The ideal culmination of this assessment is a public argument before a "Supreme Court" that you have assembled. The court members should include, if at all possible, judges and attorneys who will understand the constitutional and legal issues, will take time to read the students' legal briefs, and who will challenge the students during their oral arguments with questions and challenges in a manner that is authentic and representative of Supreme Court proceedings. A rubric has not been included for this task, as every student at this level should have been able to complete all previous tasks at the proficient or exemplary level. The focus of this enrichment task is engagement, realism, and passion for a point of view. Because this is an appellate court, there are no witnesses or evidence, but only written and oral arguments.

Note to Students: Consider this scenario: Kathy Lebowitz, a 7th grade student at Campus Middle School, went to the local Carnegie Library to find a book that had been recommended to her by a friend. She was surprised to find that the book had been removed from the shelves because of a protest from a member of the community who said that it was "inappropriate and did meet our community standards." Kathy has come to you, a noted Constitutional Lawyer, to argue her case. You took the case, and sued the library in the case of *Lebowitz v. Carnegie Library*. Unfortunately, you lost the case in the district court, so you appealed. Then you lost in the Court of Appeals. So you appealed to the United States Supreme Court. Your classmate, another capable Constitutional Law attorney, has been assigned to defend the Carnegie Library. As you know, the obligation of the lawyer is to defend the interest of the client, not the personal point of view of the lawyer.

Directions: The teacher will assign you to a team to represent either Kathy Lebowitz or the Carnegie library. You will prepare a written legal brief to outline the arguments for your side of the case. Then you will conduct an oral argument before the "court" that your teacher will construct. Ideally, the court will include people who are judges and attorneys from your community. In preparation for this assignment, you may wish to view videotape or personally observe a state supreme court in order to observe the conduct of their proceedings. You should also view examples of legal briefs. Your library/media center specialist can help you find examples of actual legal briefs and additional information to support your side of the case. An Internet search of "banned books" will also yield a number of court decisions, articles, and other research resources to help you complete this task.

Design the Ideal School

ASSESSMENT #MSMA61

Benchmark Grades

Middle School

Content Areas Addressed

Math, Language Arts

Task Description

This assessment asks students to use math skills as they imagine their ideal school. Students may benefit from working in teams, but the assessment can be done as an individual project.

For the students who complete Tasks 1 through 5 ahead of the rest of the class, there are two enrichment tasks provided at the end of the assessment.

Task Instructions

Your job is to design the perfect school. Let your imagination soar. What would the perfect school look like? Would it have plenty of room for schoolwork and play? Would it have room for soccer, baseball, and other sports? Would it be designed so that every student— even those who cannot see, hear, or walk—can easily take advantage of every part of the school?

You (and your team members) are going to design an ideal school. Even though you may like your school as it is, you have probably thought of some ways it can be better.

This assignment is an opportunity to try out your ideas. The tasks help you organize your ideas. It's important to check with your teacher after you complete each task. Then, when your teacher has evaluated your work, go to the next task.

Design the Ideal School

Standard Addressed

Arkansas Language Arts Standard AREN5
(Reading) Students will read independently for a wide range of goals and

Arkansas Mathematics Standard ARMA2.3
(Geometry) Students will be able to solve problems that involve geometry and its application to other topics in mathematics or to other fields.

Arkansas Mathematics Standard ARMA3.1
(Measurement) The student will use measurement attributes (length, capacity, weight, mass, area, volume, time, money, temperature, scale and angle) to describe and compare mathematical and real-world objects.

Arkansas Mathematics Standard ARMA3.3
(Measurement) The student will apply measurement concepts to solve problems.

Link this assessment to your state or district standards.	
Subject	Standard(s)

Task 1

Write a description of your ideal school.

Please be specific. Think about what a school should be. What are your ideas about an ideal school? Think about the school building, for example, the size of the building, the number of stories, the different types of rooms and amenities in the building. Make a list of issues that you would want to consider in designing your school, then use it to write exactly what the school will have and why you think that these things are important. Later on, you will have the opportunity to ask additional questions and improve your model based on them.

Scoring Guide – Task 1

4 Exemplary

Students describe in complete detail the elements of their ideal school. A rational explanation for all aspects of the description is provided. The paper is free of spelling and grammatical errors.

3 Proficient

Students describe in general detail the elements of their ideal school. Most of the aspects of the school have a rational explanation. Spelling and grammatical errors do not significantly affect the communication of ideas.

2 Progressing

Students have a general idea of the school, but the details are unclear. The written expression contains minor errors, which make the writing difficult to understand.

1 Not meeting the standards

Neither the ideas nor the written communication is clear.

Task 2

Draw a picture of your ideal school.

Based on the description in Task 1, you should first draw a rough draft of the school and then draw a scale drawing. A "scale drawing" means that the lines you use on the paper must represent a certain number of feet for the actual building. Your scale drawing should look as if you are viewing the building from the top down (also known as "bird's-eye" view) and will show only the length and width of the rooms and hallways of the school. You do not need to show height. It may be helpful to use graph paper to draw your scale model.

After you have finished your scale drawing, calculate the total number of square feet in the building. Provide the details of your calculation.

Scoring Guide – Task 2

4 Exemplary

Both the picture and the scale drawing are clear, neat, and directly related to the written description in Task 1. The scale is mathematically accurate and consistent and a key is provided. It shows an appropriate level of detail to convey the ideas in the written description. The calculation of square footage is done correctly and enough detail is provided to see that the calculation is consistent with the drawing.

3 Proficient

Both the picture and scale drawing are clear and generally neat. The scale is generally free of mathematical errors. The drawing shows sufficient detail to convey the ideas in the written description. The calculation of square footage is done correctly and enough detail is provided to see that the calculation is consistent with the drawing.

2 Progressing

The picture and scale drawing have good ideas but are not clearly related to the written description. The scale contains some mathematical errors, which make the drawing inaccurate in its representation of the students' ideas. The calculation of square footage is incorrect, or not consistent with the drawing.

1 Not meeting the standards

The picture and scale drawing are inconsistent with the written description. The scale drawing uses an inconsistent scale. The calculation of square footage is not related to the drawing.

Task 3

Evaluate your model.

As you review your model of the ideal school, consider how you have addressed each of the following issues. Not all of these questions may apply to your school, but you must either show how your model addresses the question, or explain why the question is irrelevant to your school.

All of these questions require some idea of how many people will use the building. So, make an estimate of how many teachers, staff, and students will use your building.

- How much space is needed for indoor and outdoor athletic facilities?

- How much space is needed for a parking lot, and how many cars will actually be able to park there?

- How wide are the hallways?

- How big is a classroom, and how many classrooms do you need?

- How much space is needed for classes that have special equipment such as shop classes, auto classes, chemistry labs, art studios, and drama and band classes?

- How many books and other media should the library have and how much space do you need for that?

- If some of your classmates have physical disabilities and need extra space (for example, to get a wheel chair through a door) or need special help (for example, to have library shelves within reach), then how will this affect your design?

Make a list of questions that can be answered either by conducting your own research or asking an expert.

Scoring Guide – Task 3

4   Exemplary

Responds to all questions in the task, with either explanations of how the issue was addressed, why no information is needed, or with a list of specific questions for research. Includes at least one additional question for research based on design of the school. The questions are comprehensive, specific, and clear. The questions will easily guide the research in the next task. An estimate of the people using the building is made that is consistent with the drawing of the school. Estimates of the number of teachers and staff are consistent with the number of students.

3   Proficient

Responds to all questions in the task, with either explanations of how the issue was addressed, why no information is needed, or with a list of specific questions for research. The questions are specific and clear, though there may be one or two additional questions the student must address before conducting research in the next task. An estimate of the people using the building is made that is consistent with the drawing of the school.

2   Progressing

Responds to most of the questions in the task, with either explanations of how the issue was addressed, why no information is needed, or with a list of specific questions for research. The questions are not sufficiently specific or they are unclear. The questions must be worded more clearly before the student can successfully conduct research. The estimate of the people using the building is plausible in itself, but may not be related to the drawing of the school.

1   Not meeting the standards

Does not respond to a majority of the questions in the task. Specific questions for research are not related to the needs of the project. The estimate of people using the building is not related to the sizes of schools, or the drawing is undocumented.

Task 4

Conduct research.

Based on the questions you identified in Task 3, spend some time in the library or media center or asking appropriate experts in order to find the answers. Provide written answers to the questions you raised in Task 3. Identify your sources of information.

Note: Look at Task 5 before you do your research, so you can possibly save time by researching both questions together.

Scoring Guide – Task 4

4   Exemplary

The answers are clear, comprehensive, detailed, and specific. The student can easily proceed to the next task. All sources are correctly identified. There are no grammar, spelling, or punctuation errors.

3   Proficient

The answers are clear and specific, though some additional research may be required. All sources are correctly identified. Any errors in grammar, spelling, or punctuation do not hinder the reader's understanding of the content.

2   Progressing

The answers are not sufficiently clear to be used by the student in the next task. Additional research is necessary. Some sources are correctly identified. Errors in grammar, spelling, or punctuation hinder the reader's understanding of the content.

1   Not meeting the standards

The answers are not related to the questions, or contain many errors in information, grammar, spelling, and punctuation. No sources are identified.

Task 5

How much do schools cost?

Conduct research to find out how much money was spent to construct schools in your community. Find the total cost of construction and how many students the buildings support. If you can find one or more that were built recently, you can use that information directly. If you can only find schools built a long time ago, you will have to "inflate" the cost to current dollars. You can do this by finding out how much inflation there has been since the school was constructed and multiplying the original cost by the inflation factor. The result is an estimate of how much it would cost now.

Calculate the cost per student of the school or schools for which you found data. Use the number of students your school will hold to calculate an estimate of the cost of your school.

Prepare written answers. Document your sources and your work.

Scoring Guide – Task 5

4   Exemplary

Researches in detail the cost of school construction, finding more than one school on which to base the calculations. Research is accurately documented. Calculates cost per student of previous construction, inflating costs to current dollars if necessary. Calculation is based on information sources, is done correctly, and details are provided. Calculates correctly an estimate of the total cost of the proposed school consistent with data of previous tasks. Suggests other factors to adjust cost (such as additional facilities new schools have) or incorporates expansion of older schools into estimates of construction costs.

3   Proficient

Researches the cost of school construction. Research is documented. Calculates cost per student of previous construction, inflating costs to current dollars if necessary. Calculation is based on information sources, is done correctly, and details are provided. Calculates correctly an estimate of the total cost of the proposed school consistent with data of previous tasks.

2   Progressing

Estimates the cost of construction. Calculates cost per student of previous construction, inflating costs to current dollars if necessary. Calculations may have minor errors, or lack details. Calculates correctly an estimate of the total cost of the proposed school consistent with data of previous tasks.

1   Not meeting the standards

Does not document sources, or uses inappropriate sources. Calculations contain conceptual errors.

Task 6

Modify and improve your model.

Based on your research, make appropriate changes to your model. Include explanations or calculations to decide how big various spaces should be.

For example, the size of the parking lot is related to the size of a car and the number of cars that will park there. And the number of cars is related to how many people use the school.

Scoring Guide – Task 6

4 Exemplary

The revised model is accurate in scale and design and represents a clear and significant improvement from the first model. The improvements are rich in detail and based on the research and questions designed by the student. The sizes of spaces relate to the number of people who will be using them. Calculations are shown to document the needs for various spaces.

3 Proficient

The revised model is accurate with only minor errors in scale and design. It represents a clear improvement from the first model. These improvements are based on the research and questions designed by the student. The sizes of several spaces relate to the number of people who will be using them. Correct calculations are shown to document the needs for some of the spaces.

2 Progressing

The revised model is an improvement, but contains errors in mathematical scale and lacks a clear relationship to the research conducted by the student. The size of at least one space relates to the number of people who will be using it.

1 Not meeting the standards

The revised model is not an improvement over the first draft.

Enrichment Task 1

Based on your improved drawing in Task 5, create a three-dimensional model of your ideal school. Using materials approved by your teacher, create a model sturdy enough to be moved around. You may notice some additional changes you want to make in your model. If so, be sure to document those changes so that your model on paper and your three-dimensional model are consistent with each other. Give an oral presentation of your model with descriptions of why you designed the project in this way.

Scoring Guide – Enrichment Task 1

4 Exemplary

The model is accurate in all dimensions and the oral presentation is complete, well-researched, persuasive, well-organized, and clear.

3 Proficient

The model is accurate in virtually all respects and the oral presentation reflects that significant student research was accomplished. The presentation is persuasive and well-organized.

2 Progressing

The model is accurate in two dimensions, but the third dimension departs significantly from the written plan. The oral presentation is not clearly based on student research and is unclear.

1 Not meeting the standards

The model is not an accurate representation of the student's design. The presentation is not clearly linked to the model.

Enrichment Task 2

Share your model with an architect or engineer. Ask this professional to review your design and make recommendations for further improvement. Your presentation should include all the tasks of the project, from the initial consideration of your criteria for the ideal school through the improvements and changes you made. Show how you conducted research to support your final design. Based on the feedback you receive from the professional, write your reflections on what you would do differently if you were to approach this project again.

Scoring Guide – Enrichment Task 2

4 Exemplary

The student's reflection is clear and well-reasoned. It identifies specific actions that could be considered in the future to improve the project and reflects that the student listened carefully to the advice of the professional.

2 Proficient

The student's reflection is clear and well-reasoned, and includes some specific actions to improve the projects. Most of the professional's advice is incorporated in the student report.

3 Progressing

The student's reflection is unclear and does not reflect attentive listening to the professional.

1 Not meeting the standards

The student's reflection is unrelated to the advice from the professional.

Check, Check, and Double Check

ASSESSMENT #ELSC27

Benchmark Grades

Can be adapted for upper elementary grades.

Content Areas Addressed

Science, Language Arts

Summary

Students will write instructions on how to get to a "secret" destination on school grounds. Others will follow these instructions and evaluate them. The original instructions will be revised and followed again. Students will then write a paragraph telling how scientists use this method.

Keywords

Evaluation
Field trials
Observation
Scientific method
Writing skills

Check, Check, and Double Check

Information for the Teacher

Task Description

This assessment asks students to conduct a series of "field trials" that allow them to practice the basic scientific procedures of preparing an experiment that can be replicated. They will work in pairs, but they will be scored individually. Students demonstrate their ability to measure, record information, follow directions, evaluate data, and recognize the importance of replicating a procedure.

Each student pair will be comprised of a trailblazer and a follower. The follower will complete Task Two while the trailblazer does the third part of Task One. For Task Four, have all the trailblazers switch followers, so that new pairs are created.

You may want to repeat the entire assessment so that students who were followers get to be trailblazers, and vice versa.

Required Materials

Students will need to leave the classroom and go to various destinations on the school grounds. Students will need to be supervised as they write their instructions to various destinations outside of the classroom.

Standard Addressed

California Language Arts Standard CALA4.4

Writing Strategies: Students write clear and coherent sentences and paragraphs that develop a central idea. Their writing considers audience and purpose. They successfully use the stages of the writing process (i.e., pre-writing, drafting, revising, and editing successive revisions).

California Language Arts Standard CALA4.5

Writing Applications (Genres and their characteristics): Students write compositions that describe and explain familiar objects, events, and experiences. Student writing demonstrates a command of standard English and the drafting, research, and organizational strategies outlined in Writing Standard 1.0.

California Language Arts Standard CALA4.6

Written and Oral English Conventions: Students write and speak with a command of standard English conventions that are appropriate to each grade level.

California Science Standard CASC3.5

(Investigation and Experimentation) Scientific progress is made by asking meaningful questions and conducting careful investigations. As a basis for understanding this concept, and to address the content of the other three stands, students should develop their own questions and perform investigations.

California Science Standard CASC4.6

(Investigation and Experimentation) Scientific progress is made by asking   meaningful questions and conducting careful investigations. As a basis for understanding this concept, and to address the content of the other three strands, students should develop their own questions and perform investigations.

California Science Standard CASC5.5

(Investigation and Experimentation) Scientific progress is made by asking meaningful questions and conducting careful investigations. As a basis for understanding this concept, and to address the content of the other three stands, students should develop their own questions and perform investigations.

Link this assessment to your state or district standards.	
Subject	Standard(s)

Check, Check, and Double Check

Assessment Introduction: Here is what you will do...

An important part of science is the ability to repeat (replicate) tests so that others can get the same results. This is one reason why it is important to be able to write instructions that others can follow easily. What would happen if an experiment was done over again and the scientist got different results each time? That would not be a very helpful experiment.

A scientist's goal is not just to get the results she wants. She also wants an experiment to show the same results even if someone else conducts it.

For the next several tasks, you are the scientist. You will need to be able to tell others what you have done and be clear enough so that they can repeat it and find the same results.

You will have a partner for these tasks. One of you will be the "trailblazer" who writes instructions to a destination. The trailblazer will also write questions for observations at the destination.

The other partner will be the "follower" who will try to follow the instructions and answer the questions. This partner will also give advice to the trailblazer on ways he or she can change the first set of instructions and questions to make them easier to follow.

It sounds simple. But giving clear instructions is harder than you may think!

Task 1: Blazing a trail for others to follow

First Part: Choose the destination. Write your instructions.

You, the trailblazer, are going to pretend you are blazing a trail for others to follow. You will write a set of instructions to your secret destination for your partner. Be sure to record measurements accurately, but do not describe the place you are going. For example, write "Turn left and walk 15 steps." Explain where to start and how to get to the secret destination. Be specific.

Second Part: Write down several questions for your follower to answer.

At the destination, think about some things that your follower can see. Find about five things that you can ask your follower about once he or she gets to your destination.

Remember to be specific. For example, "How many street lamps do you see?" Be sure you ask questions about things that will always be there. (Don't ask how many cars you see because they can move.)

Write down the answers to your questions. You'll need them for Task Two.

Third Part: Give directions and questions to your follower and conduct the first field trial of your instructions.

Observe your follower while he or she completes Task Two, but do not help. Get an idea of how clear your directions are and places you may need to change them.

Give your teacher three things:

- The list of directions to your secret destination

- The list of questions for the follower to answer based on what he or she observes

- The follower's answers to your questions

Remember that the destination is a secret, so don't tell anyone!

Scoring Guide - Task 1

4 Exemplary

Criteria for the Proficient category have been successfully completed, and more advanced work is done, such as the following:

❑ The student takes notes on his or her observations of the follower.

❑ The student predicts any possible confusion by making a list of possible problems with his or her directions or questions.

3 Proficient

❑ The student chooses a destination and writes instructions that are clear and specific.

❑ The student includes an exact starting point and has easy steps to follow.

❑ Several questions are written that are clear and specific. The questions ask about things that will not change.

❑ The follower uses the directions.

❑ The teacher is given the directions, questions, and answers to the questions.

2 Progressing

❑ Four of the criteria in the Proficient category have been met.

❑ More work is needed.

1 Not meeting the standard(s)

❑ Fewer than four of the criteria in the Proficient category have been met.

❑ The task should be repeated.

Task 2: Following the trailblazer's instructions

You, the follower, will be given a set of instructions that the trailblazer has written for you. Follow these instructions as carefully as you can.

While you do this, the trailblazer will be observing you and completing Part Three of Task One.

After following the instructions and arriving at the destination, answer the questions the trailblazer has given you.

When you have finished answering the questions, ask the teacher to give you the answers the trailblazer has for you.

Evaluate the trailblazer's instructions and questions. List any problems or questions you had using the instructions. Suggest ways to improve their instructions. If you did not get the same answers, explain why you think the answers are different.

Scoring Guide - Task 2

4   Exemplary

Criteria for the Proficient category have been successfully completed, and more advanced work is done, such as the following:

❑   The student makes special note of the positive points of the trailblazer's directions.

3   Proficient

❑   The student follows the instructions and attempts to arrive at the destination using the instructions thoughtfully.

❑   The questions are answered according to the instructions, if possible.

❑   The student evaluates the instructions and describes what was clear and what was not.

❑   The student suggests ways to make the directions more clear.

❑   The response includes a fair and careful evaluation of ways to improve the instructions.

2   Progressing

❑   Four of the criteria in the Proficient category have been met.

❑   More work is needed.

1   Not meeting the standard(s)

❑   Fewer than four of the criteria in the Proficient category have been met.

❑   The task should be repeated.

Task 3: The trailblazer sees how the follower did

How did you do at writing clear steps? You will be given the report that the follower made.

Evaluate the follower. Did he or she follow your instructions? Does he or she have any suggestions for you?

Can you improve your instructions? Should they be more specific and clear? Did you measure distances correctly? Was there a place that confused the follower?

One way to find out is to study what the follower wrote and did. That should give you ideas for improving your instructions.

Now you're ready to make revisions and improvements!

Based on what the follower wrote, change your original instructions to make them better. Go through your instructions one more time to make sure someone else can arrive at your destination.

Scoring Guide - Task 3

4 Exemplary

Criteria for the Proficient category have been successfully completed, and more advanced work was done, such as the following:

❏ The student walks through his directions to the destination to double check that they are accurate.

3 Proficient

❏ The student evaluates how the follower did at following his or her steps.
❏ The original instructions are changed as needed.
❏ Instructions and questions are clear and can be followed.

2 Progressing

❏ Two of the criteria in the Proficient category have been met.
❏ More work is needed.

1 Not meeting the standard(s)

❏ Fewer than two of the criteria in the Proficient category have been met.
❏ The task should be repeated.

Task 4: A new follower takes your trip

Are you ready? Here we go again! You are going to do the same thing you did in Task 1, but now you will give your revised instructions to a new follower who does not know the destination.

Finally, give the instructions and observe the follower. When you are finished with this final field study, answer these questions:

- Are these instructions easier?

- What makes you think that they are easier?

- Was the follower able to arrive at the final destination?

Write a paragraph comparing what you did in this task with what a scientist does in an experiment. Explain why it is important to write and follow clear instructions in science.

Remember your rules for writing, such as correct spelling, grammar, and punctuation.

Scoring Guide - Task 4

4 Exemplary

Criteria for the Proficient category have been successfully completed, and more advanced work is done, such as the following:

- ❑ There are no errors in grammar, spelling, or punctuation.
- ❑ The student lists specific examples of the ways a scientist would use this process, and clearly details why this is important.
- ❑ The student suggests other practical applications (besides scientific experiments) of the scientific method.

3 Proficient

- ❑ The revised instructions are given to another follower and the student observes the follower.
- ❑ The follower arrives at the student's destination and reports that the instructions are clear and easy to follow.
- ❑ The student answers the questions in the task completely. He or she reports on what was clear and what was not clear in the instructions to the follower.
- ❑ The paragraph tells how this task is like the work scientists do.
- ❑ The paragraph contains no more than three errors in grammar, spelling, or punctuation.

2 Progressing

- ❑ Four of the criteria in the Proficient category have been met.
- ❑ More work is needed.

1 Not meeting the standard(s)

- ❑ Fewer than four of the criteria in the Proficient category have been met.
- ❑ The task should be repeated.

Reading Cultural Literature: Walk in Someone Else's Shoes

ASSESSMENT #HSLA10

Benchmark Grades

9-12

Summary

Students read a book about someone from a cultural or ethnic background different from their own, analyze the story's main character, design artwork that illustrates the book, and write their own cultural story.

Keywords

Analyzing literature
Culture
Ethnicity
Literary elements
Mood
Plot
Setting

Reading Cultural Literature:
Walk in Someone Else's Shoes

Information for the Teacher

Task Description

This assessment asks students to demonstrate their understanding of a contemporary work of cultural literature. They learn about the experiences of people from other cultures by reading literature about people from ethnic groups and cultures other than their own.

Compile a list of fiction books representative of the variety of cultures found in the United States. The books should be accessible to students and appropriate for their reading level. The following are some examples of books you might include:

African-American: Childress, Alice. *Rainbow Jordan*. Putnam/Coward-McCann or Avon (paperback), 1981.

Hispanic: Buss, Fran Leeper. *Journey of the Sparrows*. Lodestar, 1991. Haseley, Dennis. *Ghost Catcher*. Illustrated by Lloyd Bloom. HarperCollins Children' Books, 1991.

Jewish: Aleichem, Sholom. *The Nightingale* or *The Saga of Yosele Solovey the Cantor*. Trans. by Aliza Shevrin. Plume, 1985.

Native American: Hillerman, Tony. *Skinwalkers*. HarperCollins,1987.

Asian American: Crew, Linda. *Children of the River*. Delacorte, 1989.

The list should be diverse enough to give students a choice of cultures from which to read. Groups of students (three to five per group) will read the same book. Therefore, you will need access to multiple copies of each book.

In Task 1, students are asked to read about someone from a culture different from theirs. They are then asked to write letters that tell what the book is about and what their response to the book was.

Students are asked to write a book review in Task 2.

---

[1] Book suggestions from Rochman, H. (1993). *Against Borders: Promoting Books for a Multicultural World*. Chicago and London: American Library Association. Also from Manna, A. L., & Brodie, C. S. (Eds.) (1992). *Many Faces, Many Voices: Multicultural Literary Experiences for Youth*. Fort Atkinson, Wisconsin: Highsmith Press.

In Task 3, you will need to form small groups of students who have read the same book. Group members will discuss the book and, in Task 4, chart the opinions of various group members and summarize the group's overall opinion of the book.

Students express and share their reactions to the book by creating a work of art in Task 5. You will need to help students choose an appropriate art medium and help them locate materials. This task recognizes differences in multiple intelligences and learning styles by encouraging students to demonstrate what they have learned in an artistic product.

Finally, in Task 6, the students write their own cultural story. This task is designed to recognize and affirm the value of every individual's cultural history and heritage.

Required Materials

- A list of books about people (preferably young people) from various cultures and/or ethnic groups.

- Multiple copies of books about people from various cultures and/or ethnic groups.

- Handouts on literary elements—plot, setting, mood, point of view, etc.

- A variety of art materials.

Reading Cultural Literature:
Walk in Someone Else's Shoes

Assessment Introduction: Here is what you will do...

People are like snowflakes; no two are alike. In all of the history of the world, there has never been, nor will there ever be, anyone quite like you.

Your hair, eyes, and skin are certain colors. You walk a certain way or talk a certain way. Maybe you have a distinctive way of thinking about things. Maybe you feel that everyone else in the world is normal, except you. Or perhaps, on the other hand, you feel that everyone else in the world is weird and that you are the only normal one.

But no matter what you look like or walk like or think like, you didn't become who you are overnight. You inherited certain traits from your parents. Other members of your family have probably influenced you in other ways. Maybe people are always saying that you laugh just like Uncle Buddy or sound just like Cousin Judy.

Part of who you are comes from your family. And part of who you are comes from your culture, the group of people you grew up with and/or live with today. Your culture, whether you're Korean or Cherokee or African or Irish, plays a big role in who you are.

Have you ever wondered what it would be like to be from another culture? Have you ever thought about how you would be different if you had grown up with different people, in a different location or country, or among a different cultural or ethnic group?

In this assessment, you'll get your wish. You'll get to see what the world looks like through the eyes and ears of someone who lives in a culture different from your own. There's an old saying that you can't really know another person until you have "walked a mile in his or her shoes." In this assessment, you'll get a chance to do just that.

Task 1: Read and write to someone who seems different

Your journey in someone else's shoes begins now. Get a list of books about people from different cultures from your teacher. Maybe you've always had an interest in a certain culture or have friends or neighbors from a culture that's different from yours. Choose a book about someone from a culture that interests you.

Find a quiet place, and read the book. Pay special attention to the main character in the book. Try to feel what it's like to be that person. What does the world look like to that person? What might the main character think about you? What influence does culture have on the main character? Let your imagination run wild. Pretend you're the character in the book.

As the main character, write a letter to one of the other characters in the book. The character you choose to write to could be a friend, family member, even a person the main character hasn't met in the book. Use your imagination.

In this letter, tell your literary pen pal the following things:

- Name and describe the other major characters in the story.
- Tell what part you think the other major characters played in the overall story.
- Describe the setting (where the story took place).
- Discuss any conflicts that occurred in the story. Explain how these conflicts were resolved.
- Say something about the mood of the events you are describing. Were they depressing, happy, inspiring? What created this particular mood?
- Tell from whose point of view the story is written.

Give reasons and examples to explain your opinions and impressions. Include quotations from the book if you think that they help you make your point better

It may help you to use something similar to one of the following sentences to begin your letter:

- "You'll never believe what happened to me today…"
- "I'm writing this letter because I want to discuss last year's events with you…"
- "I wanted to tell you more about my childhood…"

Your letter should be at least two pages in length, and you should use proper writing technique. When you have finished it, someone else should be able to read your letter and get a clear picture of what the book is about.

---

[2] Suggestions for how to read a book in this assessment are adapted from Adler, M. J. & Van Doren, C., (1940, 1967, 1972). *How to Read a Book: The Classic Guide to Intelligent Reading.* New York: Simon & Schuster.

Scoring Guide - Task 1

4 Exemplary

Criteria for the Proficient category have been successfully completed, and more advanced work is done, such as the following:

❑ The letter also discusses sub-plot lines.
❑ The student reads another book about the same culture and compares the stories of the two main characters.
❑ There are no errors in spelling, grammar, or punctuation.

3 Proficient

❑ The letter accurately describes the plot of the book.
❑ The letter is at least two pages long.
❑ The letter is organized and uses effective transitions.
❑ The letter clearly and accurately describes the main characters and the roles they play.
❑ The letter uses concrete details to describe the setting.
❑ The letter describes any major conflicts in the book and explains how these conflicts were resolved.
❑ The letter identifies the mood of the book.
❑ The letter tells from what point of view the book is written.
❑ Any errors in spelling, grammar, or punctuation do not hinder the reader's understanding of the letter.

2 Progressing

❑ Seven of the criteria in the Proficient category have been met.
❑ More work is needed.
❑ Errors in spelling, grammar, and punctuation make the letter difficult to understand.

1 Not meeting the standard(s)

❑ Fewer than seven of the criteria in the Proficient category have been met.
❑ The letter is impossible to understand.
❑ The task should be repeated.

Task 2: Would you recommend the book to others?

In Task 1, you demonstrated your ability to read and analyze cultural literature. In Task 2, you will write a book review. A review critiques a book, tells whether the book is worth reading or not.

Start by finding two book reviews in newspapers and magazines. These will give you examples to work from as you write your own book review.

In your book review, you will critique the book you have read. Tell whether you liked the book or not and explain why. Also, describe the effect that the book had on you. Did it help you to learn anything new? If so, what did you learn? How did the book make you feel? Why? Is this a good book for others to read? Why or why not?

Your book review should be at least two pages long. Explain all of your answers and write a convincing review that would persuade your best friend to either read the book or return it to the library right away.

Scoring Guide – Task 2

4 Exemplary

Criteria for the Proficient category have been successfully completed, and more advanced work is done, such as the following:

- ❑ The student brings in three or more copies of reviews.
- ❑ The review contains no errors in grammar, spelling, or punctuation.
- ❑ The student researches reviews of the specific book he or she has read to determine other people's reactions to it, then compares and contrasts his or her own opinions to those of the reviewers.

3 Proficient

- ❑ The book review is at least two pages long.
- ❑ The review contains 3 or fewer errors in grammar, spelling, and punctuation.
- ❑ The book review tells whether the student liked the book or not and provides specific reasons.
- ❑ The student explains how the book made him/her feel, explains why, and uses specific references from the book as examples.
- ❑ The book review answers all of the questions posed in the task.
- ❑ The book review has a distinct beginning, middle, and end.
- ❑ Concrete evidence is used to support all opinions.

2 Progressing

- ❑ Six of the criteria in the Proficient category have been met.
- ❑ More work is needed.

1 Not meeting the standard(s)

- ❑ Fewer than six of the criteria in the Proficient category have been met.
- ❑ The task needs to be repeated.

Task 3: Compare your opinion with classmates

Get together with a small group of your classmates who read the same book that you did. Your teacher will help you with this. Discuss the following questions with the other members of your group:

- What was the book about?

- How did you feel about the book?

- Were you able to identify with any of the characters in the book? If so, which character(s) and why? If not, why not?

- What did you learn about a different culture from reading the book?

- What did you learn about yourself and your culture as a result of reading the book?

Scoring Guide - Task 3

4 Exemplary

Criteria for the Proficient category have been successfully completed, and more advanced work is done, such as the following:

- ❑ The student takes on a leadership role in the discussion and makes sure the group stays on the topic and that every member of the group participates.
- ❑ The student takes detailed notes of the proceedings for use in Task 4.

3 Proficient

- ❑ Student shares opinions about each question with group.
- ❑ Student shows respect for other group members and their ideas.
- ❑ Student listens carefully when other group members speak.
- ❑ Student asks questions when another group member's point is not understood.
- ❑ Student uses specific examples from the book as evidence for opinions.
- ❑ Student encourages others, particularly the quieter students, to share their opinions.

2 Progressing

- ❑ Four or five of the criteria in the Proficient category have been met.
- ❑ More work is needed.

1 Not meeting the standard(s)

- ❑ Fewer than four of the criteria in the Proficient category have been met.
- ❑ The task should be repeated.

Task 4: What is the bottom line?

As a result of your group discussion, you may have found that some people felt the same way you did about the book. Other classmates may have had different opinions about the book.

Create a chart to summarize your group's discussion. Draw a vertical line down the center of a piece of notebook paper. At the top of the left-hand column, write the word, "Opinions." At the top of the right-hand column, write the word, "Reasons." List at least five opinions of other group members in the "Opinions" column. Next to each opinion, in the "Reasons" column, explain why you think your classmates had that particular opinion or response to the book.

At the bottom of your chart, write several sentences that summarize the group's overall reaction to the book. Write whether or not the group felt the same way about the book that you did. Write whether or not other group members had the same or a different understanding of the book from the one that you had. Give reasons for your answers.

Scoring Guide - Task 4

3 Exemplary

Criteria for the Proficient category have been successfully completed, and more advanced work is done, such as the following:

❑ The student compares and contrasts each opinion with his or her own.

2 Proficient

❑ The chart accurately lists at least five responses of group members.
❑ The chart gives logical reasons for group opinions.
❑ The chart is detailed, specific, and readable.
❑ The summary accurately tells what the overall opinion of the group was.
❑ Specific reasons are given for the group's opinion.
❑ The summary contrasts the student's opinion with the opinions of other group members.

2 Progressing

❑ Five of the criteria for a Proficient score have been met.
❑ More work is needed.

1 Not meeting standard(s)

❑ Fewer than five criteria for a Proficient score have been met.
❑ The task should be repeated.

Task 5: Design artwork for the book

So far, you've had a chance to write about cultural literature. In this Task, you'll have a chance to create some artwork that expresses what the book is about. You can draw something, paint something, create a collage, design artwork on the computer, take a series of photographs, or mold something out of clay. Your own imagination and creativity are the only limitations. Work with your teacher to find an art form that will highlight your talents and help you find the art materials you will need.

Design your artwork to show someone else what the book is about. Your artwork should include visual images that express how culture influenced characters in the book. Create your artwork so that it also shows what you learned about this particular culture from reading the book.

Scoring Guide – Task 5

4   Exemplary

Criteria for the Proficient category have been successfully completed, and more advanced work is done, such as the following:

❏ The artwork compares and contrasts the student's own culture with that of the characters in the book.

3   Proficient

❏ Artwork clearly shows what happened in the book and how the student felt about the book.

❏ Artwork clearly shows the influence of culture on major characters in the book.

❏ Artwork clearly depicts what the student learned about the culture.

❏ Artwork has been carefully prepared and shows originality and creativity.

2   Progressing

❏ Three of the criteria in the Proficient category have been met.

❏ More work is needed.

1   Not meeting the standard(s)

❏ Fewer than three of the criteria in the Proficient category have been met.

❏ The task should be repeated.

Task 6: What's your cultural story?

Whether people identify themselves with a particular ethnic group or not, everyone grows up and lives in some kind of culture. Use what you have learned about cultural literature to write your own story, based on the culture you were reared in or live in now. (It can be a short story rather than an entire book!)

You will be the main character of your cultural story. As you are writing your story, pay attention to setting, characters, plot, conflict, mood, point of view, and the other literary elements that you have learned about.

Your story should be at least three and no more than five pages long. Be sure to follow proper writing guidelines. Make your story as detailed and descriptive as possible so that your reader can get a clear picture of who you are, how your culture has shaped who you are, and what you have learned because you grew up in your particular culture.

Scoring Guide – Task 6

4 Exemplary

Criteria for the Proficient category have been successfully completed, and more advanced work is done, such as the following:

❑ The story documents the student's family tree in detail.

❑ The story includes or is based on interviews with an older family member, such as a grandparent, who can detail the family's cultural history.

❑ The story contains no errors in grammar, spelling, or punctuation.

3 Proficient

❑ A narrative cultural story of 3 to 5 pages long is written.

❑ Detailed setting, characters, plot, and conflict are used to effectively tell the student's own story.

❑ Through the use of literary elements, the story clearly shows the influence of culture.

❑ What the student has learned from his/her culture is woven into the story line.

❑ The story shows originality and creativity.

❑ Any errors in grammar, spelling, or punctuation do not hinder the reader's understanding of the story.

2 Progressing

❑ Five of the criteria in the Proficient category have been met.

❑ More work is needed.

1 Not meeting the standard(s)

❑ Fewer than five of the criteria in the Proficient category have been met.

❑ The task should be repeated.

APPENDIX B

Internet Links to State Standards

Alabama: http://www.alsde.edu/ver1/section_detail.asp?section=54

Alaska: http://www.eed.state.ak.us/qschools/standards.html

Arizona: http://www.ade.state.az.us/standards/contentstandards.htm

Arkansas: http://arkedu.state.ar.us/standard.htm

California: http://goldmine.cde.ca.gov/board/

Colorado: http://www.cde.state.co.us/index_stnd.htm

Connecticut: http://www.state.ct.us/sde/dtl/curriculum/index.htm

Delaware: http://www.doe.state.de.us/DPIServices/Desk_Ref/DOE_DeskRef.htm#This

Florida: http://www.firn.edu/doe/curric/prek12/frame2.htm

Georgia: http://www.glc.k12.ga.us/qstd-int/homepg.htm

Hawaii: http://165.248.10.190/HCPS/L2/hcps6.nsf/

Idaho: http://www.sde.state.id.us/osbe/exstand.htm

Illinois: http://www.isbe.state.il.us/ils/

Indiana: http://doe.state.in.us/standards/welcome.html

Iowa: http://www.state.ia.us/educate/index.html

Kansas: http://www.ksbe.state.ks.us/Welcome.html

Kentucky: http://www.kde.state.ky.us/oapd/curric/Publications/Transformations/
vol1into.html

Louisiana: http://www.doe.state.la.us/DOE/asps/home.asp?I=HOME

Maine: http://janus.state.me.us/education/g2000/linktool.htm

Maryland: http://www.mdk12.org/mspp/standards/index.html

Massachusetts: http://www.doe.mass.edu/frameworks/current.html

Michigan: http://cdp.mde.state.mi.us/MCF/default.html

Minnesota: http://cfl.state.mn.us/GRAD/gradhom.htm

Mississippi: http://www.mde.k12.ms.us/curriculum/

Missouri: http://www.dese.state.mo.us/standards/

Montana: http://www.metnet.state.mt.us/Montana%20Education/OPI/
          School%20Improvement/HTM/Mtstandards.shtml

Nebraska: http://www.nde.state.ne.us/Issu/AcadStand.html

Nevada: http://www.nde.state.ne.us/Issu/AcadStand.html

New Hampshire: http://www.ed.state.nh.us/CurriculumFrameworks/curricul.htm

New Jersey: http://www.state.nj.us/njded/cccs/index.html

New Mexico: http://sde.state.nm.us/divisions/learningservices/schoolprogram/
            standards/csnb.html

New York: http://www.emsc.nysed.gov/ciai/pub.html

North Carolina: http://www.dpi.state.nc.us/curriculum/

North Dakota: http://www.dpi.state.nd.us/standard/content.shtm

Ohio: http://www.ode.state.oh.us/ca/ci/

Oklahoma: http://sde.state.ok.us/publ/pass.html

Oregon: http://www.ode.state.or.us//TchgLrngStds/intro.htm

Pennsylvania: http://www.pde.psu.edu/regs/chapter4.html

Rhode Island: http://www.ridoe.net/standards/frameworks/default.htm

South Carolina: http://www.state.sc.us/sde/test123/standard.htm

South Dakota: http://www.state.sd.us/deca/ContentStandards/index.htm

Tennessee: http://www.state.tn.us/education/ci/cicurframwkmain.htm

Texas: http://www.tea.state.tx.us/teks/

Utah: http://www.uen.org/cgi-bin/websql/utahlink/CoreHome.hts

Vermont: http://www.state.vt.us/educ/stand/framework.htm

Virginia: http://www.knowledge.state.va.us/main/sol/sol.cfm

Washington: http://www.k12.wa.us/reform/EALR/default.asp

West Virginia: http://wvde.state.wv.us/igos/

Wisconsin: http://www.dpi.state.wi.us/standards/index.html

Wyoming: http://www.k12.wy.us/publications/standards.html

Standards Implementation Checklist

Classroom Checklist

Professional Practice	Exemplary	Proficient	Progressing	Remarks
1. Standards are highly visible in the classroom. The standards are expressed in language that the students understand.				
2. Examples of "exemplary" student work are displayed throughout the classroom.				
3. Students can spontaneously explain what "proficient" work means for each assignment.				
4. For every assignment, project, or test, the teacher publishes in advance the explicit expectations for "proficient" work.				
5. Student evaluation is always done according to the standards and scoring guide criteria and *never* done based on a "curve."				
6. The teacher can explain to any parent or other stakeholder the specific expectations of students for the year.				
7. The teacher has the flexibility to vary the length and quantity of curriculum content on a day-to-day basis in order to insure that students receive more time on the most critical subjects.				
8. Commonly used standards, such as those for written expression, are reinforced in every subject area. In other words, "spelling always counts" – even in math, science, music and every other discipline.				
9. The teacher has created at least one standards-based performance assessment in the past month.				

Classroom Checklist (cont'd)

Professional Practice	Exemplary	Proficient	Progressing	Remarks
10. The teacher exchanges student work (accompanied by a scoring guide) with a colleague for review and evaluation at least once every two weeks.				
11. The teacher provides feedback to students and parents about the quality of student work compared to the standards – not compared to other students.				
12. The teacher helps to build a community consensus in the classroom and with other stakeholders for standards and high expectations of all students.				
13. The teacher uses a variety of assessment techniques, including (but not limited to) extended written responses, in all disciplines.				
Other professional practices appropriate for your classroom:				

School Checklist

Professional Practice	Exemplary	Proficient	Progressing	Remarks
1. A Standards/Class matrix (standards across the top, classes on the left side) is in a prominent location. Each box indicates the correspondence between a class and the standards. Faculty members and school leaders discuss areas of overlap and standards that are not sufficiently addressed.				
2. Standards are visible throughout the school and in every classroom.				
3. The school leaders use every opportunity for parent communication to build a community consensus for rigorous standards and high expectations for all students.				
4. Information about rigorous standards and high expectations is a specific part of the agenda of every faculty meeting, site council meeting, and parent organization meeting.				
5. The principal personally evaluates some student projects or papers compared to a school-wide or district-wide standard.				
6. The principal personally evaluates selected student portfolios compared to a school-wide or district-wide standard.				
7. Examples of "exemplary" student papers are highly visible.				

School Checklist (cont'd)

Professional Practice	Exemplary	Proficient	Progressing	Remarks
8. Job interview committees explicitly inquire about the candidate's views on standards, performance assessment, and instructional methods for helping all students achieve high standards.				
9. A "jump-start" program is available to enhance the professional education of new teachers who do not have an extensive background in standards and assessment techniques.				
10. Every discretionary dollar spent on staff development and instructional support is specifically linked to student achievement, high standards, and improved assessment.				
11. Faculty meetings are used for structured collaboration with a focus on student work, not for the making of announcements.				
12. The principal personally reviews the assessment and instructional techniques used by teachers as part of the personnel review and evaluation process. The principal specifically considers the link between teacher assessments and standards.				
13. Other professional practices appropriate for your school:				

District/State/System Checklist

Professional Practice	Exemplary	Proficient	Progressing	Remarks
1. The system has an accountability plan that is linked to student achievement of standards, not to the competition of schools with one another.				
2. The system has a program for monitoring the "antecedents of excellence," that is, the strategies that schools use to achieve high standards. The monitoring system does not depend on test scores alone.				
3. The system explicitly authorizes teachers to modify the curriculum guides in quantity and emphasis so that student needs for core academic requirements in math, science, language arts, and social studies are met.				
4. The system publishes the "best practices in standards-based assessment" on an annual basis, recognizing the creative efforts of teachers and administrators.				
5. The system has established an assessment task force to monitor the implementation of effective and fair assessments, and to distribute models of educational assessments for use throughout the year.				
6. The system provides timely feedback on district-level assessments so that all assessments can be used to inform instruction during the current school year. Assessments that are not used for the purpose of informing instruction and improving student achievement are not used.				

District/State/System Checklist (cont'd)

Professional Practice	Exemplary	Proficient	Progressing	Remarks
7. The system reports to the public a comprehensive set of student achievement results throughout the year.				
8. The system uses multiple methods of assessments for system-wide assessments. It never relies on a single indicator or single assessment method to represent student achievement.				
9. There is a clearly identified senior leader at the system level who is responsible for standards, assessment, and accountability, and who communicates this information clearly to all stakeholders.				
10. Commitment to standards is a criterion in all hiring decisions at all levels.				
11. The system monitors the investment of resources, including staff development, technology, and capital expenditures, for a consistent and clear link to student achievement of standards. System leaders can provide explicit examples of changes in resource allocation decisions that reflect this commitment.				
12. Evaluations of schools and of building leaders are based on student achievement, not based on competition or any other norm-referenced system.				

District/State/System Checklist (cont'd)

Professional Practice	Exemplary	Proficient	Progressing	Remarks
13. The system does not take into account ethnicity and socio-economic level in determining its expectations of student performance. These variables, along with linguistic background, learning disabilities, and other factors, are included in resource allocation decisions and the development of instructional and assessment strategies.				
14. The system allocates resources based on student needs and a commitment to the opportunity for all students to achieve standards. Resources are not allocated merely on the basis of student population; the objective is equity of opportunity, not equality of distribution.				

APPENDIX D

Staff Development Curriculum

Knowledge and Skills Required for Teachers

Understand the importance of standards and how to assess in a standards-based environment

Professional Development Workshop Description:

Making Standards Work: Designing and Developing Standards-Based
Assessments . . . . (Two 6-hour workshops)

Result:

Participants create a complete standards-based assessment, including four tasks with a scoring guide for each task. The assessment can be immediately used in the classroom and shared with colleagues.

Understand the layers of standards, from general academic content standards to specific classroom requirements

Professional Development Workshop Description:

Unwrapping the Power Standards . . . .(One 6-hour workshop)

Result:

Participants begin with an academic content standard and identify the essential questions that must be asked by the teacher and answered by students to provide evidence that the standard has been achieved.

Understand and apply effective teaching strategies in the standards-based classroom

Professional Development Workshop Description:

Effective Teaching Strategies in the Standards-Based Classroom . . . .(One 6-hour workshop)

Result:

Participants understand the research foundation behind specific strategies for effective teaching, practice these strategies, and immediately apply them in the classroom.

Understand the relationship between test data at the state, district, and classroom levels and successful curriculum and teaching practices

Professional Development Workshop Description:

Data-Driven Decision Making . . . .(One 6-hour workshop)

Result:

Identify specific goals for student achievement, teaching strategies to achieve those goals, and measurable indicators that allow educators to provide monthly evidence of student improvement.

Understand aspects of writing instruction and how to establish a cohesive professional development plan to address needs of teachers as they learn effective teaching strategies

Professional Development Workshop Description:

Writing Excellence Part I: Administrators/Curriculum Leaders . . . . (One 6-hour workshop)

Result:

Participants understand the research supporting program development and learn what teachers and building principals need to be able to establish and sustain either district or school changes related to improving student achievement in the area of writing.

Understand aspects of writing instruction, assessment, analytic traits, best practices, and effective teaching writing strategies in content areas

Professional Development Workshop Description:

Writing Excellence Part II: Teachers . . . . (Two 6-hour workshops)

Result:

Participants understand the research supporting specific and effective instructional and assessment techniques.

Understand and prepare for writing instruction using modes (Persuasion, Descriptive, Expository, Narrative)

Professional Development Workshop Description:

Writing Excellence Part III: Teachers . . . . (One 6-hour workshop)

Result:

Participants acquire specific knowledge of different modes of writing, how to create meaningful writing prompts for students, and how to critically assess student writing.

Glossary

Academic (or Content) Standards

The knowledge and skills expected of students at certain stages in their education. In other words, academic content standards describe what students should know and be able to do.

Accountability

The obligation of reporting, explaining, or justifying standards, making them responsible, explicable, and answerable.

Assessment

An appraisal or evaluation.

Assignment

A particular task or job given to a student for a specific purpose.

Central Tendency

The score of a typical individual in a group. The mean (or average), median, and mode are measures commonly used to report the central tendency of test scores.

Concurrent Validity Tests

Comparison of district-wide tests (involving a sample of students) with the Standards Achievement Report for those students. If the teacher-designed assessments are based on the same standards of performance as the district assessments, the results should be consistent in a high percentage of cases. Any disparities should be investigated.

Evaluation

An appraisal (examination or test) to determine progress of a student toward meeting academic standards.

Inter-Rater Reliability

A term used to describe the relationship of the scores (ratings) among two or more judges (raters). This can be computed in a variety of ways from simple correlations to percentage of agreement. The larger numbers indicate a greater degree of agreement.

Modeling

Teaching methods and resources that serve as an example for imitation and comparison.

Network

A widespread, organized system of people who can serve as a resource for standards implementation.

Norm

A designated standard average performance.

Performance Assessment

An evaluation (or examination) used to determine a student's progress toward meeting academic standards.

Performance Standards

The levels of performance of tasks that students must reach to demonstrate they have met the Content Standards—or that they are on their way toward meeting them. Performance Standards can be distinguished from Content Standards because Performance Standards have levels (e.g., 4 = exemplary, 3 = proficient, 2 = progressing, 1 = not meeting the standards).

Reliability

In order for a measure to be reliable it must be consistent.

Reliability Coefficient

A measure of how two or more judges score the same exam. A reliability coefficient of 1.0 means they are in complete 100% agreement.

Psychometrician

A person who designs mathematical and statistical tests to measure psychological variables such as intelligence, aptitude, and emotional disturbance.

Pilot Project

An experimental or trial undertaking of standards implementation prior to full-scale use.

Rubric

The specific rules within the scoring guide. For example, one Language Arts rubric might be to "read and recognize literature as an expression of human experience." These also appear on the Standards Achievement Report (see Chapter 9).

Scenario

An outline or dramatic plot or situation.

Scoring Guides

The documents used to determine whether the work is exemplary, proficient, progressing toward the standard, or not yet meeting the standard. A Standards Achievement Report (SAR) is an example of one such guide.

Standard

A model that is used as a basis of judgment.

Standards Achievement Report (SAR)

One type of scoring guide designed to replace the traditional report card, consisting of the rubric (e.g., for Language Arts, "read and recognize literature as an expression of human experience"), a description of the Performance Standard (e.g., 4 = exemplary, 3 = proficient, 2 = progressing, 1 = not meeting the standards), teacher and parent comments, and a plan for meeting the standard.

Task Force

A temporary grouping of people, formed for the purpose of implementing, evaluating, analyzing, investigating, or solving a specific problem in the establishment of educational standards.

Validity

A reflection of the intended measure. Validity means that we are testing what we think we are testing.

Bibliography

Baron, J.B. & Wolf, D.P. (Eds.). (1996). *Performance-based student assessment: Challenges and possibilities*. Chicago: University of Chicago Press.

Center on Learning Assessment and School Structure [CLASS]. (1995). *CLASS Summer Institute on Assessment Reform*. Princeton, NJ: CLASS. (**Note:** To order this publication, contact: CLASS, 648 the Great Road, Princeton, NJ 08540.)

Cobb, N. (Ed.). (1994). *The future of education: Perspectives on national standards in America*. New York: The College Board.

Crocker, L. & Algina, J. (1986). *Introduction to classical and modern test theory*. New York: Holt, Rinehart and Winston.

Daggett, W.R. & Kruse, B. (1997). *Education is not a spectator sport*. Schenectady, NY: Leadership Press.

Damon, W. (1995). *Great expectations. Overcoming the culture of indulgence in our homes and schools*. New York: Free Press Paperbacks.

Darling-Hammond, L., Einbender, L., & Frelow, F. et al. (1993, October). *Authentic assessment in practice: A collection of portfolios, performance tasks, exhibitions, and documentation*. New York: National Center for Restructuring Education, Schools, and Teaching.

Educational Testing Service[ETS]. (1995). *Performance assessment: Different needs, difficult answers*. Princeton, NJ: ETS. (**Note:** To order this publication, contact: ETS, 1425 Lower Ferry Rd., Trenton, NJ 08618, Phone 609-771-7670, Fax 609-771-7906.)

Ellis, A.K. & Fouts, J.T. (1999). *Research on educational innovations* (2nd ed.). Larchmont, NY: Eye on Education.

Gardner, H. (1991). *The unschooled mind: How children think and how schools should teach*. New York: Basic Books.

Gardner, H. (1993). *Frames of mind: The theory of multiple intelligences*. Boulder, CO: Basic Books.

Goleman, D. (1995). *Emotional intelligence: Why it can matter more than IQ.* New York, Bantam Books.

Goodlad, J.I. (1990). *Teachers for our nation's schools.* San Francisco: Jossey-Bass.

Hirsch, E. D. (1988). *Cultural literacy: What every American needs to know.* NY: Random House.

Hirsch, E. D. (1997). *What your kindergartener needs to know: Preparing your child for a lifetime of learning (Core Knowledge Series).* NY: Dell.

Hirsch, Jr. E.D. (1996). *The schools we need and why we don't have them.* New York: Doubleday.

Hanson, F.A. (1993). *Testing testing: Social consequences of the examined life.* Berkeley: University of California Press. (**Note:** This offers a fascinating historical critique of tests.)

Howard, R. (Ed.). (1993). *The learning imperative: Managing people for continuous innovation.* Boston: Harvard Business School.

Howe, K.R. (1994, November). Standards, assessment, and equality of educational opportunity. *Educational Researcher, 23*(8), 27-32.

Keillor, G.A. (1974). *Prairie home companion.* Minneapolis, MN: American Public Radio Network. (**Note:** Garrison Keillor first began this broadcast in 1974. This program can presently be heard throughout the U.S. on National Public Radio Stations.)

LeMahieu, P.G., Gitomer, D.H., & Eresh, J.T. (Fall 1995). Portfolios in large-scale assessment: Difficult but not impossible. *Educational Measurement: Issues and Practice,* 11-16.

Marsh, H.W. (1984). Students' evaluations of university teaching: Dimensionality, reliability, validity, potential biases, and utility. *Journal of Educational Psychology, 76,* 707-54.

Marzano, R.J. & Kendall, J.S. (1996). *A comprehensive guide to designing standards-based districts, schools and classrooms.* Alexandria, VA: Association for Supervision and Curriculum Development.

Miller, B. & Singleton, L. (1995, January). *Preparing citizens: Linking authentic assessment and instruction in civic/law-related education.* Boulder, CO: Social Science Education Consortium.

Mitchell, R. (1996). *Front-end alignment: Using standards to steer education change—A manual for developing standards.* Washington, DC: The Education Trust. (**Note:** To order this 58 page book, contact: Publications Orders Desk, American Association for Higher Education, One Dupont Circle, NW, Suite 360, Washington, D.C., 20036-1110, Telephone 202-293-6440, ext. 11, Fax 202-293-0073.)

Mitchell, R. (1992). *Testing for learning: How new approaches to evaluation can improve American schools.* New York: The Free Press.

Mitchell, R., Willis, M., & The Chicago Teachers Union Quest Center. (1995). *Learning in overdrive: Designing curriculum, instruction, and assessment from standards.* Golden, CO: North American Press.

National Educational Goals Panel. (1995). *The national education goals report: Building a nation of learners.* Washington, D.C.: U.S. Government Printing Office.

Naftulin, D.H., Ware, J.E., & Donnelly, F.A. (1973). The Doctor Fox lecture: A paradigm of educational seduction. *Journal of Medical Education, 48,* 630-635.

Perkins, D. (1995). *Outsmarting IQ: The emerging science of learnable intelligence.* New York: The Free Press.

Powell, B. & Steelman, L.C. (Spring 1996). Bewitched, bothered, and bewildering: The use and misuse of state SAT and ACT scores. *Harvard Educational Review, 61*(1), 27-59.

Ravitch, D. (1995). *National standards in American education (a citizens guide).* Washington, D.C.: Brookings Institution Press.

Reeves, D. B. (2000). *Accountability in action: A blueprint for learning organizations.* Denver, CO: Advanced Learning Press.

Reeves, D. B. (2001). *Holistic accountability: Helping students, schools, and communities.* Thousand Oaks, CA: Corwin Press.

Rothman, R. (1995). *Measuring up: Standards, assessment, and school reform.* San Francisco: Jossey-Bass.

Shepard, L.A. & Bliem, C.L. (1995, November). Parents' thinking about standardized tests and performance assessments. *Educational Researcher,* 25-32.

Slavin, R. (1994). *Educational psychology* (4th ed.). Boston: Allyn and Bacon.

Sykes, C.J. (1995). *Dumbing down our kids: Why American children feel good about themselves but can't read, write, or add.* New York: St. Martin's Press.

Index

A

ability groups 29
above average 30, 32
absenteeism 141
academic achievement 33, 157
academic content standard(s) 12–13, 14, 17, 19, 41, 52, 119
academic core curriculum 11
accountability 53, 71, 88, 153–155, 157, 159–160
accountability plan 155
accountability system 158
accuracy 46
activity 111
analysis 119
analyze 121
anonymous questionnaires 135
arts 114
assessment(s) 8, 60, 85–88, 111, 130
assignment 106, 111
attendance 10, 11
augmentation 139
average 26
average score(s) 31, 36

B

behavior 28, 74–75
bell curve 8, 30, 38
benchmark(s) 18–19, 106
best practices 53, 55, 149, 164
bias 36
board of education 63–64, 68–69, 155, 173
bureaucracies 43

C

central office 57
central tendency 120
challenges 173
clarity 139
   of evaluation 133
   of instructions 133, 135
class participation 11
classroom management 122

interdisciplinary 142
International Performance Assessment System 126

J

Johns Hopkins University 28
Jordan, Barbara 176
journal 54

K

Keillor, Garrison 154

L

leadership 166
LeMahieu, Robert 30
lesson plans 104
letter grade(s) 11, 71–73
leverage 110
Los Angeles Unified School District 26

M

Marsh, Herbert 135
mean 119–120
median 119–120
memorization 118
Milwaukee Public Schools 38
mode 119–120
model responses 130
modeling 144
money 68, 70
motivation 141
multidisciplinary 114
   assignment(s) 109, 112
multiple choice 84
   questions 36
   test(s) 39, 82, 88, 121, 168, 171
multiple intelligences 73
multiple measures 87
multiple opportunities 10, 22

N

Naftulin, D.H. 97
national standards 89
national standards movement 7
networking 173, 175
non-academic electives 13
norm(s) 25–26, 28–29, 32
norm-based assessments 36
norm-referenced tests 30
not meeting standards 125, 126

number 17, 19
numerous drafts 127

O

objective 168
"one shot" 22
oral presentations 122
ownership 63, 69

P

parent(s) 33, 75–76, 143–145
parental involvement 143
passing grade 10, 14
peer coaches 29
percentile 26
performance assessment(s) 39, 82, 121, 129,
   132, 134, 136, 168, 169
performance-based test(s) 169
Perkins, D. 32
personal responsibility 173–174
Peters, Tom 173
pilot program(s) 65–66, 70
planning period 67
policy 64
power standards 110
pre-test/post-test analysis 133
primary standard 109, 111, 114
principal(s) 57–59, 61–62
process 46
professional development 49, 51, 60, 97
   sessions 50
proficiency 11, 18, 26–28, 30, 109, 129
proficient 34, 53, 125–126, 128
progress 60
progressing 125, 126
protection 68, 70
public reporting 166
pull the weeds 52, 61, 104, 107, 108

R

racial prejudice 31
random samples 87
range of difficulty 109
ranking 33
realism 141–142, 145
recognition 62, 66, 149
reflections 54
reflective evaluations 54
relevance 47
reliability 81, 82, 83, 85, 88, 159
report card(s) 71, 72, 73, 74

Resources for Improving Student Achievement

Other books by Advanced Learning Press

Accountability in Action: A Blueprint for Learning Organizations
by Douglas B. Reeves, Ph.D.

Design a comprehensive accountability system that includes more than just test scores. This guide gives educational leaders a clear framework and specific steps to developing an accountability system that is fair, rigorous, and meets the needs of the school system. Each chapter has worksheets and discussion questions to structure the process. Appendices include sample accountability reports, hundreds of sample indicators, templates, checklists, and resource lists for accountability research. Dr. Reeves is a leading expert in educational accountability. (317 pages)

101 Questions & Answers about Standards, Assessment, and Accountability
by Douglas B. Reeves, Ph.D., Edited by Allison W. Schumacher

This easy-to-use reference book provides clear answers to commonly asked questions about the most pressing issues in education today. Standards and standardized tests, writing and student achievement, accountability systems, interventions for under-performing students, standards and the arts, motivation, leadership issues, plus many more topics are addressed in this handbook for educators. Dr. Reeves clearly articulates responses to questions he has received over the years during teacher workshops and national presentations, while facilitating K-12 accountability task force meetings and working with students in the classroom, and as the Test Doctor on the Internet. This book is a helpful reference for understanding the issues and improving communication among teachers, parents, students, and all stakeholders in school communities. (208 pages)

www.makingstandardswork.com   **800-844-6599**

Performance Assessment Series
(Elementary or Middle School Edition available)

by the Center for Performance Assessment
Foreword by Douglas B. Reeves, Ph.D.

Timesaving tools and ready-to-use materials for classroom assessment. These books help teachers and administrators plan and teach by providing performance assessments and scoring guides for the K-12 standards-based classroom. Each edition includes:

- Standards-based performance assessments for the four core subject areas

- Model scoring guides (rubrics) for composition, research papers, oral presentations, and more

- Frequently asked questions and answers about assessments

- Teacher tips for implementation

- Tools for teacher self-assessment

- Performance assessments that 1) are aligned to standards; 2) include essential questions, concept-based activities, and enrichment ideas; 3) include 4 or more tasks, each with a four-point scoring guide (rubric); and 4) are models that you can build on

- Template and scoring guide for assessment design

(Elementary - 161 pages, Middle School - 171 pages)

Five Easy Steps To A Balanced Math Program

by Larry Ainsworth and Jan Christinson

Developing a balanced math program is the answer for teachers who want to ensure that their students are receiving the full range of mathematical understanding and skills. The purpose of this book is to share with other teachers the methods that the authors have successfully developed for doing this. The reader follows a step-by-step process that goes through each of the five components in this balanced math program model and learns an easy-to-follow sequence of how to implement the program successfully in the primary, intermediate, and middle school classroom. (171 pages)

www.makingstandardswork.com   **800-844-6599**